ROUTLEDGE LIBRARY EDITIONS:
DEVELOPMENT

ECONOMIC INTEGRATION IN AFRICA

ECONOMIC INTEGRATION IN AFRICA

PETER ROBSON

Volume 54

Routledge
Taylor & Francis Group

LONDON AND NEW YORK

First published in 1968

This edition first published in 2011
by Routledge
2 Park Square, Milton Park, Abingdon, Oxon, OX14 4RN

Simultaneously published in the USA and Canada
by Routledge
270 Madison Avenue, New York, NY 10016

Routledge is an imprint of the Taylor & Francis Group, an informa business

© 1968 George Allen & Unwin Ltd

Printed and bound in Great Britain

British Library Cataloguing in Publication Data
A catalogue record for this book is available from the British Library

ISBN 13: 978-0-415-58414-2 (Set)
eISBN 13: 978-0-203-84035-1 (Set)
ISBN 13: 978-0-415-59373-1 (Volume 54)
eISBN 13: 978-0-203-83836-5 (Volume 54)

Publisher's Note
The publisher has gone to great lengths to ensure the quality of this reprint but
points out that some imperfections in the original copies may be apparent.

Disclaimer
The publisher has made every effort to trace copyright holders and welcomes
correspondence from those they have been unable to contact.

ECONOMIC INTEGRATION IN AFRICA

AFRICA
SHOWING COMMON MARKETS

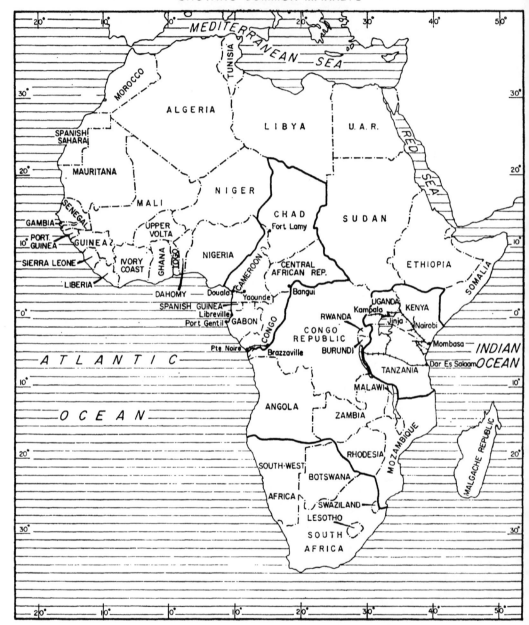

ECONOMIC INTEGRATION
IN AFRICA

BY

PETER ROBSON

Professor of Economics,
University College, Nairobi

London
GEORGE ALLEN AND UNWIN LTD
RUSKIN HOUSE   MUSEUM STREET

PRINTED IN GREAT BRITAIN
in 11 on 12 pt Times Roman type
BY PURNELL AND SONS LTD
PAULTON (SOMERSET) AND LONDON

PREFACE

THIS book is a brief study for Africa of the opportunities and problems of economic integration between independent states. It begins with a brief survey of the present scope of integration in Africa. This is followed by a review of some leading aspects of the theory of economic integration, with particular reference to less developed countries. The theory of the subject is a large and growing field, and the discussion in Chapter 2 is confined to aspects which are salient and particularly relevant to the discussion of later chapters. Those who wish to pursue the theoretical analysis further will find on page 313 a brief annotated reading list which indicates some of the most important literature. Chapter 3 contains a general survey of the African economic setting within which actual and projected integration arrangements must operate and considers some of the factors on which the size of the opportunities from integration may depend. The remaining chapters are taken up by empirical studies of the operation of integration arrangements in various parts of Africa together with a brief consideration of initiatives which have failed and of projected arrangements.

The book is limited to a discussion of economic considerations. This does not mean that the author regards political factors as unimportant in the integration process. All experience suggests the contrary, and the further progress of integration in Africa no less than in other areas will presumably be influenced to a considerable degree by the interplay of political forces. Nevertheless, the purely economic issues involved are sufficiently large and complex in themselves to warrant separate treatment. In the same way, the book contains no reference to administrative problems though these too are of great importance.

I am indebted to the Editor of the *Bulletin of the Oxford University Institute of Economics and Statistics* for permission to use in Chapter 3 material from my article entitled 'Africa and EEC', which appeared in the *Bulletin*, Vol. 27, no. 3; and to use in Chapter 4 material from my article entitled 'The Shiftability of Industry and the Costs and Benefits of the East African Common Market; Some Further Considerations', *Bulletin*, Vol. 30, no. 2. I am also grateful to the Editors of the *Journal of Modern African Studies* for permission to use in Chapter 6 material from my articles entitled 'The Problem of Senegambia', *Journal*, Vol. 3, no. 3, and 'Economic Integration in Southern Africa', *Journal*, Vol. 5, no. 4. An earlier version of Chapter 4 first appeared as part of a collection of essays edited by Arthur Hazlewood and published by Oxford University Press, entitled *African Integration and Disintegration*. I am grateful for permission to make use of this. Mr Ali Ganda of Freetown was kind enough to permit me to quote a quatrain from his calypso in Chapter 2.

In writing this book I have incurred many debts. I should like in the first place to acknowledge generous financial assistance from the Rockefeller Foundation which made possible research in various parts of Africa on which Chapter 5 and parts of Chapter 6 are based. Dr Rothchild read the Introduction and Chapter 5. Mr K. Savosnick was kind enough to read Chapter 1. I am particularly grateful to Mr W. T. Newlyn of Leeds University, to Dr B. F. Massell, formerly of University College, Nairobi and now of Stanford, and to Professor H. G. Johnson of London University, for reading and commenting most helpfully on a draft of the whole book. I am also grateful for stimulus and comment to the members of the Staff Seminar in Economics at University College, Nairobi. Finally, the help of my wife has been invaluable. She has prepared many of the statistics, removed innumerable infelicities, and in countless ways has greatly improved the presentation. Errors and shortcomings, of course, are entirely the responsibility of the author.

Nairobi 1967.

CONTENTS

CHAPTER 1

INTRODUCTION

1 THE RATIONALE OF INTEGRATION

ECONOMIC integration between sovereign states has some claim to be regarded as one of the leading aspirations of international economic policy in the mid-twentieth century, so much so that this era has been termed 'the age of integration'.[1] In the developed world, the desire for integration is reflected in the formation of such groupings as the European Economic Community (EEC), the European Free Trade Area (EFTA), the Council for Mutual Economic Assistance (COMECON), and in initiatives in the South Pacific. In the less developed world, interest in integration is even more widespread. In Latin America it has given rise to the Central American Common Market and the Latin American Free Trade Association (LAFTA); in the Middle East it has produced the Arab Common Market.

A similar interest is also found in Africa and is expressed in a variety of existing arrangements and in plans for others. The concern of African countries with integration, like that of countries elsewhere, derives not only from economic considerations, but in part from political and social factors as well, which cannot easily be disentangled from each other. At the political level, the basic motivation for integration, or at least for co-operation, springs from the assumption that for all but a few larger African states, considerations of modernization and genuine independence render some form of international co-operation or interdependence inescapable. During the colonial period, this co-operation took the form of a dependence of African states upon foreign powers. In post-colonial Africa there exists a fairly widespread desire to free the continent from its external dependence and to provide the safeguards and benefits of interdependence through a continental, or at any rate, a wide geographical, system of institutions capable of harmonizing the common interests of African states and

11

presenting a united front in external affairs. For some African leaders these political objectives are buttressed by a Pan-African ideology[2] which encourages outlooks fostering wider political unity.

Although the interplay of political interests, including a desire for greater international bargaining power, undoubtedly accounts for some of the widespread interest in integration between African states at the present time, the primary motives are commonly economic. The end of colonial rule has led to the creation of a large number of African states, many of which offer little prospect of a satisfactory standard of life. Integration is seen as a means of helping to overcome the disadvantages of small size and of making possible a greater rate of economic growth and development. Integration makes it possible on a basis of reciprocity, to exploit economies of scale and to take advantage of differences in comparative advantage in the production of commodities. Furthermore, wider markets may make it possible to attract more foreign capital and to increase employment. Other advantages include the diversification of output which, it is hoped, may contribute to economic stability as well as to growth.

If, instead, each country tries to develop separately behind its own national tariff barriers, low per capita incomes, small populations and narrow resource bases will in many cases make the achievement of their objectives more costly, if not impossible. Some of those economic objectives, like the political objectives mentioned earlier, could doubtless be achieved by the maintenance of close links with countries outside Africa. There is, however, a fairly widespread belief that if economic growth is to be accelerated, external links must be substantially supplemented by strengthened intra-African links. In any case, a reduction in external economic dependence is seen as a necessary condition, not only for the kind of economic diversification aimed at, but also for the attainment of economic autonomy.

Given the objectives of economic policy in many African states, there can be little doubt that integration can create potential opportunities for their more effective attainment. Many African leaders realize this and some also find ideological support for integration in the doctrines of Pan-Africanism. In so far as this is the case, the limited extent to which these considerations have been reflected in widespread and close economic links may appear surprising. Although there are a number of important examples of integration in Africa, the gap between aspiration and achievement is large.

In part no doubt, the explanation lies in the fact that, although integration is certainly advantageous to the members of the group as a whole, benefits are not automatically reaped by each single member. This consideration is likely to be especially important where integration involves the grouping of countries which are at somewhat different stages of development, for in this situation, market forces may direct the benefits of integration mainly towards the more advanced members, to the possible detriment of the more backward members. In such conditions, bargaining for a share of the new industry made possible by integration, or for some redistribution of its gains by fiscal means may be a precondition for an equitable distribution of benefits, and hence for the formation and maintenance of integration arrangements. Yet dependable estimates of the effects of integration are difficult to make and divergent assessments on the nature and distribution of the resulting gains may render negotiations protracted and difficult.

Moreover, although economic integration or co-operation in trade or monetary matters may be feasible without political links, opportunities for substantial gains may in some cases depend upon assurances of the durability of the arrangements; these may be difficult to provide in the absence of some cession of sovereignty. Similarly, in the case of common services, where a practicable alternative exists, the extra cost of which is not too high, there may be reluctance without political confidence to rely on other countries for vital services such as telecommunications, power and transport, however important the economic gains.

Evidently, the progress of integration will be dependent upon a complex process of international negotiation. But the nature of the political process in many of the new African states is such that in practice energies tend to be absorbed by domestic issues. In many of these states, national cohesion is fragile, and its consolidation is given priority over initiatives involving international co-operation. An unwillingness to contemplate the sharing of power may reinforce this tendency. Also domestic political considerations make it necessary to evaluate national economic interests very carefully; in addition, potential future benefits resulting from a wider economic unity may be heavily discounted in comparison with the advantages of promoting development now.

In relation to the progress of economic integration, national considerations based on its promise of prospective economic benefits are no doubt important. These are unlikely to prevail, however, except where a majority of those who make political decisions in the countries in question identify their personal and group interests with the interests which integration would promote, and also where the prospective benefits are sufficiently large to overcome the obstacle presented by the inevitable uncertainties which major changes in economic policy necessarily entail. The lack of fulfilment of these conditions in many cases suggests that although there is good reason for supposing that integration will be a perennial concern of African states for a long time to come, it is unrealistic to suppose that its progress will be either smooth or rapid.

2 THE SCOPE OF ECONOMIC CO-OPERATION IN AFRICA

Aspirations towards unity and co-operation in Africa currently find institutional expression in a variety of organizational arrangements for co-operation and in initiatives for others. The new intergovernment political organizations of independent Africa may be first mentioned because commonly their objectives have included the promotion of measures for economic co-operation. Of these organizations, the Organization for African Unity (OAU) which was founded in 1963 is the most inclusive. Its formation represents the first comprehensive attempt to organize continent-wide African co-operation on a permanent footing. OAU is not, of course, a supra-national organization but an inter-governmental body whose concern is to promote the common interests of member states and, in particular to foster the building up of African unity. Intended

14

to replace all existing sub-regional political groupings, its formation was in fact accompanied by the liquidation of the Casablanca[3] and Monrovia groupings[4], the Pan-African Movement for East and Central Africa (PAFMECSA)[5], and the Ghana-Guinea Union.

The Brazzaville group[6] made up of the French speaking African countries south of the Sahara except Congo (Kinshasa) was reluctant to wind up its regional grouping known as the Union Africaine et Malgache (UAM), apparently fearing to lose the opportunities it afforded for more intimate regional co-operation. And although UAM was disbanded, its members' dissatisfaction with the working of OAU soon led them (in 1965) to establish a successor, known as the Organisation Commune Africaine et Malgache, (OCAM).[7] The Conseil de l'Entente which grouped five members of UAM, did not disband at all, and still functions. It now seems to be accepted that at the present stage of Africa's evolution regionally based political organizations cannot be dispensed with.

Intergovernmental arrangements for co-operation at the economic level in Africa are much more numerous than at the political level. There may first be mentioned some institutions of continental scope which are concerned with planning. These include the specialized commissions of the OAU, which were set up to co-ordinate and harmonize the policies of the member states in a number of fields of economic policy. At its first meeting in Niamey in 1963, the Economic and Social Commission of OAU adopted a very ambitious programme of activities which included co-ordinating and harmonizing national development plans; setting up a free trade area between member states; establishing African internal conventions on transport and communications by land, sea and air; creating an African tele-communications union for the continent as a whole; studying the problems of payments agreements between African countries until the setting up of an African payments and clearing union; standardizing a common external tariff among member states; and setting up a monetary zone and a central bank of issue. Of these, the first five points were selected for special priority.[8]

Whatever action can be taken in these matters will probably have to depend very heavily on the African-wide United Nations

Economic Commission for Africa for the necessary preliminary studies, for the OAU itself lacks the necessary personnel. The work of ECA, like that of its sister regional organizations in Asia and the Far East and Latin America, is in fact concerned almost exclusively with expert studies; it is not in a position to finance or administer any development projects which it may advocate. In recent years ECA has been one of the most ardent advocates of economic integration in Africa.

At a sub-regional level expert studies were to have been among the functions of the Organisation Africaine et Malgache de Co-opération Économique (OAMCE), but in practice its staffing has been insufficient to enable it to undertake many of these. Its functions in this and other areas have now been absorbed by OCAM, which has in addition taken over responsibility for the specialized agencies for functional co-operation of the former UAM, like the Union Africaine et Malgache des Postes et Télé-communications (UAMPT)[9], and the Organisation Africaine et Malgache du Café (OAMCAF).

Although intergovernmental planning organizations may have an important role to play in preparing the ground for integration, in the end the exploitation of its potential benefits depends on the willingness of governments to commit themselves to integration and to embody this commitment in executive institutions and working arrangements, such as customs unions and common markets, the co-ordination of industrial development, the provision of common services and monetary co-operation. A number of African governments have in fact committed themselves to such arrangements and others are projected. This introduction concludes with a brief survey of existing arrangements and of initiatives for others.

Within French speaking Africa there is much experience with forms of economic co-operation. Throughout most of the colonial period, the member states of the two big administrative federations of French West Africa (AOF) and French Equatorial Africa (AEF) enjoyed close economic links in the fields of trade, finance and common services. When their constituent states became independent, they were encouraged to continue these economic links. A first outcome, in 1959, was the establishment of a West African Customs Union (UDAO) comprising Dahomey,

16

Ivory Coast, Mauretania, Niger, Senegal, Soudan (now Mali) and Upper Volta. In the following year an Equatorial Customs Union (UDE) was formed by Congo, Gabon, Chad and the Central African Republic (CAR). These arrangements for market integration were soon complemented by the establishment of new central banks for each of the areas which preserve their monetary unions in suitably modified form. In addition to these forms of co-operation, new inter-state organizations were created to make possible the continued common operation of services such as transport.

From the outset the West African Customs Union ran into difficulties, mainly over the allocation of import duties; before long customs barriers were established at the frontiers; indirect taxes were imposed on inter-regional trade and the union became largely ineffective.

Within francophone West Africa, the smaller grouping known as the Entente has made various attempts at economic co-operation. Initially the Entente consisted of Ivory Coast, Upper Volta, Niger and Dahomey but Togo was induced to join in 1965. Although the Entente was established chiefly as a political grouping[10] it also had limited objectives in the field of economic co-operation. Thus, its agreement provided for the establishment of a customs union and also for some redistribution of revenues to support the poorer members. In addition the harmonization of development plans was envisaged. The achievements of the Entente in economic matters have so far been limited, but lately a number of changes have been made which may foreshadow its evolution into a more effective instrument of economic co-operation.

On the whole, in francophone West Africa and in the smaller Entente area, the achievements of integration initiatives in the field of trade and industry have been negligible. On the other hand, in the monetary sphere, continued co-operation in the area has proved to be workable. Moreover, the more important arrangements for co-operation in the provision of common services, mainly transport, have continued to function successfully.

In equatorial Africa, attempts to preserve and develop former economic links have been more successful. In 1960 a Customs

Union was established between Congo (Brazzaville), Gabon, Chad and the Central African Republic. A common central bank (which included Cameroon) and an interstate transport agency were also set up. These arrangements have been maintained and have been expanded into an economic union with a wider geographical base, having Cameroon as its fifth member.

North of the Sahara, integration has not yet progressed far, but steps have recently been taken to strengthen economic co-operation among the three Maghreb countries of Morocco, Tunisia, and Algeria, with which Libya is associated. The objectives are to harmonize trade policy and to co-ordinate development plans. A ministerial council for economic affairs was formed in 1964, together with a secretariat, and there is provision for common services in the field of statistics and tourism.[11] Also it is proposed to handle the external marketing of certain agricultural products jointly and a specialization agreement for an iron and steel plant is envisaged. Attempts have also been made to draw up lists of products which would be exempt from duty in trade between the four countries. Another Arab country, the United Arab Republic, has sought its economic links outside the continent in the shape of the Arab common market which includes Egypt, Irak, Jordan, Kuwait and Syria.[12]

Among English-speaking countries the major example of integration is the long established East African Common Market which includes Kenya, Uganda and Tanzania. A high degree of monetary co-operation also exists in this area and several important common services are jointly operated. In the last few years these forms of co-operation have been subject to many stresses, but with the formal establishment of the East African Economic Community in 1967, these appear to have been largely surmounted.

In Southern Africa a customs union and a *de facto* currency union between South Africa and the three High Commission territories of Basutoland, Swaziland and Bechuanaland has operated since 1910. These arrangements have been retained as these countries have progressed to independence but a revision of the customs agreement is in prospect. In 1956 the High

Commission territories entered into a customs agreement with the Federation of Rhodesia and Nyasaland which continues to operate with Rhodesia. Other integration agreements in Southern Africa which may be mentioned include the trade agreement which was made between Rhodesia and Malawi in 1964 after the break up of the Federation of Rhodesia and Nyasaland. This provided for the payment of fiscal compensation for the partner losing customs revenue[13] as a result of its importation of the other's products. After the break up of the Federation, a *de facto* common market between Rhodesia and Zambia was maintained for some time though with some restrictions on the Zambian side. Rhodesia's declaration of independence in 1966 brought both of these arrangements to an abrupt end.

Outside former French and British Africa, customs unions exist amongst the Portuguese colonies (and between them and Portugal) but, as between the African components, they are unlikely to be of any practical significance, because of the wide separation of the territories. Until January 1964 a customs and currency union also existed between Ruanda and Burundi.

A few attempts have been made to develop customs unions or other forms of economic integration between English and French speaking countries. Of these, the 1961 Ghana-Upper Volta Customs Union agreement and the Ghana-Guinea agreement of 1961 were the first, but neither appears to have had much practical effect. During 1963 and 1964 there were initiatives aimed at bringing about the economic integration of Gambia and Senegal, but these were largely unproductive.[14] In 1964 proposals were put forward for a West African Free Trade Area to include Ivory Coast, Guinea, Liberia and Sierra Leone. These countries have since set up at Freetown an Organization for West African Economic Co-operation which is studying the problems and possibilities of closer co-operation.

In the last few years proposals have also been made which envisage extensive subregional economic integration or co-operation on a very broad geographical basis. This co-operation would in some cases be based on existing trade groupings but generally would go well beyond them. An example is the scheme for an Eastern African Community to include the English speaking countries of East and Central Africa and adjoining countries, which was recommended at the Lusaka ECA Conference in October–November 1965. The governments of six countries of the subregion (Ethiopia, Kenya, Malawi, Mauritius, the United Republic of Tanzania and Zambia) subsequently accepted the conference recommendation and signed general Draft Articles of Association. In May 1966 an Interim Council of Ministers met and discussed a Draft Treaty.[15] No further action has occurred on this, but four members of the community (the three East African countries and Zambia) subsequently cooperated in the establishment of a multinational shipping line. In West Africa articles of association for a West African Economic Community were considered at a meeting in Niamey in October 1966[16] and in Accra in April–May 1967[17]. They have not yet been signed by the governments concerned, but an Interim Council of Ministers has been set up.

Suggestions for a Southern African Common Market based on South Africa, Rhodesia and Malawi and including the Portuguese territories of Angola and Mozambique have also been discussed but have been ruled out as impracticable by the South African Government[18].

In conclusion certain other forms of integration, actual or projected may be briefly mentioned. An African Development Bank was established in 1964 in Abidjan. Proposals for an African Clearing and Payments Union have also received detailed discussion. Interstate authorities to plan and oversee the development of various lake and river basins have been set up for the Senegal, Niger and Mono rivers and for the Chad Basin.[19] Other organizations for functional economic cooperation include the Union Africaine et Malgache des Postes et Télécommunications and the Organisation Africaine et Malgache du Café mentioned already. A measure of industrial cooperation in the establishment of joint industries is being attempted between Togo and Dahomey. Another proposal envisages the establishment of a West African Iron and Steel Community. This idea was first discussed at the conference on industrial co-ordination in Bamako in October 1964[20] in terms of the establishment of a large integrated iron and steel plant

20

on the Liberian coast, together with a less important plant in Mali. Following the acceptance in principle of the idea of co-ordinated development of iron and steel in West Africa a fourteen-country provisional committee was formed in 1965 to study the possibility of the formation of the community, but the prospects of effective co-operation do not seem bright. Although Liberia and Mali naturally support the idea, countries whose claims to plants have been disregarded are not co-operating. Thus Guinea has decided to build its own plant, and Nigeria has also announced plans for an independent iron and steel works.

In relation to the various forms of economic co-operation in Africa, both actual and projected, many important questions are suggested. What is the source of their economic benefits? How extensive are these benefits likely to be? Can economic association without political unity maximise the gains from integration? Under what circumstances is economic association likely to develop into some kind of political association? Is economic integration a stable form of organization, or does its continuance seem likely to demand some degree of political unity? Several of these questions are for the political scientist rather than the economist, and will not be considered in this book.

The scope of this book is much more limited. After examining the economics of integration, with special reference to less developed countries, it considers some salient features of the African economic setting within which actual and projected schemes must operate. There follows a survey of the experience of existing arrangements for economic integration between independent African states. Finally some new initiatives which are under discussion or are taking shape receive brief mention. Ultimately the character and pace of economic development in Africa may be considerably influenced for the better by the consolidation and development of economic integration arrangements. But although the long term economic objectives of most African states can best be served by economic co-operation, short term interests often lead to independent action. The future of economic co-operation in Africa will depend on which of these considerations becomes dominant.

REFERENCES: CHAPTER 1

1 See G. Haberler, Integration and Growth in the World Economy in Historical Perspective, *American Economic Review*, March 1964, page 1.

2 For a useful account of Pan Africanism see Colin Legum, *Pan-Africanism. A short Political Guide*, Pall Mall Press, London 1962. An account of recent developments is contained in the same author's 'The Changing Ideas of Pan-Africanism', *African Forum*, Vol. 1, No. 2, 1965, New York.

3 This neutralist group resulted from a meeting at Casablanca in January 1961 between the heads of state of Egypt, Ghana, Guinea, Mali and Morocco together with representatives or observers from certain other countries including Algeria. In July 1961 the group agreed on far-reaching measures of political and economic co-operation, including the creation of a common market over a period of five years, beginning in January 1962, and the setting up of an African payments union, an economic development bank and a joint air and shipping line. These measures were never implemented. Within the Casablanca group, still closer relations had already been planned between Ghana, Guinea and Mali at a meeting in December 1960. The three countries proposed inter alia, 'To establish the union of our three states; and to promote a common economic and monetary policy'.

4 In May 1961 a conference of heads of independent African States was held at Monrovia. It had been hoped that the outcome would be a reconciliation of growing divergencies between the Casablanca group and other African countries. In the event the Casablanca group decided not to take part because of wide differences of opinion over current developments in the former Belgian Congo. The Monrovia group thus consisted of the members of the Brazzaville group together with Ethiopia, Liberia, Libya, Nigeria, Sierra Leone, Somalia, Togo and Tunisia. At a later meeting in July 1961 the group produced an economic programme similar to that of the Casablanca countries, including the creation of a common market and an economic development bank.

5 See Richard Cox, *Pan-Africanism in Practice* (*PAFMECSA 1958–1964*), Oxford University Press, London 1964, for Institute of Race Relations.

6 The Brazzaville group which established the Union Africaine et Malgache at Brazzaville in December 1960, subsequently met at Dakar in January–February 1961 and agreed on a treaty establishing OAMCE (l'Organisation Afro-Malgache de Co-opération Économique) with the following members: Senegal, Ivory Coast, Cameroon, Central African Republic, Dahomey, Gabon, Upper Volta, Madagascar, Mauritania, Niger, Chad and the former French Congo. The main objective in the first instance was economic co-operation, principally with a view to strengthening their negotiating position vis-à-vis the EEC and other trading partners.

7 On the evolution of these organisations, see 'From UAM to OCAM', by Diakha Dieng, in *African Forum*, Vol. 1, No. 2, 1965.

See also K. Panter-Brick, The Union Africaine et Malgache, in (ed.) D. Austin and H. N. Weiler, *Inter-State Relations in Africa*, Freiburg i. Br. 1965.

8 See C. Legum, The Specialized Commissions of the Organization for African Unity, *Journal of Modern African Studies*, Vol. 2, No. 4, pp. 587–90, Cambridge 1964.

9 See Dieng, op. cit., pp. 29–35.

10 Some aspects of its operation are discussed in Chapter 5.

11 See *Report of the Sub-Regional Meeting on Economic Co-operation in North Africa*, E/CN.14 NA/Ecop. 11 (24.6.1966).

12 See M. Diab, *Inter-Arab Economic Co-operation 1950–1960*, American University of Beirut, 1963. Also, Diab, The Arab Common Market, *Journal of Common Market Studies*, Vol. IV., No. 3.

13 On this, see A. Hazlewood, The Rhodesia-Malawi Trade Agreement, *Bulletin of the Oxford Institute of Economics and Statistics*, May, 1965.

14 See Chapter 5 for a discussion of this initiative.

15 See *Report of the First Meeting of the Interim Council of Ministers of the proposed Economic Community of Eastern Africa*, May 1966 (E/CN/14/352).

16 See *Report of the Sub-Regional Meeting On Economic Co-operation in West Africa*, Niamey, 10–22 October 1966, E/CN.14/366, E/CN.14/INR/144, 11 November 1966.

17 See *Report of the West African Sub-Regional Conference on Economic Co-operation*, E/CN.14/399. 24.5.1967.

18 See Statement by Dr Diederichs, Minister of Economic Affairs, reported in East African Standard, September 19, 1965. See also 'Can a Free Trade Area be operated in Southern Africa?' In *Optima*, Johannesburg, No. 3, September 1965 by F. J. C. Cronje.

19 See *UNECA Natural Resources Newsletter* (*Addis Ababa*), No. 5, 1965, for a note on the Chad and Niger authorities. See also M. Seck, L'aménagement du bassin du fleuve Senegal, in *Europe—France Outre-Mer*, Paris, No. 412.

20 See *Report of the Conference on Industrial Co-ordination in West Africa*, Bamako, 5–15th October, 1964, E/CN.14/INR/78.

CHAPTER 2

THE ECONOMICS OF INTEGRATION AMONG LESS DEVELOPED COUNTRIES

Our Salvation
Is economic co-operation
With this Free Trade idea
African unity now is here.
                    West African Calypso

1 INTRODUCTION

'ECONOMIC integration' is a term to which economists have attached a variety of meanings, but most would agree that it embraces several forms of international economic co-operation including at least free trade areas, customs unions, common markets and economic unions. These arrangements represent successively higher degrees of integration. In a *free trade area*, tariffs and quantitative restrictions are abolished on trade in local products between the participants but each country retains its own tariff against imports from non-members. A *customs union* involves not only free trade between its members but also a common external tariff. The *common market* is a more developed form of integration in which, in addition to free trade, obstacles to the movement of some or all of the factors of production within it are also removed. In the still more advanced form which is termed *economic union*, fiscal, monetary and other instruments of economic policy are also harmonized or integrated.

All these forms of economic co-operation share two essential characteristics; first they facilitate expanded specialization and exchange between a group of independent countries by means of the elimination or substantial reduction of barriers to trade among them; secondly they entail discrimination against non-

25

members of the group. These characteristics are fundamental to free trade areas, customs unions, common markets and economic unions. Since they are likewise fundamental to other actual or planned institutional arrangements which are termed integration by both politicians and economists, these characteristics will be taken to delimit the arrangements which form the subject matter of this book. Integration may be defined as a situation having these characteristics. It is normally attained as a result of a process, extending over time, during which progressive adjustments are made with the object of bringing about a state of affairs in which, within the group, specialization, and exchange are expanded.

Integration is of course a means, not an end. The economic incentive for independent states to embark on a process of integration is its anticipated economic benefits. In principle these may be derived from a number of different sources. These include: (i) the specialization of production according to comparative advantage which is the basis of the classical case for the gains from trade; (ii) economies of scale; (iii) changes in the terms of trade; (iv) forced changes in efficiency due to increased competition; and (v) a change in the rate of economic growth. As Lipsey notes, 'the theory of customs unions has been almost entirely confined to an investigation of (i) above, with some slight attention to (ii) and (iii), (v) not being dealt with at all, while (iv) is ruled out of traditional theory by the assumption (often contradicted by the facts) that production is carried out by processes which are technically efficient'.[1] It is nevertheless convenient to begin this discussion of the economics of integration in less developed countries by outlining briefly some of the salient aspects of the traditional theory of customs unions. This is primarily concerned with considerations relating to the efficiency of resource allocation under static assumptions, and it analyses the circumstances under which gain may be derived from expanded trade among the members of a customs union when trade barriers among them are eliminated.

2 THE TRADITIONAL THEORY OF CUSTOMS UNIONS

The term 'traditional theory of customs unions' may be taken to refer to a fairly recent body of writings from Viner to Meade which analyses under static assumptions the circumstances under which a customs union leads to gain.[2] In its simplest form, the theory employed to elucidate this question makes the same basic assumptions as the static theory of comparative advantage[3]. It thus deals with a situation in which the inputs of factors of production, the state of technical knowledge, tastes and the forms of economic organization are all treated as constant or as autonomous variables. Trade within each country is assumed to be perfectly competitive, and external economies and diseconomies are disregarded, so that domestic grounds for interference with the operation of the price system can be ignored. Full employment is implied. Problems of adjustment which in practice would be involved in the formation of a customs union are disregarded.

Following Viner, the criterion of gain from customs union has been whether its formation is, on balance, trade creating or trade diverting. Trade creation refers to an increase of trade among the members of a customs union, and trade diversion to a reduction of trade with the rest of the world, both of which may follow the removal of trade barriers between the members of a union.

Suppose that two countries A and B form a customs union, and there are no quantitative restrictions on trade between them. The removal of tariffs makes possible the replacement of high cost domestic production of one member by lower cost production from another which was prevented beforehand by the existence of the duties. After integration, each country will expand the production of commodities it can manufacture at lower cost. This is trade creation. It results in an increase in the income of the members of the union.

But the formation of the customs union also means that the rest of the world, which may be termed C, will be discriminated against within the union. Before the formation of the union, the producers of country C faced the same tariff barrier in country A as did B's producers; after integration, C will have to surmount the common external tariff of the union while B pays no duty. Assuming constant costs, if the rest of the world C supplied A with a particular commodity prior to integration, but the sum of its production costs and the common tariff of the union exceeds the cost of production in member country B, the latter will supplant C as supplier of the commodity in question to country A. In other words A's demand is diverted from a lower cost producer, which is the rest of the world, to a higher cost producer within the union. This is trade diversion. It results in a reduction in world income, and, given the terms of trade, in the income of the members of the union.

The following examples illustrate the two cases of trade creation and trade diversion for a given product. For simplicity, transport costs are assumed to be zero. Costs are constant, so that within the union a producer will either satisfy the whole of the market for a given product, or will not produce it at all.

TABLE 2:1

Trade Creation as a Result of a Customs Union between A & B

	Production cost per unit	Non-Discriminatory Tariff of 100%	Price in A with A–B Customs Union
A	20	20	20
B	16	32	16
Rest of world	12	24	24

In this case, before the customs union is formed, A does not import the product in question. Its consumers buy A's product at the price of 20 which is less than the price including duty of the product from the alternative suppliers. If now, A and B form a customs union, the duty on B's product is eliminated, and, as shown in the third column, its price in A will be 16. A's consumers will now buy B's product instead of their own. This represents an economic and efficient expansion of B's lower-cost industry at the expense of A's higher cost industry.

A second case may now be considered in which the formation of a customs union between A and B leads instead to a less efficient use of resources in the production of the given commodity. This is illustrated in Table 2:2. It is assumed that the costs of production in the three areas are as before, but there is now, initially a tariff of only 50 per cent on imports into A. In this case the price of the imported goods from the rest of the world before the union will be 18, that of B's product 24, and that of A's product 20. Before the union, A's users will import the product of the rest of the world which will be cheapest in cost and price. If now B's product is exempted from duty in A as a result of the formation of a customs union, it will become cheapest to A's users who will consequently divert their demand from the rest of the world. The result of the formation of the customs union will be an uneconomic diversion of output from the lowest cost producer, which is the rest of the world, to B's higher cost industry. This is termed trade diversion. It results in a reduction in world income and, also, given the terms of trade, in the income of the members of the union.

TABLE 2:2

Trade Diversion as a Result of a Customs Union between A & B

	Production cost per unit	Non-Discriminatory 50% tariff	Price in A with A–B Customs Union
A	20	20	20
B	16	24	16
Rest of world	12	18	18

The amount of trade created or diverted, however, is not in itself an adequate representation of the gains or losses from a customs union, because it takes no account of the size of the differences in the production costs of different commodities in different countries. Effectively the gains and losses derived from the establishment of a customs union are represented by savings in costs resulting from the shift of purchases from higher cost to lower cost sources of supply within the union, whereas the loss relates to the extra costs of producing a commodity in the partner country instead of in the rest of the world. Thus, as Meade notes,[4] in order to ascertain whether the formation of a union represents on balance, a net gain or loss, it is necessary to consider not only the total volume of trade on which costs have been lowered and the total volume of trade on which costs have been increased, but also the extent to which costs have been raised or lowered on each unit of created or diverted trade. Taking this into account, the test becomes whether on balance the 'production' effects of integration are positive or negative.

In the limiting case where all elasticities of demand are zero and all elasticities of supply are infinite, the gains and losses can be measured by multiplying the value of each category of diverted trade by the rise in cost per unit of the trade so diverted, and multiplying the value of each category of newly created trade by the fall in the cost per unit of the trade so created.[5] In other cases the analysis becomes much more complex, and it becomes necessary to take account of intercommodity substitution and consumption effects.[6]

A second source of gain from integration which receives much less attention in the traditional theory derives from economies of scale. By producing an enlargement of the market, integration may have a three-fold effect upon the operation of individual industries. In the first place, as the size of the market increases, larger plants may be built where costs can be lowered by so doing. In the second place, a widening of the market for particular products may make it possible to reduce the variety of products in individual plants and to lengthen production runs. In the third place, in a larger market, productive processes formerly integrated in a single plant can be separated in individual plants. An increase in the size of the market can thus make possible the establishment of larger plants and also horizontal and vertical specialization, from which economies of scale can be derived.[7] Gains from such specialization can be obtained even in the absence of differences in comparative costs. If two countries produce two commodities on a small scale and at equal costs, both may gain from specialization if this makes possible the exploitation of economies of scale in the industries concerned. Since the exploitation of economies of scale may involve either a transformation of the methods of production of existing industries in the area, or a substitution of imports from outside the area, it too may be a source of trade creation or trade diversion.

3 THE RELEVANCE OF THE TRADITIONAL THEORY OF CUSTOMS UNIONS TO ECONOMIC INTEGRATION AMONG LESS DEVELOPED COUNTRIES

The traditional theory of customs unions thus considers the gains which may be achieved from reallocating given inputs of

30

existing resources under the static assumptions set out on page 27. The theory was evolved with the cases of Benelux, European integration, and thus, the more developed countries in mind. This does not necessarily mean that the theory has no relevance to less developed countries. Nevertheless, the question must be posed, as to what extent the theory is relevant also to the problems of integration among less developed countries. This may be regarded partly as a question of the extent to which on balance, trade creation can be expected to result in the conditions of less developed countries, and partly a question of whether these are the gains on which to focus attention in such countries.

In recent years there has been a growing criticism of 'conventional economics', and, in particular, of static trade theory on the grounds of its alleged irrelevance to less developed economies. For example, Seers maintains that in economies which are underdeveloped '. . . purely static propositions are mostly irrelevant, if not actually misleading'.[8] Among the writers who have specifically examined the problem of integration in less developed countries, Balassa takes the view that: 'The traditional theory of customs unions will . . . be of little usefulness for evaluating the desirability and the possible consequences of integration among less developed countries'.[9] In a similar vein, Mikesell affirms: 'I seriously question the applicability of the generalizations of the theory of customs unions which relate to complementarity, competitiveness and trade patterns, to the potential gains from regional trading arrangements for developing countries'.[10]

From the first standpoint, the question is whether the theoretical possibilities of gain from a customs union which have been discussed are in practice significant, having regard to the conditions prevailing in less developed countries. Although as Meade, Viner and others have emphasized, no prior judgements can be made about the possible effects of a hypothetical customs union, nevertheless a variety of considerations have been cited as important in determining the likely extent of the trade creating and the trade diverting effects of a customs union in particular circumstances.

Among these considerations, one of the most important is

that trade creation is thought likely to result when the member countries have little external trade in proportion to their internal production, but undertake a high proportion of that external trade with their prospective fellow members. It has also been demonstrated that the strength of the effects will depend on the sensitiveness of the trade pattern to tariff changes, and on the extent of the differences in the pattern of relative prices at which protected products are produced. Trade creation is also thought more likely, the higher are each member's pre-union duties on the others products, which is a proposition illustrated in tables 2:1 and 2:2 above.

To the extent that these propositions are valid, the immediate gains from integration in less developed countries could certainly be expected to be small. Typical less developed countries have a large external trade in relation to their domestic production whereas the actual volume of trade amongst them is small. In Chapter 3 it is noted that the exports of African countries are one fourth of total production; imports one third. On the other hand, trade among African countries is less than one-tenth of their total trade, and even within existing common markets it generally constitutes only a small fraction of the trade of the member countries with the outside world. Moreover, since the bulk of the exports of less developed countries consists of primary products which are not generally produced under protection, and which freely compete on world markets, integration cannot be expected to bring about a reallocation of resources within the union for these products. Also, a very large part of imports consist of intermediate products and capital goods (one half to two thirds) which are not produced at all in many less developed countries. In a static context, it is inappropriate to talk about trade diversion in relation to these products. It is true that there is some protected industrial production in which less developed countries are competitive with each other and for which costs may vary considerably, but its present extent is small and any short-run gains must also be small. The general conclusion is that in terms of the criterion of gain of traditional theory, a customs union among typical less developed countries would be likely to offer small opportunities of gain. Indeed the conclusion suggested by the static theory taken in conjunction with these facts is that less developed countries ought to form customs unions, if at all, with some of the advanced industrial countries. It is with these countries that they do most of their trade and the advanced countries have a big comparative advantage in most kinds of manufacture. Critics of the traditional theory do not conclude from these considerations that regional integration among less developed countries is not justifiable, but rather, that its analytical categories have limited relevance to the problems of less developed countries. On this view there are gains, but they are not the gains of static customs union analysis. It is contended that by its concentration upon the reallocation of existing resources, and on shifts in existing trade patterns, and by its purely static interpretation of comparative advantage, static theory is of little use for evaluating the desirability and consequences of integration in less developed countries.

4 DYNAMIC ARGUMENTS FOR ECONOMIC INTEGRATION AMONG LESS DEVELOPED COUNTRIES

The approach of such writers to the economics of integration among less developed countries rests on the proposition that it is necessary to look beyond existing patterns of production to what is likely to emerge in the future, when comparative advantage and trade patterns are likely to be different. Their arguments for integration are basically concerned with its contribution to economic growth and to the structural transformation of less developed countries. The approach is 'dynamic', in the sense that inputs of factors of production, in particular, of capital and labour, are taken to be variable, and the character and effectiveness of factors are assumed to be bound up with the character of production. Actual trade flows and the actual degree of competitiveness or complementarity are regarded as largely irrelevant to the opportunities of such unions, since they are not necessarily indicative of their potentialities.

This approach to integration relies in its turn on a rejection of the traditional static case for free trade with its emphasis on maximizing world productive efficiency under static conditions. In the post war world it has been widely contended that the classical theory of international trade does not illuminate the structural and dynamic problems of the less developed countries and there has been a corresponding growth of interest in analyses which seek to justify protection[11] in less developed countries in terms of its effects on growth and development.

Economic arguments for protection have a long history. In the shape of the traditional 'infant industry' arguments, justifications of protection go back at least as far as List, J. S. Mill and Carey in the nineteenth century. Well-established static arguments have been based on the existence of external economies and on the possibility of using tariffs to influence the terms of trade. Thus, the theory of the optimum tariff rests on the proposition that if a country possesses monopolistic power in world markets, appropriately chosen import and export duties can equate the relative prices of goods to domestic producers and consumers to their relative opportunity costs in international trade.[12] A much more recent static argument for protection is based on the alleged fact that in underdeveloped economies wages in manufacturing industry exceed the opportunity cost of labour which is taken to be represented by the average productivity of labour in the agricultural sector.[13] Most of the afore-mentioned arguments operate substantially within the static resource allocation analysis; they accept its analytical categories and provide merely limited qualifications to it.

Writers such as Nurkse, Myrdal, Prebisch and Seers on the other hand, justify protection and industrialization in less developed countries on the basis of a 'dynamic' approach which not merely qualifies the static analysis but claims to depart fundamentally from it in the assumptions employed.[14] Among the arguments employed by this group of economists, leading notions include the need to consider changes other than purely marginal ones operating within the existing structure, since it is contended that the problem is one of fostering structural transformation of these economies; a disposition to interpret comparative advantage as something which is not only changing but which can forcibly be changed; emphasis on the existence of unemployed resources which the traditional theory disregards; emphasis on a persistent trend towards external imbalance, dramatically portrayed in the statistical estimation of the 'trade gap'; arguments for reducing export dependence in the interests of promoting domestic stability; and in particular the favourable effects of protection on the inflow of capital. Their analysis is also typified by its emphasis on a range of factors, not readily susceptible to the tools of economic analysis, such as the contribution which industrialization can make to the development of new skills and growth facilitating changes in personal attitudes, and by its refusal to rule out purely sociological considerations.

Out of the many examples of these propositions, two may be cited here for purposes of illustration. The Raisman Commission which was set up to consider the operation of the East African Common Market contended that with respect to less developed countries 'the growth of industry under protection, displacing imports . . ., does not simply divert resources from one productive use to another equally (or perhaps) less productive, as may happen when protection is applied in a highly developed country. It draws into employment labour which would otherwise be largely unproductive, brings in capital from abroad, and generally stimulates activity'.[15]

The 'trade gap' argument for protection may be illustrated from calculations made recently by the United Nations.[16] These claim to show that, on the basis of present economic structures and policies in the developing countries, the achievement of an annual compound rate of increase of 5 per cent in their gross domestic product as a whole would imply a hypothetical current payments gap with the rest of the world of 20 billion US dollars by 1970. For Africa, the deficit would amount to 6 billion dollars. These calculations take no account of the net inflow of long term capital and aid to the developing countries. If allowance is made for these on the basis of experience in the 1960's the aggregate hypothetical gap would still amount to 11 billion dollars for the developing countries as a whole. This gap cannot materialize in fact; but to prevent it will entail increased aid, increased exports, or reduced imports entailing a reduced rate of growth. The UN-Prebisch thesis is that the less developed countries need to develop industrial exports and import substituting industries within regional groupings if the import requirements necessary to meet the assumed growth targets are to be afforded.

Taken together the group of arguments mentioned above represents the new conventional wisdom in development economics.[17] They underlie the policies advocated by the United Nations Economic Commission for Latin America (ECLA), the Economic Commission for Africa (ECA) and by the United Nations Commission for Trade and Development (UNCTAD). They are widely accepted in many less developed countries as justifying protection for the purpose of accelerating industrial development which, initially, must rest on the development of industries which produce substitutes for imports.

Integration is seen, in this context, as reinforcing these growth effects in as much as it makes it possible to undertake a given degree of industrial development more economically by taking advantage of the economies of scale and specialization within the region. In this context the concepts of trade creation and trade diversion have diminished relevance. Trade creation involves a movement towards free trade *vis-à-vis* the world as a whole; trade diversion on the other hand involves the opposite. But the very basis of the dynamic case for integration is protection, which is assumed to have growth effects. Nevertheless, while it may be inappropriate in this context to judge an integration scheme according to whether on balance it is actually or prospectively trade creating or trade diverting, the case for integration *per se*, as opposed to the case for protection, rests on the growth reinforcing effects of precisely those factors which are the subject matter of the traditional theory of customs unions, namely, specialization and economies of scale, to the extent that these are given scope to operate within the region. In this wider framework, however, both trade diversion from the outside world, and trade creation within the union can be a source of gain.

Basing the case for integration on a prior case for protection does have a very important theoretical advantage which must at this point be noted. This is that it provides a logical foundation for regional integration which is otherwise lacking. If there is no case for protection, there is in terms of pure theory, no case for integration.

5 THE DEPENDENCE OF ARGUMENTS FOR INTEGRATION ON THE CASE FOR PROTECTION

This logical difficulty has been noted by H. G. Johnson, with reference to the traditional theory. If the possibility is ruled out that integration may produce favourable changes in the terms of trade with the outside world (which is rarely a relevant consideration for less developed countries), then, as Johnson puts it, 'These arguments (however) are equally arguments for unilateral tariff elimination, which would have the advantage of entailing no losses from trade diversion".[18] Thus, although it is possible that a customs union may result in a gain in real product for the union as a whole, an even larger gain could be achieved through a simple elimination of the common external tariff. In terms of conventional customs union analysis, a customs union produces gain through trade creation—which essentially means through a movement towards free trade. On the other hand, income will be reduced through trade diversion, which means a more protectionist policy. The theory does not explain why, if trade creation is the only source of gain, a rational economic policy would not demand a move to complete free trade, if necessary, by unilateral tariff reductions. The introduction of scale economies does not remove this difficulty for if economies of scale permit economic production, it should be possible to export the product, in which event the size of the domestic market is irrelevant.[19] Thus the basic arguments do not provide a rationale for the formation of regional customs unions since, in theory, national product could be made higher by a further move to free trade. Arguments for regional economic groupings must therefore rest on a framework of analysis which either provides a rationale for protection as an aim of policy, or accepts it.

Evidently industrial development and the achievement of a more balanced industrial structure *are* major policy objectives in most African countries. This is mainly because these objectives are seen as the best way of achieving economic growth and greater stability. Nevertheless, non-economic reasons involving nationalist aspirations are also important and it is possible that many less developed countries may be willing to accept a reduction in their real product or its rate of growth, to achieve increases in industrial output or industrial employment because of the widespread identification of industrialization with welfare.

This suggests the possibility of basing an analysis of customs unions and economic integration upon such a preference for industrial production and of treating protection as a legitimate policy objective. Such a starting point has recently been made the basis of an economic theory of nationalism[20]; it also under-lies the reformulation of customs union theory undertaken by H. G. Johnson, and later, by Cooper and Massell.[21] In purely theoretical terms it suggests defining the community welfare function so as to include utility from the collective consumption of industrial production. Assuming rationality in government decision taking, this leads to the proposition that the common market authorities will tend to carry protection to the point at which the value of the marginal collective utility derived from the collective consumption of domestic industrial activity is just equal to the marginal excess private cost of protected industrial production. In doing so they will maximise the region's real income, in the sense of utility enjoyed from both private and public consumption, though not necessarily its real product (defined as total production of privately appropriable goods and services) since the maximizing of real income may require the sacrifice of a certain amount of real product to gratify the preference for collective consumption of industrial production.[22]

For the purposes of this study of integration, a rather similar standpoint will be adopted. No attempt will be made to evaluate the arguments briefly mentioned above, which contend that, in particular on dynamic assumptions, protection results in a larger product or rate of growth than free trade. To examine the conditions under which a protectionist policy would have these consequences would demand a survey of much of the theory of international trade. To examine its relevance to the countries of Africa would demand an empirical survey of its economies which would go far beyond the scope of a book on integration. Doubtless, for particular African countries, employing particu-lar kinds and levels of protection and tariff structures, such consequences would follow. But this is not a matter on which general statements can usefully be made. This problem will be avoided in this chapter by accepting protection and accelerated industrial development as legitimate policy objectives. In this way, the problems of integration *per se* can be placed in sharper focus. Thus the potential opportunities of integration will be looked at in purely relative terms. For example, the standard against which integration schemes will be assessed will be the alternative situation or process which would result if each country chose to attain its desired level or rate of growth of industrial production independently.[23]

Against this background, the case for regional integration in Africa, as in most other less developed areas, rests squarely on the proposition that, by specialization within the region, it may enable these objectives to be achieved more effectively. At the present stage of economic development of most African countries, industrialization must rest on the basis of import substitution. The small scale of most national markets renders this as an expensive process beyond a point which is soon reached. Because integration makes possible specialization on the lines of comparative advantage within the union, and also the exploitation of economies of scale, gains are possible as compared with the situation which would be reached if instead each country tried to achieve a given expansion of industry separately. Except in the unlikely special case in which the countries have identical economic structures and there are no economies of scale, integration can make possible a potential increase of real income to the region. Regional integration makes the frame of reference of import substitution the regional, rather than the national, market; it should therefore increase the potential rate of growth of manufactured output for any given level of protection. In this way it should contribute to economic growth directly and indirectly.

The factors determining the magnitude of the basic potential gain from a customs union in this context may, in this light, be briefly summarized as follows. They will be larger: (i) the stronger the preference for industry in the region; (ii) the more steeply the private cost of industrial development rises with the rate of industrial development; (iii) the greater the differences in the cost ratios of producing industrial goods in the different countries; (iv) the larger the economies of scale. To these basic gains there must be added any 'dynamic' gains which are associated with the accelerated industrial development made possible by integration.

An important implication of an approach to economic integration which accepts a preference for industrial development as a legitimate policy objective, is that it is no longer necessarily appropriate to evaluate integration schemes in terms of whether trade creation outweighs trade diversion, for gains from integration can be produced even in the context of a net balance of trade diversion for the region as a whole. To put the matter in another way, integration makes it possible for trade diversion, which may be a valid objective of policy, to be undertaken in a more efficient way.

This approach is clearly consonant with the possibility that trade diversion may be an efficient way of stimulating the rate of growth of real product in the long run. If protection makes possible an increase in real product and its rate of growth in the long run, integration may make it possible to increase the potential product or growth rate still further. On the other hand, if protection implies real costs, integration can reduce these, and thus increase real product or its rate of growth. Despite the fact that trade diversion is, in this framework, no longer a relevant concept as a criterion of gain, the central point of the traditional analysis remains. This is that specialisation produces productivity gains. These remain fundamental and basic to the case for regional economic integration, even in a dynamic context, though the standard of reference admittedly changes.

6 THE DISTRIBUTION OF THE BENEFITS AND COSTS OF INTEGRATION

The previous sections have reviewed some arguments which have been put forward in support of the view that 'traditional' theory of customs unions needs qualification before it can usefully be employed for evaluating the opportunities for regional integration among less developed economies. A further reason for qualifying the traditional theory, is that it takes no account of the way in which the potential benefits from regional integration may be distributed among the member states. But although integration may promise potential benefits to the region as a whole, the additional industries which result, and the potential income and product gains from the greater rate of growth, may be unevenly distributed among its members in the absence of deliberate measures to bring about an equitable distribution. If each member of a planned or existing union is assumed to be concerned with its own gains in terms of industry, product or growth, rather than with the gains to the region as a whole, feasible arrangements will demand the assurance of an equitable distribution of benefits. This may be necessary even on static assumptions which assume full employment, if there is a preference for industry. On dynamic assumptions this becomes even more necessary because in this framework it is conceivable that individual members of a customs union may suffer a loss of real product and real income from their membership, so that they would be better off outside. The formation of new unions is improbable unless each prospective member sees the prospect of gain. Similarly existing unions are unlikely to be durable unless each member feels it would be better off inside the union than outside in the long run, even if not during every short time period.

Such distributional considerations are in fact central to the reformulation of customs union theory undertaken by Johnson and by Cooper and Massell, and which appears to be of particular relevance to the analysis of integration among less developed countries. The preference for industry, which forms a key assumption of these analyses, is assumed to operate in each member state, so that the distribution of industry within the region is not a matter of indifference. Not the least of the merits of their approach is that, unlike traditional theory, it is able to provide a coherent explanation of why customs union negotiations are conducted as they are. For instance it explains why, in contemporary discussions of customs unions the replacement of domestic consumption by cheaper imports is commonly regarded as a cost rather than as a benefit, whereas benefits are expected to result both from trade diversion and from trade creation in favour of domestically produced products.

On the assumption that each country is concerned with its own gains in terms of industry and product, rather than those of the region as a whole interest attaches to an analysis of the circumstances under which and the extent to which market forces will bring about an equitable distribution of the costs and benefits of integration. Recent theorising on customs unions in less developed countries has been much concerned with this issue. A central theme of these analyses has been the proposition that except in favourable circumstances, natural forces operating within a free trade area or customs unions may tend to produce an inequitable distribution of its benefits in the absence of countervailing policy measures. This is because it is believed that within a single market area, the growth of manufacturing industry and its dependent economic activities, tends to become highly localised. Moreover this process is thought to operate cumulatively, so that increasing inequality is generated. To the extent that this is so, where integration is accompanied by import substitution behind a common external tariff, although the direct burden of any higher costs of production due to trade diversion will be borne by all member countries in proportion to their consumption of the product in question, the benefits, whether consisting of a larger amount of industrial development or of a growth in real income, will accrue largely to the country in which the development is concentrated.[24]

These forces have been much discussed by economists in the last few years. Myrdal refers to them as 'backwash effects', whereas Hirschman terms them 'polarization effects'[25]. Briefly the polarization effect is the process by which, after the formation of the customs union, the growth of income, industry and employment tends to concentrate in one country. The process of polarization is bound up with the determinants of locational decisions. In explaining these decisions, modern location theory tends to stress four groups of factors—natural resources, nearness to markets, transportation costs and external economies as the major determinants of industrial location. Of these, external economies are generally thought to play a dominant role where secondary manufacturing industry is concerned— whose development provides a major part of the case for regional integration. External economies are those generated by existing industries, and include such factors as the availability of public utility services, a skilled or semi-skilled labour force, and the presence of subsidiary and service industries such as banking, finance, distribution, etc. They influence location decisions partly through their indirect cost reducing effects, and partly through non-economic factors.

The initial location of industry in any region is determined by a variety of historical and economic factors. But once it has started, new industries tend to locate in the same area so as to enjoy the external economies provided by the initial industrial development. Further industrial growth strengthens these economies and makes it increasingly difficult for competing industries to operate as efficiently elsewhere. In due course, these effects are reinforced as all kinds of social facilities come to be provided in the growth centre on a more lavish scale than elsewhere—in part because of the concentration there of high income earners. In turn the availability of these facilities tends to influence the locational decisions of new investors, particularly those from overseas, and so the process feeds upon itself.

Within East Africa, Nairobi provides a striking example of the operation of this principle. The original settlement owed its location in the midst of an unprepossessing swampy plain to the accident that it was a convenient place for construction of the Uganda Railway to stop while the engineering difficulties of building over the escarpment into the Great Rift Valley of East Africa were tackled. Later on, it became the seat first of local, and then of central administration. An inflow of labour, capital and industry followed, and the Nairobi region has become today Kenya's major pole of development and a preferred location for new industries serving the whole of the East African market.

In the context of a preference for industry, these considerations suggest that customs unions are most likely to be negotiable among countries which, apart from having a similar preference for industry, have a similar degree of comparative advantage in industrial production, or, as it is sometimes put, which are countries at a similar stage of economic development. This is partly because in such circumstances, membership is likely to afford a good prospect of obtaining a share in any increase in aggregate industrial production made possible by union, and little chance of any undue loss of industrial production to other members, and partly because these circumstances are likely to facilitate agreement on the initial common tariff level. This is a different, and more realistic conclusion from that suggested by the traditional theory.

In practice, of course, the operation of the forces making for polarization between countries may be limited by a variety of factors, which may produce growth centres in each country. These include the existence of several concentrations of fixed natural resources which may serve as growing points for industrial and commercial complexes; limits to the mobility of the population; distribution costs, and finally, of course, public policy. Apart from these influences, the spontaneous dissemination of the economic benefits of economic and industrial development in a common market beyond the countries which enjoy the initial growth centres will depend on what Myrdal and Hirschman respectively term 'spread effects' and 'trickle down effects'.[26] The most important of these is the increase of the developing country's purchases from the lagging area which may be expected to take place if the economies of the region are to some degree complementary. These may offset the polarization effects wholly or in part, and will determine jointly with them the net benefits received by the less developed members of the union. The operation of these factors is discussed in detail in Chapter 3, Section 7.

Despite the operation of the polarization effect, if regional integration can produce substantial potential productivity gains to the region as a whole, it should be possible to redistribute these in such a way that all members of the region are better-off over a long run, if not necessarily in each short time period if the costs of redistribution are not too high. Incentives can thus be provided to maintain existing markets and to establish new ones. The distribution of the total market gains which would be brought about by market forces may be altered by two main means. The first is by direct income transfers from the country or countries which would otherwise benefit most. For instance a part of the tax on incomes generated in manufacturing industry located in the industrializing country may be redistributed to the exchequers of the others. However, if there exists a strong preference for industry in all member countries, such a transfer within practicable ranges of fiscal redistribution may not be acceptable as compensation for foregone industrial development. In this event, cohesion may require that the common market authorities agree on tax, investment or other policies to influence the location of industry within the market so that polarization effects are reduced—although of course, in some favourable situations where all the members of the market are at a comparable level of development, the polarization forces may not be strong, and intervention may not be necessary.

Experience in Africa certainly suggests that sharing the additional industrial growth made possible by the formation of common markets is likely to be a necessary condition of their establishment and cohesion. If additional private costs are involved in a distribution of industry policy for the region as compared with locations which would otherwise be selected, the net total market gains from integration will clearly be reduced and if the additional costs are substantial it is even conceivable that there may be no opportunities for potential gain from integration. Nevertheless, if a regional distribution of industry policy is carried out with discretion, and if the gains from integration are large enough, it should be possible to arrange things so that all members of an integration scheme would be better off than if they were to impose trade barriers against their neighbours.

The basic condition for exploiting gains from integration in a static or a dynamic context, is economic specialization within the union. Specialization makes it possible to exploit economies of scale as well as any gains from trade afforded by differences in relative costs due to divergent natural resource endowments within the region or other factors. But potential gains from productivity and growth will not necessarily be fully achieved merely as a result of abolishing tariffs and quantitative restrictions on inter-country trade. In practice a variety of other instruments will have to be harmonized, if the basic gains from market integration are to be maximized. In this survey it is possible only to comment briefly on a few which seem to be of particular relevance to African conditions. Those chosen have to do with fiscal policies, monetary policy, and policies in relation to the development of manufacturing industry and of the infrastructure, including communications and power. We shall briefly discuss aspects of these in turn. Labour mobility between the member countries of a union is disregarded in this discussion since it appears to be of small, and diminishing relevance in Africa today.

Since the distribution of benefits must be taken into account, it is necessary to consider the non-market requisites of effective integration discussed below, with this in mind. In this light for instance, optimal fiscal harmonization need not imply uniformity and it becomes desirable to think of fiscal policy as a means of influencing the location of new enterprises within the region towards locations jointly agreed by the member countries which initially may involve higher private costs. In the same way, investment concessions may be determined so that, within the region, they contribute by planned differentials to the desired distribution of industry. Likewise the loan and investment policies of development corporations and other semi-public financial institutions may be formulated with the same objective in mind. Finally, it may be that the imposition or retention of some fiscal barriers to trade between member states is a defensible policy instrument even though, from the standpoint of maximizing the productivity gains from regional specialization, it is desirable to minimize interference with free trade. This must be borne in mind in the following discussion, which for simplicity disregards these important considerations.

7 FISCAL INTEGRATION

An important policy instrument for which related integration measures are required if the primary gains from market integration are to be achieved, concerns domestic taxation and investment concessions. Fiscal integration or harmonization of methods and rates of domestic taxation is normally a requisite for effective integration because taxation differences—or even their possibility—may effect the spatial allocation of resources in a common market, and thus prevent productive resources being used in the place and on the scale which is optimal.[27] In addition, large differences in certain kinds of taxation may give rise to smuggling, and so to internal revenue losses and gains amongst the participating countries.

Some of the problems involved may be briefly illustrated with reference to indirect taxes on particular products and taxes on business profits. Apart from import duties, which are uniform in a customs union, these two kinds of taxes are the most important sources of revenue in most African countries. Considering first production taxes, a need arises on efficiency grounds for harmonising the *methods* of levying such taxes, if the rates are to be allowed to diverge in the various countries.

The two alternatives are to levy such taxes in accordance with either the principle of origin or the principle of destination. Where the principle of origin is applied, taxes are levied in the country of origin on both production for home consumption and exports to partners at the rates imposed in the producing country. Where the destination principle is applied, the tax is levied according to the tax rates appropriate to the consuming country.

If, within a union, there are markedly divergent tax rates on a particular product, and the origin principle is applied, production will be discouraged in the country imposing the higher rate. If on the other hand the destination principle is applied, then a higher tax rate in one country than in another will discourage consumption of the product there irrespective of its origin. The distribution of production between the countries of the union will therefore continue to be in accordance with comparative costs. Thus on grounds of economic efficiency, the latter system is to be recommended if tax rates are to differ, since it does not interfere with the operation of comparative advantage within the union.[28]

Nevertheless, although on efficiency grounds, the destination principle for taxation is indicated, its use does not eliminate certain practical difficulties if the members of a customs union wish to employ differing rates of production tax. The most important of these is that if large divergencies exist, smuggling will be encouraged from the area with the low tax levied on the destination principle to the area where it is high, giving rise to losses of revenue to the high taxation area. A similar problem arises if origin principle taxation is employed. If smuggling is very profitable, inter-territorial movements of goods will have to be policed which will reduce one of the administrative savings of a customs union. Thus whether destination or origin principle taxation is employed, tax differences will have to be kept down to limit the profitability of smuggling, or confined to articles whose movement can be controlled.

The taxation of business profits and the provision of investment concessions is a second area in which a need for harmonization arises in a regional integration scheme, because differences in these areas are likely, if large, to affect the initial location of new firms, and the location decisions of existing firms which contemplate expansion. Other things being equal, member countries whose business tax provisions are relatively harsh will be less attractive for new investment. Even in a simple customs union in less developed countries, this consideration may be important to the extent that investment depends on outside capital,[29] but it is likely to be particularly so in a common market since in this case tax-avoiding movements of local capital may be encouraged by tax differences.

Thus for a combination of reasons relating to economic efficiency, revenue and administrative considerations, effective regional integration normally requires some degree of harmonization of internal taxation, both as to methods and rates, if integration gains are to be optimized. But harmonization creates its own difficulties by reducing the freedom of choice of the participating countries as to the means they can employ to increase tax revenues, since major unilateral tax increases of the major taxes are then ruled out. In a union where the budgetary needs of the different countries diverge markedly, the resultant 'fiscal strait jacket' may give rise to stresses.

In the interest of effective integration it is not merely existing tax policies that must be harmonized. It is even more important to provide assurances that harmonization will continue in the future. If a firm is to establish a plant of optimal size to serve the market as a whole, it needs to be assured that its competitive position in the markets of the other member countries will not be upset by differential tax measures introduced subsequently. This argues for embodying any fiscal harmonization arrangements in an inter-state convention which might provide better safeguards against *ad hoc* unilateral fiscal changes, and so help to reduce the uncertainties which must inevitably exist in a regional integration scheme not supported by a supra-national political authority.

8 MONETARY INTEGRATION

It is possible for market integration to operate without monetary union, and for monetary union to exist and to serve useful purposes without market integration.[30] Nevertheless, there are several reasons for supposing that the full beneficial effects of market integration will only be obtained if there is, if not monetary union, at least a harmonization of monetary policies. The reasons are in part similar to those put forward already to justify fiscal harmonization. If a regional market is to have its full beneficial effects on productivity and growth it must modify the nature, scale and distribution of economic activity, and in particular of manufacturing industry. Ultimately it does this by affecting the level, and character of public and private investment. Since investment decisions are of a long-run nature, they will only be influenced in a manner which will maximize gains if those making them are assured that a free regional market will continue at least for some minimum time period, and that the region's economic relations will not be disturbed or disrupted by trade restrictions, exchange control, or exchange rate changes introduced to counter balance of payment difficulties. Thus, effective integration demands an assurance of freedom of payments—at least for current transactions, and preferably for capital transactions too—at stable rates of exchange.

The best guarantee that these conditions would be satisfied in a regional economic grouping would be provided by the use of a common currency which involves monetary union. Apart from providing certainty to business men which is an important consideration in relation to the promotion of trade and investment, such a union may also offer potential efficiency gains. For example, in a monetary union surplus resources can be transferred from one area to another where there may be a seasonal need for credit. This was exemplified in East Africa, where, towards the end of the calendar year, banking funds moved massively from Tanzania and Kenya into Uganda to assist in financing the harvesting and sale of the export crops and then moved out when the season was over. Similarly the big commercial firms could move their funds, usually concentrated in one place, to finance their branches and subsidiaries elsewhere as required. They might also borrow in one place their net requirements of credit for East Africa as a whole. Similarly, the East African Currency Board was able to provide for East Africa a very inexpensive currency service. During the last three years of its life its costs of administration averaged less than £EA200,000 per annum.

If monetary union is not practicable, then some minimal harmonization of the monetary policies of the members will be important if confidence is to be engendered in the maintenance of the above-mentioned conditions.

In principle, the monetary arrangements which accompany market integration may range from complete autonomy to complete integration. One end of the spectrum would be represented by the case of complete autonomy where each economic unit has its own currency and autonomous monetary authority. Trade between each integrated unit and with other members of the region and rest of the world is then settled ultimately through the supply of and demand for foreign exchange. Each monetary authority maintains its own external reserves and pursues its own credit and interest rate policies, subject only to its over-riding need to maintain equilibrium, in the long run, on its external account.[31] The other end of the spectrum is represented by a complete monetary union with a single monetary authority, a common currency and pooled and unallocated reserves of external assets. Between these two extremes a number of variants is conceivable including arrangements involving a common currency and harmonized monetary policies but independent external reserves, and arrangements where monetary policies are harmonized, but separate currencies and external reserves are maintained.

Where separate currencies exist, the need for harmonization of monetary policy if market integration is to be fully effective is easy to appreciate. Given free trade and convertible currencies, it would not be possible for one country in a common market indefinitely to follow a much more expansionary monetary policy than the others, relative to its supply conditions. If it tried to do so, it would find its inter-territorial imports rising as its incomes, and perhaps prices, rose faster than those of its neighbours, giving rise to a loss of its foreign exchange reserves to its partners—and possibly to some flight of capital to them. A degree of independence may be achieved to the extent that a country might employ external controls different from those employed in the rest of the region, and possibly also different quantitative restrictions on external trade, but the scope for major differences in these instruments would be limited in the absence of the detailed supervision of intra-regional transactions. If this is ruled out as inconsistent with the aims of market integration each country will be obliged in the long run to limit credit to government and commerce to an amount which is consistent with overall external balance, given the level of the common external tariff, the common exchange rate, and the (largely uniform) extra-regional trade and exchange restrictions. This would amount to *de facto* harmonization.

Even where a monetary union exists, with a single central bank, agreement among the members on the credit policies to be pursued in each separate country by the monetary authority is still needed. If credit is expanded in one member country, either as a result of granting credit to government or as a result of increasing commercial credit, this will ordinarily be accompanied in the first instance by an increase in that country's imports from the outside world (and possibly from its partners) and a reduction in the common reserves. Thus part of the burden of a more vigorous development policy by one member of the union will fall on the other members. Since there is likely to be competition for fiduciary finance and since the ultimate limitation upon its provision and, in general, on an expansion of credit will be the size of the external reserves,[32] inter-governmental agreement on credit creation in different parts of the union will be necessary. Where a common currency exists, and external reserves are not separately identified, this agreement would have to prescribe, as a minimum, the division of any fiduciary issue—i.e. central bank credit to the member governments. A more flexible approach would entail the limitation of credit creation in each member of the monetary union to whatever amount would preserve external balance in the national monetary balance of payments, over a period of years,[33] but this cannot be operated without separate identification of the currency circulation in each country and other calculations. If such a criterion were followed, the monetary situation would be similar to one with separate currencies and monetary harmonization, but the existence of the common currency in the case of the union should provide a greater assurance of the continuance of the harmonization arrangements.

9 THE NEED FOR PAYMENT AND CREDIT AGREEMENTS

Although monetary harmonization on the lines just discussed should ensure long-term equilibrium from the payments side, arrangements for extensive trade liberalization and customs unions may need the support of payments and credit arrangements in order to enable countries in temporary difficulties in their balance of payments to honour their commitments without recourse to escape clauses involving the use of quantitative or other restrictions against their partners. The elimination of trade restrictions within an integration scheme should help to strengthen the trading position of the group as a whole with the outside world to the extent that it stimulates trade expansion and the direction of production along more rational and economic lines. But the benefits may not, at the outset, be distributed equally among the participating countries. The new economic opportunities may lend themselves to more immediate exploitation by some countries than by others. Until the necessary reallocation of resources has been carried out through a redistribution of investment, a rationalization of production and, possibly, by exchange rate adjustments, some participants may suffer adverse changes in their payments positions.

To cope with transitional situations of this kind, and also with temporary disequilibria in established common markets, escape clauses from liberalization commitments must be available to countries in difficulties, but it is desirable that recourse to them should be avoided or minimized. The provision of temporary financial assistance to countries in difficulties by members who benefit most, or most rapidly, from the integration arrangements and who have the strongest interest in their maintenance may be a means of avoiding the need to introduce trade restrictions among the members.

Since indefinite credit cannot be provided to a country in persistent deficit, borrowing rights can hardly be automatic, except for moderate amounts and on a short term basis. Moreover, mutual credit provisions must not hinder any basic policy adjustments which may be needed to ensure an ultimate restoration of equilibrium in the member's payments position.

Equilibrium should not imply bringing about a payments balance between each member country and the other members of the region on the one hand, and with the rest of the world on the other, because normally the most economic and desirable trade pattern of any country involves the multilateral off-setting of deficits with some trading partners against surpluses with others. Likewise borrowing rights and lending obligations should not be related exclusively to a country's deficits or surpluses within the common market. It would thus be undesirable for a member to be debarred from borrowing, or on the other hand required to lend, solely because it exports more to its neighbours than it imports from them. The adoption of intra-regional balance of payments criteria to determine the borrowing rights and lending obligations of member states would not operate satisfactorily for less developed countries where both at present and for a long time to come members of a regional grouping are likely to carry on only a small part of their trade and capital transactions with other members, so that their overall payments position will depend mainly on their transactions with countries outside the common market. Moreover the adoption of criteria for lending and borrowing based on payment balances might result in requiring the poorer countries to lend to the richer, merely because the former happen to be in surplus. Finally, particularly if the credit arrangements were anything more than short term, there is a danger that such a system might, through its financial incentives and deterrents, promote a distortion of economically desirable trade patterns. For these reasons, member countries' needs for assistance or their ability to provide assistance to partners would have to be determined by their overall payments and reserve positions rather than their positions within the common market.

10 THE HARMONIZATION OF INDUSTRIAL POLICY

Another important area in which economic co-ordination is desirable if the benefits from market integration are to be fully exploited concerns the member countries' policies towards the operations and the development of manufacturing industries and towards the development of the economic infra-structure.

With respect to the development of manufacturing industry the need for co-ordination derives (apart from the distributional considerations discussed in Section 6 above) from the need to provide an appropriate framework for competition. Much of modern manufacturing industry is in the terminology of Sargent Florence[34] 'footloose'—which means that it is capable of being operated in a wide range of alternative locations at comparable costs. As Dell puts it: 'except in industries tied closely to highly specific natural resources that are expensive to ship, the advance of modern technology has greatly reduced the natural advantages of siting manufacturing activities in one place rather than another. By now, the advantages of one site over another are largely man-made rather than nature-made. And if advantages are made by man, they can also be changed by man in accordance with rational and deliberate planning criteria.'[35] Although this may be true, this statement disregards what is normally the real problem, which is the cost of infra-structure investment necessary to make such industries viable.

Nevertheless, where a suitable infra-structure exists, since footloose industries may lack any important natural locational advantages, they may not be set up on the scale made feasible by their access to protected markets in the other countries of the group unless there is some assurance that similar enterprises will not be encouraged by artificial inducement to establish themselves in those countries until the market has grown sufficiently large to support the additional output. In the East African Common Market there are several examples of artificially induced competition. With government encouragement, wheat mills, and pyrethrum factories have been replicated even though the original factories located in Kenya could for a long time have continued to serve the common market. For similar reasons several cement works, all operating at less than full capacity, now exist in East Africa.

To avoid the waste of resources entailed in this kind of situation, which must ultimately have a bearing on the character of future investment decisions, an agreed pattern of investment concessions may be of help. But since there are many less direct ways of bringing about the same ends, the avoidance of this kind of development would demand co-ordination of policies in several fields. It would be necessary, for instance, to ensure that the investment decisions of public development corporations are guided by economic considerations and that their operations are not made a vehicle for the subsidization of unprofitable enterprises. Likewise, in relation to development undertaken wholly by the private sector, it would be necessary to ensure that such factors as unilateral quantitative restrictions, or a threat of their imposition, are not employed to foster developments which would not be profitable, given the agreed common level of tariff protection.

One way of providing the necessary assurances would be for the countries forming the union to operate a system of industrial licensing to back up an agreed sharing of industries in which economies of scale were important. Joint governmental financial participation in common-market based industries, either directly or through a regional development bank, might also be of value in limiting the unilateral provision of artificial inducements to the establishment of industries. Ultimately the establishment of a comprehensive code of trading conduct may be the best solution if the operation of the common market from this point of view were to be as fully beneficial as possible, though the administrative and judicial problems of operating such a code would doubtless be enormous. Such a code might also deal with monopolistic practices by private and public enterprises, which again may hinder the full exploitation of the primary gains from regional integration. On grounds such as these some co-ordination of the policies of the separate governments towards the operation and the establishment of private manufacturing industry is called for if the gains from scale are to be fully exploited, and indeed, the gains from specialization.

On different grounds it can be argued that a co-ordination of

55

development plans in the public sector is also desirable in order to facilitate the co-ordinated development of complementary resources made possible by the development of the common market. This is particularly important in relation to infrastructure investment in communications, power, and water development, etc. These are activities in which economies of scale, external economies and interdependences are likely to be large, so that co-ordination may affect the viability of particular projects. Co-ordination of key projects may enable a group of projects to be undertaken profitably for the regional market if carried out simultaneously, whereas in isolation, none would be feasible. For instance, it may not be worthwhile carrying out a power project in one country, and a railway construction in a second unless industry is developed in a third to make use of the railway and the power. But the industrial development in the third country may itself not be feasible unless the infra-structure facilities are provided. In isolation none of these projects may be started because of the risk that the others may not be undertaken at the appropriate time. In this kind of situation joint planning of development to co-ordinate initiatives and the phasing, character, and location of development has obvious merits. A variety of possible ways of effecting such co-operation may be devised ranging from a regional investment board, jointly financed, which would have the responsibility of planning and undertaking investment in infra-structure, and possibly in some industries which serve the common market, to joint boards established to deal, on a regional basis, with particular kinds of activity such as power, irrigation, etc. But if each country insists on retaining sole responsibility for planning, financing and operating its own development projects, a minimum condition for the effective exploitation of integration gains will be consultation and harmonization with respect to key development projects.

11 CONCLUSION

The traditional theory of customs unions is only of limited applicability for understanding the rationale and problems of integration in less developed countries in terms of its criterion of gain. There are several reasons why this is so.

Firstly, the traditional static theory does not provide a logical basis for choosing integration rather than free trade. Arguments for integration in less developed countries must rest on a case for protection. Such a case may be built on the basis of static considerations, but, as the theory of integration has developed in relation to less developed countries, the case is mainly a dynamic one. Thus the theory minimizes the gains from integration with respect to the allocation of existing resources, and concentrates attention upon the effects of integration on such factors as the inflow of foreign investment, external economies, the level of utilization of growing supplies of factors, balance of payments considerations and general dynamic factors concerned with innovation and enterprise.

Secondly, in the context of a case for protection, or assuming this to be a legitimate policy objective in less developed countries, it is evident that the central criterion of benefit in the static model which turns on the distinction between trade diversion and trade creation, is inappropriate. Within a protectionist context, trade diversion is of the essence and, particularly when the assumptions are 'dynamic', the emphasis on income gains becomes a factor of importance which in some cases may outweigh any considerations of diversion.

Thirdly, the traditional theory of integration has little to say about the distribution of benefits within the union. In the theory of integration in less developed countries however, this aspect is central, for the members are primarily concerned with their own welfare, rather than with that of the group. In practice, customs union or integration arrangements commonly contain provisions designed to ensure that the growth of production in the union does not concentrate in one or a few countries at the expense of the rest.

Nevertheless, the fact that the traditional theory of customs unions has been largely directed towards the analysis of integration problems under static assumptions does not mean that it has no relevance for less developed countries where the focus of interest is growth and development. The effects of integration in a dynamic context, as opposed to the effects of protection *per se*, rest essentially on the contribution which economic specialization can make within the region; this is also the rationale of the static theory. In a dynamic context, integration provides *within the area* for the more effective operation of the principle of comparative advantage, and the exploitation of scale economies.

So long as these economies are not absorbed by uneconomic industry locations within the region, this should enable any given degree of industrialization to be carried out at lower cost and for any direct or indirect growth effects of protection to be reinforced. Resource allocation considerations are not to be discounted even in a dynamic context. In the case of integration, the additional potential gains which it may produce as compared with the outcome in separately protected markets, are dependent on the basic gains from specialization. Thus, although the criterion of gain for customs union analysis may be different for less developed economies in the sense that the balance of 'trade creation' and 'trade diversion' may be irrelevant, the basic source of gain is the same. The contrast between the traditional theory of integration and what is alleged to have replaced it cannot usefully be drawn too sharply.

REFERENCES: CHAPTER 2

1 See R. G. Lipsey, 'The Theory of Customs Unions: A General Survey', *The Economic Journal*, September 1960, p. 496.

2 There is a large literature on this subject. The basic works are: J. Viner, *The Customs Union Issue*, Carnegie Endowment for International Peace, New York, 1950; J. E. Meade, *The Theory of International Economic Policy*, Volume 11: Trade and Welfare, Oxford University Press, London, 1955; J. E. Meade, *The Theory of Customs Unions*, North Holland Publishing Company, Amsterdam, 1965. Apart from Lipsey (*op. cit.*), one of the most useful recent general surveys is H. G. Johnson, 'The Economic Theory of Customs Unions', in *Money, Trade and Economic Growth*, Allen and Unwin, London, 1962.

3 For an exposition of this basic aspect of trade theory, see, for instance, J. Viner, *Studies in the Theory of International Trade*, Harper, New York, 1937.

4 Meade, *Theory of Customs Unions*, pp. 34–6.

5 Meade, *op. cit.*, p. 36.

6 This refinement is due to Lipsey, Meade, Gehrels and others. It is not discussed here. See, however, Meade, *op. cit.*, pp. 37–43; Lipsey, *op. cit.*; F. Gehrels, 'Customs Unions from a Single Country Viewpoint', *Review of Economic Studies*, No. 63, 1956–7. Lipsey has argued that, taking

these effects into account, trade diversion can raise welfare. See, however, C. A. Cooper and B. F. Massell, 'A New Look At Customs Union Theory', *Economic Journal*, December 1965, for a convincing critique of Lipsey's analysis.

7 Economies of scale may be derived from a change in the size of the firm or industry, given the aggregate supply of factors (economies internal to the firm or industry) or they may be bound up with the growth of the economy as a whole (external economies). Economies of scale thus provide a bridge between an analysis on static assumptions and an analysis on dynamic assumptions of the kind discussed below, in which factor supplies and the level of employment as a whole are treated as variables.

8 D. Seers, 'The Limitations of the Special Case', *Bulletin of the Oxford Institute of Economics and Statistics*, May 1963, p. 83.

9 B. Balassa, *Economic Development and Integration*, CEMLA, Mexico, 1965, p. 35.

10 See R. F. Mikesell, 'The Theory of Common Markets as Applied to Regional Arrangements Among Developing Countries', in *International Trade Theory in a Developing World*, edited by Roy Harrod and D. C. Hague, Macmillan, London, 1963, p. 213.

11 The term protection is usually interpreted to mean a tax on imports. However, the term may appropriately be applied to any policy which raises the price received by domestic producers of an importable commodity above the world market price. This result can be achieved by a variety of devices such as import restrictions, exchange controls, multiple exchange rates and export subsidies. These devices are not equally efficient in terms of their effects on productivity and welfare. In practice, export subsidization, which may be the most efficient device to employ, may be ruled out by international obligations under GATT, or other practical limitations. We shall assume that the protective device to be employed to stimulate industrialization is an import tariff.

12 For a brief discussion of these arguments and citations see, for example, G. Haberler, *A Survey of International Trade Theory*, Princeton University, International Finance Section, Department of Economics, 1961, pp. 52–6.

13 On these and other arguments for protection based on domestic distortions, see H. G. Johnson, 'Optimal Trade Intervention and Domestic Distortions', in *Trade, Growth and the Balance of Payments*, Essays in Honour of Gottfried Haberler, North-Holland Publishing Company, Amsterdam, 1965.

14 See, for example, R. Nurkse, *Patterns of Trade and Development*, Blackwell, Oxford, 1962; Gunnar Myrdal, *Economic Theory and Underdeveloped Regions*, Duckworth, London, 1957; UNECLA, *The Economic Development of Latin America and its Problems*, New York, 1950; Seers, 'A Model of Comparative Rates of Growth in the World Economy', *Economic Journal*, March, 1962. There are, of course, many differences of emphasis in the various arguments.

15 See *East Africa, Report of the Economic and Fiscal Commission*, 1961, London, HMSO Cmnd: 1279, p. 24, para. 81.

16 See *UN Conference on Trade and Development*, New York, 1964, Vol. VI, Part 1, pp. 92–7.

17 The term 'conventional wisdom' is J. K. Galbraith's (see *The Affluent Society*).

18 See H. G. Johnson, 'An Economic Theory of Protectionism', *Journal of Political Economy*, June 1965, p. 280.

19 If economies of scale would reduce costs below the level reached on the national market, but not below the world level, there is a special kind of trade creation-trade diversion problem.

20 See A. Breton, The Economics of Nationalism, *Journal of Political Economy*, August 1964.

21 See H. G. Johnson, *op. cit.*, *Journal of Political Economy*, and C. A. Cooper and B. F. Massell, 'Toward a General Theory of Customs Unions for Developing Countries', *Journal of Political Economy*, October 1965.

22 See H. G. Johnson, *An Economic Theory of Protection*, p. 259. The distinction between real product and real income is a useful heuristic device, but it leaves some important problems aside.

23 Clearly there is in practice not just one alternative situation or process but a whole range, depending in part on the structure and level of the tariff which is assumed to be otherwise chosen. This is one of the problems which makes customs unions and economic integration so difficult to evaluate. In the discussion of the existing East African Common Market in Chapter 4, the alternative employed is a hypothetical situation in which each of the three countries imposes a tariff identical with that of the existing common market. It therefore gives its results on the basis of the existing tariff structure. This is a convenient simplification, but it is most unlikely that the optimal tariff from the standpoint of Tanzania or Uganda for, instance, would be identical with the present common market tariff.

24 It is sometimes said that the second reason for an uneven distribution of benefits is that with import substitution all countries lose customs revenue but, depending on the fiscal arrangements, the revenue gains from the taxes on income generated from domestic development may accrue largely to the country in which the development is concentrated. This way of putting the matter obscures the issues. Any primary loss is due to the higher costs of protected industrial production. In a simple model this will be equal to the loss of customs revenue. For African countries in general, customs revenue derived from imports from outside Africa represents merely a transfer of income from the taxpayer to the government. It must not be overlooked, however, that the formation of a customs union normally entails a reduction in the customs revenue raised by the countries forming the union, irrespective of whether real product is increased or lowered. Given the administrative obstacles which may exist to the develop-

ment of an effective system of income taxation, the development of other forms of taxation to replace this lost revenue may be difficult especially in the context of a parallel need for fiscal harmonization.

25 See G. Myrdal, *op. cit.*, Chapter 3, p. 27. Also A. O. Hirschman, *The Strategy of Economic Development*, Yale University Press, Newhaven 1958 Chapter 10, pp. 187–190.

26 See Myrdal and Hirschman, loc. cit.

27 The whole question of tax harmonisation is a difficult one and there is a growing literature. Carl S. Shoup (ed.), *Fiscal Harmonisation in Common Markets*, Vol. 1 and 2, Columbia University Press, 1967. Chapter 1, Vol. 1 by D. Dosser, *Economic Analysis of Tax Harmonisation*, is particularly important.

28 A detailed analysis of the problems may be found in '*Rapport sur les problèmes posés par les taxes sur le chiffre d'affaires dans le marché commun*' (The Tinbergen Report, Luxembourg, 1963).

29 Whether differences in business taxation in a common market will affect the spatial distribution of foreign investment will depend on the treatment of overseas income in the foreign investor's home country. Many countries (UK, USA, Japan and Germany) permit foreign income taxes to be credited fully against their own taxation. The result is that where the effective rate of taxation in the taxpayer's home country is greater than the effective rate in the country in which the investment is undertaken, and the income originates, the total income tax burden borne is the same regardless of its geographical origin. The importance of differences in business taxation in a common market therefore depends on the source of the foreign investment and the nature and extent of double taxation arrangements.

30 Outside Africa, economic integration without monetary union is found in both EEC and in Latin America. The former British colonies in West Africa shared a currency union under the Currency Board System, but there was no market or fiscal integration. Likewise the former French West African Colonies currently have a monetary union but there is little economic integration. The advantages of monetary union include economy in the use of reserves and economies of administration.

31 After taking into account long term capital imports.

32 For a discussion of the factors to be taken into account in determining the desirable level of foreign exchange reserves, see The Adequacy of Monetary Reserves, *Staff Papers*, International Monetary Fund, Washington D.C., October 1953.

33 This approach is followed in UDEAC. See Chapter 5, pp. 201–8.

34 See P. S. Sargent Florence, *The Logic of British and American Industry*, Routledge and Kegan Paul, London, 1953, p. 40.

35 See Sidney Dell, *A Latin American Common Market*, Oxford University Press, London, 1966, p. 69.

CHAPTER 3

THE ECONOMIC SETTING IN AFRICA AND THE PROBLEMS OF INTEGRATION

1 INTRODUCTION

The previous chapter discussed the economics of integration in less developed countries in quite general terms. A realistic appreciation of the opportunities, problems and prospects of economic integration in Africa whether on a continental or a regional basis must be based upon a knowledge of the continent's economic structure and its recent economic and political development. This chapter focuses attention on those aspects which have an important bearing on economic co-operation.

In terms of physical conditions the most striking features of Africa are its vast size and great diversity of climatic conditions and topography. Including Madagascar and the other African islands it has a total area of about eleven million square miles which makes it slightly larger than the whole of the North American continent including Greenland or as large as South America and Australia combined. Within its bounds one finds glacier topped mountains and tropical beaches, rain forests and deserts, and a large amount of elevated savannah capable, under favourable conditions, of supporting semi-tropical and temperate agriculture. In 1964 the population of Africa was about 300 million or about 9 per cent of the total world population. Population densities are fairly low but much of the continent is desert or arid land and cannot support a large population.

The most striking feature of Africa's political geography is the large number of independent states which it contains. Nearly all of these have been established in the course of the post-war withdrawal of the former colonial powers. It is astonishing to recall that as late as the early 1950's there were only four independent states in Africa—Egypt, Ethiopia, Liberia and the Union of South Africa. At the end of 1966 there were forty and

TABLE 3:1

Africa: Basic Economic Data

	Population (1964)		AREA (a)			Gross National Prod. per Capita (b) £	Electric Power per Capita 1964 KWH per Year	Literacy (a)	Pupils as % of Pop. 1963	Health—People per Doctor 1963	Export Trade—Main Exports
	Total Mns.	Rate of Growth 1958/64 %	Total thousand sq. miles	% of Total Area	Acres per Capita						
ALGERIA	11·0	0·9	920	19	10	100	102	9	12	8,700	Petroleum
ANGOLA	5·1	1·4	481	n.a.	n.a.	n.a.	43	n.a.	2	8,300	Coffee
BURUNDI	2·5	2·5	11	n.a.	n.a.	21	5	n.a.	4	68,000	Coffee
CAMEROON	5·1	2·1	183	35	9	36(c)	210	5-10	12	30,000	Cocoa/coffee
CENTRAL AFRICAN REP.	1·3	2·2	238	n.a.	n.a.	45(c)	15	5-10	8	33,000	Cotton/coffee
CHAD	3·3	1·5	496	47	48	22(c)	5	5	4	62,000	Cotton
CONGO (BRAZZAVILLE)	0·8	1·6	132	n.a.	n.a.	45(c)	56	20	21	15,000	Wood/diamonds
CONGO (KINSHASA)	15·3	2·1	906	22	8	31	159	50	14	30,000	Copper
DAHOMEY	2·3	2·9	45	n.a.	n.a.	14	7	20	5	21,000	Palm products
ETHIOPIA	22·2	1·8	457	59	9	16	8	5	2	96,000	Coffee/hides
GABON	0·5	1·6	103	n.a.	n.a.	106(c)	70	5-10	15	5,700	Wood/petroleum
GAMBIA	0·3	2·4	4	n.a.	n.a.	30(d)	25	n.a.	4	16,000	Groundnuts
GHANA	7·5	2·7	92	22	2	75	69	25	16	12,000	Cocoa

GUINEA	3·4	2·8	95	n.a.	n.a.	21	43	10	6	21,000	Aluminium/bananas
IVORY COAST	3·8	3·3	125	n.a.	n.a.	66	48	20	9	19,000	Coffee/cocoa
KENYA	9·1	2·9	225	10	2	31(e)	55	20–25	10	9,700	Coffee/tea
LIBERIA	1·0	1·4	43	19	5	47	212	5–10	8	11,000	Iron ore/rubber
LIBYA	1·6	3·6	679	6	21	106	98	30	12	4,400	Petroleum
MALAGASY REP.	6·2	3·1	228	65	16	27	22	30–35	10	9,700	Coffee/vanilla
MALAWI	3·9	2·8	46	30	2	14	11	7	10	35,000	Tea/tobacco
MALI	4·5	2·3	465	n.a.	n.a.	21	6	5	3	40,000	Livestock/groundnuts
MAURITANIA	0·9	2·2	419	n.a.	n.a.	n.a.	n.a.	1–5	2	27,000	Livestock
MOROCCO	13·0	2·8	171	42	4	59	97	13	9	9,700	Phosphates
MOZAMBIQUE	6·9	1·3	302	n.a.	n.a.	n.a.	27	n.a.	6	18,000	Cotton
NIGER	3·3	3·4	489	25	12	14	5	5	1	65,000	Groundnuts
NIGERIA	56·4	2·0	357	24	1	30	18	20	6	34,000	Groundnut products
RWANDA	3·0	3·1	10	n.a.	n.a.	n.a.	4	n.a.	12	144,000	Coffee/minerals
SENEGAL	3·4	2·3	76	40	6	56(d)	58	5	7	20,000	Groundnuts
SIERRA LEONE	2·2	0·9	28	81	7	25	38	10	6	19,000	Diamonds/iron ore
SOMALIA	2·4	2·9	246	34	28	14	5	5	1	30,000	Bananas/livestock
REP. OF SOUTH AFRICA	17·5	2·4	472	83	15	160	1,738	40–45	15	1,900	Gold
SOUTHERN RHODESIA	4·1	3·3	150	17	4	74	927	20–25	15	7,700	Tobacco
SUDAN	13·2	2·8	968	12	6	36	13	10	4	29,000	Cotton
TANZANIA	10·3	1·9	363	28	11	24(e)	19	5–10	5	21,000	Sisal/cotton
TOGO	1·6	2·8	22	42	4	25	17	5–10	10	34,000	Coffee/cocoa
TUNISIA	4·6	2·0	48	40	3	62	80	25–35	14	10,000	Olive oil/wine
UGANDA	7·4	2·5	94	12	1	27(e)	46	25	8	13,000	Coffee/cotton
UNITED ARAB REP.	28·9	2·7	386	3	0·2	44	170	30	14	2,500	Cotton
UPPER VOLTA	4·8	2·5	106	n.a.	n.a.	14	4	8	2	63,000	Livestock
ZAMBIA	3·6	2·9	288	41	21	59	198	20–25	10	8,900	Copper

SOURCES: *United Nations Statistical Yearbook 1965*.

(a) From estimates made for the US Mutual Defense and Development Programme.
(b) *Ibid.* Mainly for 1962 except for items marked (c) for which see Chapter 4, (d) see Chapter 5 and (e) see Chapter 3.

65

E

only a handful of colonial territories remains. Someone has remarked that Africa has the highest ratio of frontiers to total area of any continent. Whether this is so or not, it certainly contains a number of states which are very small in terms of population and natural resources.[1] Indeed of the independent countries of Africa only eight have a population higher than ten million, more than half have a population below 5 million, and there are even several—for instance Congo (Brazzaville), Gambia and Gabon which have a population of less than a million.

For the most part the political boundaries of the new states follow those of their colonial predecessors and coincide neither with natural, geographic, economic nor ethnic divisions. They are the product simply of the arbitrary divisions which were agreed upon amongst the former colonial powers during the scramble for Africa which took place towards the end of the nineteenth century. Only in a few cases has the withdrawal of the colonial powers since the Second World War been accompanied by political changes resulting in the disappearance of arbitrary boundaries. Thus British and Italian Somaliland were joined to make the new state of Somalia. Eritrea was joined to Ethiopia, first in a federation and eventually as part of a unitary state. The three separately administered parts into which Morocco was formerly divided were joined when Morocco gained independence in 1956. The British trust territory of Togoland was absorbed by Ghana. In the British Cameroons one part—the former north—joined Nigeria, while the South became the small western member of the new two-state Federal Republic of Cameroon. On the other side of the picture, the huge administrative federations in French West Africa and French Equatorial Africa were broken up on independence into thirteen constituent states, and Ruanda-Urundi severed its economic links with the Congo and became two separate states. On balance, therefore, decolonization has so far resulted in the fragmentation of an already over-divided continent.

From the standpoint of economic co-operation, these political changes are much more serious than a mere counting of states might suggest. Of course, in colonial days, frontiers were just as artificial and almost as numerous as they are today.

66

The point is that in many cases they did not prevent close co-operation, at least among the territories of any one colonial power. The metropolitan powers could and did insist on close co-operation between their different territories in such fields as money, communications, education etc. Admittedly this was done in most cases for reasons of administrative economy rather than for the purpose of promoting economic development, but it often facilitated economic gain within the limits of the rather restricted approach to development which was then practised.

With the departure of the colonial powers, the economic disadvantages of the present boundaries become in a sense much more serious while at the same time, with independence, the pressure for development has become much more acute. The difficulties of bringing about and maintaining co-operation should not be underestimated in a situation in which it depends on having each country separately and at least in the long run, satisfied with its deal, and in which objective demonstrations of the long-term advantages of co-operation are unfortunately much more difficult to find than evidence of its short term disadvantages.

2 THE ECONOMIC CHARACTERISTICS OF AFRICAN ECONOMIES

The present economic structure of African economies on to which attempts are being made to graft fresh integration arrangements and reshape existing ones, is, of course, a product of the continent's economic history. In terms of the development of a modern economy this history is relatively short—for most parts of Africa less than a hundred years. Over this period two main patterns of development can be distinguished which have an important bearing on the present background to economic integration. One group of economies developed mainly on the basis of a growth of commercial mining or European agriculture, stimulated by large scale capital inflows. These economies were characterized by the existence of European settler communities and Africans participated in economic life mainly as wage earners. Algeria, Rhodesia, Zambia, Kenya and the Congo are countries in this category. A second group of economies, for instance, Ghana and Uganda, grew on the basis of the development of a peasant agriculture, producing cash crops for export. Of course this dichotomy is artificial and to some extent both kinds of development are found in many African countries but as a first approximation it is useful.[2]

The bearing of these different patterns of development on integration is that on the whole the economies falling into the first group have become more industrialized and have enjoyed faster rates of growth than the latter, in part because throughout the colonial period foreign capital investment was concentrated upon them.[3] The second group of economies on the other hand is characterized by slower rates of growth, simpler techniques of production and a more even income distribution. Thus within the background of the generally low level of development which characterizes the African continent there are already economies which, in terms of techniques and infra-structures, are substantially more advanced than most. Both theory and experience suggest that, with free trade, economic development could be expected further to polarize in such a situation in the absence of countervailing policy measures. Economic unions between countries of the former kind and their more backward neighbours call for safeguards if the latter are to benefit. It is no accident that Kenya, Rhodesia and some of the other more developed African economies with modern industrial enclaves have found their neighbours reluctant to integrate their markets without wider agreement on the allocation of benefits.

The divergent historical development of African states to which attention has just been drawn is evidently bound up with the great variety of climatic conditions, resource endowments and population densities which are found in the continent. Despite this great diversity, most African economies do share, in varying degree, a number of important economic characteristics.

In the first place as table 3:1 indicates, they are very poor. The total income of the continent measured in terms of what is admittedly both conceptually and statistically a rather imperfect yardstick[4] was in 1962 no more than £9,300 mn. This is about one half of the aggregate income of the United Kingdom and only twice that of Mexico. In terms of income per head this means a range (excluding South Africa) from as little as £14 in Niger to £75 in Ghana. South Africa's *per capita* income is very much higher than any of the others at £160. These estimates include subsistence production—that is, agricultural production which is produced not for sale but for consumption within the household. If only monetary income is included these figures would have to be substantially reduced, because about one third of the continent's output originates in subsistence agriculture. The individual national markets provided by cash incomes of the present order are in most cases clearly very small. Indeed, the money income for the 'median' African country is probably less than the income of an English town of 100,000 inhabitants.[5] Other indicators of economic development included in table 3:1 relate to education, health and power consumption.[6] The more complete picture gained from these indicators is varied but generally indicative of poverty.

In the second place, African market economies are heavily concentrated on primary production—mainly of agrarian products—for export. For the continent as a whole, exports amount to about one fourth and imports to one third of its output so that its overall foreign trade dependence is very high. Export output in most countries is not well diversified but highly concentrated on a few commodities. For Africa as a whole about two-thirds of export earnings come from agricultural products, and four of these—cocoa, coffee, cotton and oilseeds produce a large part of this revenue. A few minerals and metals—gold, copper and diamonds—account for most of the rest. The main exports of the different countries are summarised in table 3:1.

Bearing in mind the substantial amount of non-marketed agricultural production, the dominant importance of agriculture for most African economies is clear. A corollary of this is that industrial output is relatively insignificant. At present Africa accounts for only about two per cent of world industrial production. Much of this is concerned with the processing of mineral products, and is concentrated mainly in South Africa, Zambia, Rhodesia and the Congo. Manufacturing industry proper is still in its early stages, except in South Africa and to a lesser extent in Rhodesia. In other countries the limited range of industrial production is concerned mainly with the simple

TABLE 3 : 2

The Relative Significance of Intra-African Trade in the Trade of African Countries with the World, 1961

(In millions of US dollars and in percentages)

Countries	Imports, c.i.f.			Exports, f.o.b.		
	Total world	Africa	Per cent	Total world	Africa	Per cent
MOROCCO	446	15	3·4	342	38	11·1
ALGERIA	1,024	55	5·4	369	19	5·1
TUNISIA	210	6	2·9	110	5	4·5
LIBYA	149	4	2·7	18	0·3	1·7
UAR (EGYPT)	684	14	2·0	485	23	4·7
SUDAN	234	24	10·3	179	12	6·7
ETHIOPIA	95	2	2·1	74	6	8·1
SOMALIA	32	3	9·4	26	1	3·8
SENEGAL	171	24	14·0	149	44	29·5
MALI	47	18	38·3	39	28	71·7
MAURITANIA	44	13	29·5	14	13	93·0
IVORY COAST	173	26	15·0	182	35	19·2
UPPER VOLTA	32	12	37·5	19	17	89·5
DAHOMEY	27	6	22·2	17	3	17·6
NIGER	21	8	38·1	22	13	59·1
GAMBIA	13	1	7·7	10	0·2	2·0
SIERRA LEONE	91	2	2·2	82	0·6	0·7
GHANA	414	41	9·9	322	12	3·4
TOGO	26	4	15·3	20	3	15·0
NIGERIA	627	18	2·9	483	10	2·1
CAMEROON	96	15	15·6	98	7	7·1
EQUAT. CUSTOMS UNION	173	23	13·3	127	23	18·1
CONGO (KINSHASA)	133	13	9·8	117	14	12·0
ANGOLA	114	3	2·7	135	11	8·2
RHODESIA AND NYASALAND	434	13	3·0	579	21	3·6
MOZAMBIQUE	129	6	4·7	89	7	7·6
MADAGASCAR	103	5	4·9	78	12	15.4
REUNION	58	6	10·3	37	2	5·4
MAURITIUS	68	4	5·9	62	1	1·6
ZANZIBAR	15	5	33·3	12	1	8·3
TANGANYIKA	141	32	22·7	146	11	7·5
KENYA	255	26	10·2	164	52	31·7
UGANDA	95	22	23·2	137	25	18·2
Total listed countries	6,372	470	7·3	4,743	470	9·8

SOURCE : *United Nations Trade and Development*, Vol. VII, p. 259. N.Y. 1964.

processing of foodstuffs and raw materials for domestic consumption and export, and the production of textiles, simple household goods and construction materials such as cement. Few African countries possess any important heavy industries.

A third characteristic of African countries which is very relevant to integration and which is closely bound up with their present structural characteristics is the, on the whole, small extent of their trade with each other. Estimates[7] for 1964 put recorded intra-African trade at £210mn. or about 7 per cent of total African exports. Moreover, since 1960 there has been a tendency for this figure to drop from 9 per cent in 1960, to 7 per cent in 1963 and 1964. One of the reasons for this decline is that products like petroleum, iron ore and diamonds account for an increasing share of total African exports, but make hardly any appearance in intra-African trade.

Although intra-African trade thus plays a very modest role in the economy of Africa as a whole, it is nonetheless of major significance for several individual countries. The considerable differences in the relative importance to different countries of intra-African trade in 1961 are shown in Table 3:2. It can be seen that it is particularly important for a number of landlocked countries like Mali, Upper Volta and Niger which depend heavily on exports to neighbouring countries of such products as live animals, and fish. In addition, intra-African trade is relatively important for a few other countries, such as the three East African countries, where special institutional arrangements have encouraged it. Three other prominent features of the structure of intra-African trade are worth mentioning in conclusion. One is that a very high proportion of this trade has hitherto been accounted for by a small group of countries. Disregarding the trade of South Africa and the Rhodesia, Zambia and Malawi group, which accounts for over 40 per cent of both total exports and imports, about 35 per cent of total intra-African imports were absorbed in 1961 by four countries (Algeria, Ghana, Tanganyika and Kenya) and five countries (Kenya, Morocco, Ivory Coast, Mali and U.A.R.) were responsible for 36 per cent of total intra-African exports.[8] The second prominent feature of the trade is its marked clustering within four sub-regions—north west, north east, west and central.[9] These sub-regions are areas of the continent where population, production, and transport facilities are highly concentrated, and which are isolated from each other by reason of the poor transport links between them. The third prominent characteristic of the trade is that a large share is represented by foodstuffs. About two thirds of the total value of the trade is in foodstuffs, if South Africa is excluded. If unrecorded trade were included, the share of foodstuffs would be even higher.

TABLE 3:3

Commodity Structure of Intra-African Trade

	1960 (excluding trade to & from South Africa) %	1961 (including trade to & from South Africa) %
Food, beverages and tobacco	59	38
Crude Materials	15	15
Fuels	3	2
Manufactures	23	45
Total £75mn.	100	£190mn. 100

SOURCE: *Intra-African Trade*, E.C.A. 1963

Many of the foodstuffs are commodities of the kinds which made up the traditional intra-regional trade which came into existence in Western Africa in remote times in the course of a natural division of labour between the upland savannahs and the coastal forest belt, two areas with complementary conditions of agricultural production. When Leo Africanus arrived in Africa early in the sixteenth century, this trade was already flourishing and its extent no doubt partly explains the high degree of prosperity attained by the kingdoms of Ghana, and Mali and the Empire of Songhai.[10]

The very low level of intra-African trade to which attention has just been drawn must not be assumed necessarily to indicate the most economic allocation of the continent's productive resources. It is to some extent an historical product of an infra-structure in transportation, banking and finance which was developed primarily by European interests to promote their own food and raw material imports and to provide outlets for their exports. This is not to say that this pattern has not resulted in great gains for Africa or that any other pattern would have been possible but a correction of the colonial bias towards extra-African trade in the interests of developing trade within the continent may be overdue.

3 MONETARY AND TRADE ARRANGEMENTS IN AFRICA AND THEIR BEARING ON INTEGRATION

Two other aspects of the present economic setting in Africa which might be expected to have an important bearing on trade and integration are the diverse monetary systems and the complex system of preferential arrangements which exist between many African countries and between them and states outside the continent.

Currently, Africa is divided into about twenty-five different currency areas, most of which have strong links with a world trading currency—in most cases the franc or the pound sterling. Usually these currencies circulate in only one country but in French-speaking West and Equatorial Africa a common currency circulates in the member countries of the two currency unions. All currencies which are linked to the franc have a fixed exchange rate with the metropolitan franc and are transferable freely among many franc zone countries. The currencies which are linked to sterling likewise have a fixed exchange rate with the pound, but a more divergent pattern of exchange controls restricts their interchangeability with other sterling currencies. In East Africa there is also de facto interchangeability of the three separate currencies. African franc and sterling currencies are not freely interchangeable with each other.

At the present time most African trade—both intra-African and extra-African—is stipulated in the convertible currencies of major trading countries (sterling, francs or dollars). Thus the earnings of one country can be readily converted into other currencies needed for payments purposes. The most notable exception is that a part of the French franc earnings of the countries belonging to the franc zone is not so convertible. This does not mean that there are no payments difficulties currently hindering intra-African trade, but these have arisen in cases in which countries are in overall balance of payments difficulties necessitating exchange and trade restrictions. So far, however, such difficulties have been of small importance for intra-African trade. This is mainly because a large part of it is clustered inside areas within which there are no payments restrictions. For instance, within former French West Africa and within former French Equatorial Africa payments are free, and the same is true in East Africa.

Trade flows between countries may also be influenced by bilateral payments and trade agreements imposed for reasons of commercial policy as well as for external balance considerations. In Africa the use of bilateral trade and payments agreements as an instrument of commercial policy was in fact uncommon until fairly recently, but since 1955 a large number of agreements have been concluded.[11] While most of these have been with countries outside Africa—especially with centrally planned economies, a fairly large number concern other African countries. These have been designed to expand trade by ameliorating in particular cases the effects of quantitative restrictions and exchange controls. So far the level and structure of intra-African trade have not been significantly influenced by these arrangements.

As far as trade is concerned, the most important intra-African agreements at present cover regions where fairly active trade existed prior to the conclusion of the agreements, e.g. Sudan-UAR, Upper Volta-Ghana, and Morocco-Senegal. In most cases these agreements have been followed by some trade expansion but in absolute terms this has been small so that total intra-African trade has remained virtually unaffected.[12] Significant trade expansion between African countries is in most cases hardly to be expected without a diversification of their production structures and improvements in transport which are matters more dependent on general economic policy than on trade agreements and in any event show their effects only in the long run. Even where the economies in question are complementary and the necessary infra-structure exists, expansion of trade has often been hindered by the high cost of goods from partners which has made it difficult for them to compete with

74

goods coming from outside Africa without tariff preferences[13] even with the support of a trade agreement.

Generally, payments agreements provide for settlement in convertible currencies. The principle exceptions are the agreements between Ghana and Guinea and Mali where local inconvertible currencies have been employed. The practice of stipulating settlement in convertible currencies evidently limits the scope for trade diversion through such agreements. If, however, the trend towards more exchange control and more diverse exchange controls continues in Africa, bilateral trade and payments agreements may become more widespread. Care will then be needed to see that they do not become instruments for the encouragement of unprofitable trade diversion and that they work with, and not against, arrangements for market integration.

Of somewhat greater importance hitherto and perhaps potentially of greater importance in the future are the various trade and other economic links which exist between African countries and their trading partners *outside* Africa.

4 EXTERNAL LINKS AND ECONOMIC INTEGRATION IN AFRICA

African economic co-operation has in the past been influenced in a variety of ways by the policies of foreign governments, financial institutions and business enterprises.[14] Of particular interest in the context of the present chapter are some of the special links which exist between independent African states and foreign states outside Africa—usually the former colonial powers.

Most of the former colonial powers in Africa gave preferential access for their colonies' produce in the metropolitan country, and for many commodities and countries these preferences were of considerable economic importance. Often reciprocal preferences were granted in turn by the colonies both to the metropolitan country and to its other colonies but in many cases, before independence, international agreements (such as the Congo Basin Treaty of 1885 which provided for non-discriminatory trade policy) hindered reciprocity so that preference operated one way.[15] In themselves these long-established preferential arrangements have not hitherto been of great significance one way or the other for intra-African trade and integration. In the case of the franc zone, however, an extensive system of quotas, payments restrictions and bilateral contracts were developed in conjunction with them which in the aggregate had the effect of tying the countries of the zone very closely to France. In total these arrangements have created a situation which has a considerable bearing on the problem of integration in Africa.

Although tariff preferences formed a part of the franc zone preferential system, it relied much more on quantitative restrictions on trade and payments which were supported by a range of bilateral commodity contracts covering the African countries' main exports, notably coffee, oilseeds and sugar. Quotas for these commodities in the French market were fixed globally and apportioned amongst the different suppliers.[16] The prices so fixed were consistently above world market prices.

In purely financial terms these so-called *surprix* arrangements may, in the short run, have worked to the advantage of the participating African countries. For instance one estimate[17] put the net gain of all the CFA countries at about 350mn. French francs for 1961. Also the arrangements had the advantage of providing a degree of economic stability which might otherwise have been lacking. On the debit side, however, the system has resulted in a cost and price structure in franc zone countries which at current exchange rates is out of line with that of neighbouring non-franc countries[18]; and in the development of primary production, much of which is not economic at free market prices. Moreover, it must not be forgotten that in return for this treatment, members of the group reciprocated by buying most of their imports from France—frequently at prices a good deal higher than that of comparable goods in the world market. This was particularly so before the devaluation of the French franc in 1958. These distortions represent a potential obstacle of some importance to co-operation with English-speaking countries, where commercial policy has been much more liberal. Their existence played some part in the recent failure to bring about the integration of Gambia with Senegal.[19]

At the present time, these special arrangements are being liquidated. This is consequent upon France's membership of the European Economic Community (EEC) and the provisions for associating most of her former colonies with the whole of EEC in a wider scheme of trade preferences with which direct aid provisions are coupled. Thus by 1967 the *surprix* arrangements are to disappear and import quotas into the African countries affected are to be globalized for EEC as a whole. Provision has been made for the payment of special grants to facilitate the adjustment of these countries to their more competitive external trade position, but the required degree of adjustment for some countries is considerable and it is doubtful if it can be carried out either easily or rapidly.[20]

The arrangements for associating certain former African colonies with EEC have themselves given rise to much debate and controversy in African countries, some of it essentially politically motivated.[21] In so far as the issues are economic, the question for African countries, often lost sight of, is: assuming them to be alternatives, how does economic integration with other African countries compare with EEC ties in terms of their contribution to growth? The following section outlines the provisions for association and indicates their bearing on this question.

5 THE PROBLEM OF ASSOCIATION WITH EEC

Briefly, association under the Yaoundé convention of 1963[22] provides for preferential trade arrangements between a group of African countries (all former colonies of the Six—mainly of France) and EEC. These arrangements are coupled with provision for special financial assistance to associates through the European Development Fund. So far as trade is concerned, association means that exports from associated countries to Europe will benefit from the same elimination of duties and quotas as the community members apply amongst themselves. Thus the exports of associates will eventually be exempted from the common external tariff the height of which provides a measure of the degree of preference enjoyed by associates. At present this concession is mainly important for tropical agricultural produce which enters duty free at once[23]. Most raw materials enter the community duty free anyway. As to manufactures, few African associates export many of these at present, but the potential impact of duty-free entry into the common market could ultimately be considerable, in particular for processing activities where the *effective* degree of protection enjoyed by EEC industries is often much higher than the nominal tariff rates suggest.[24] The remaining category of African exports consists of agricultural products like sugar and oilseeds which are similar to or competitive with European agricultural products. The treatment to be received by these commodities will be settled by the Community in the course of defining its common agricultural policy. Apart from trading preferences, association also gives access to grants and soft loans from the European Development Fund which will amount, for the African states, to $730mn. over a five-year period.

In return for the privilege of duty free entry to the European markets associates are expected, in principle, to give duty free entry to imports from the Community. They may nonetheless impose duties on such imports if this is necessary for revenue or for development purposes but there must be no discrimination against members of the Community. In practice, association arrangements have generally involved the grant of some recipro-cal tariff preferences to the Community, partly in order to bring the arrangements for association unequivocally within the GATT definition of a free trade area. Associates normally grant similar tariff preferences to each other.

At present eighteen independent African states are associates and have accepted the required institutional links with EEC. In addition, the three Maghreb countries enjoy a special position which is not very clearly defined. These countries taken together account for a large part of African economic activity.

From the time of Britain's early negotiations for entry to EEC when similar arrangements were in prospect for them, the English speaking African countries have consistently objected on political and ideological grounds to the institutional links involved in association. Subsequently, they urged that the Community should extend similar tariff preferences to non-associated African countries by means of direct bilateral trade agreements outside the Convention. In 1963 the Six declared their willingness to do this for countries whose economic structure and level of development is similar to that of the associates. Any such agreements are to relate solely to trade and will not provide access to the EEC Development Fund. Nigeria has already negotiated such an agreement which came into effect in 1967. The three East African countries have commenced negotiations at Brussels with the same objective in view, while other African states, including Zambia and Sudan are also interested.

Although much has been written in general terms about the significance of these trade preferences to present, and possible future 'associates' their quantitative importance to the different countries of Africa has not been clearly brought out. Table 3 : 4 attempts to throw some light on this matter by quantifying these trade preferences for all African countries except those, like the Maghreb countries, for which special arrangements may be made. The method employed is to calculate the formal incidence of the preference arrangements. This is done for each country by weighting the present volume of trade with Europe in each commodity by the absolute margin of tariff preference and summing. The results are expressed both in absolute terms and as a proportion of total export receipts. The calculations are based on the common external tariff in the Common Market which is already in force for most tropical produce of interest to Africa.

It should not be assumed that these calculations provide any very accurate indication of the effective benefit from the trade preference arrangements to any one country or to the Continent as a whole. Certainly the tariff concessions available to present associates and, prospectively, to other African countries, should have a favourable impact upon their export earnings from the Six. This will depend in the first place on the effect the discrimination has upon their shares of the European market and on how the net price for those exports compares with what it would have been in the absence of preference. The calculations do not necessarily provide an accurate measure of the effect of these factors. Moreover, against these benefits must be set the cost (in terms of foregone import duties, impact on least cost

TABLE 3 : 4

Africa and EEC
(figures refer to 1963 except where otherwise stated)

Country	Total Exports	Total Imports	Trade with EEC as % of Total Export	Import	Trade with UK as % of Total Export	Import	Incidence of Association benefits Absolute	Relative to Total Exports	Main Commodities Benefiting	Maximum other Benefits negotiable Absolute	Relative to Total Exports	Main Commodities affected
	$000	$000					$000	%		$000	%	
1. Associates in Africa												
MAURITANIA	5,228	30,016	70	75	—	1				24	0·4	Fish
MALI	10,556	34,245	21	40	—	2	—	—		—	—	
UPPER VOLTA	8,151	36,997	18	55	1	3	—	—		—	—	
NIGER	19,706	22,712	71	57	—	2	—	—		59	0·3	Vegetable oil
SENEGAL	110,508	155,997	89	74	1	2	—	—		5,654	5·1	Vegetable oil, fish
IVORY COAST	230,330	169,737	70	76	1	2	11,392(d)	4·9	Coffee, cocoa, bananas, pineapple	248	0·1	Fish
TOGO	18,265	29,031	74	48	2	10	503	2·8	Coffee, cocoa	26	0·1	Tapioca, vegetables
DAHOMEY	12,779	33,416	85	70	1	3	49	0·4	Coffee	92	0·7	Vegetable oil
CAMEROON	118,334	108,989	84	69	2	2	4,312	3·6	Coffee, cocoa, bananas, pineapple	2,149	1·8	Aluminium(e)
CHAD (a)	22,707	29,034	67	63	7	3	—	—		—	—	
CENTRAL AFRICAN REPUBLIC (a)	21,996	26,340	54	76	1	4	297	1·4	Coffee	24	0·1	
GABON (a)	72,347	48,103	68	70	4	4	28	—	Coffee, cocoa	—	—	Vegetable oil
CONGO (BRAZZAVILLE) (a)	41,631	61,775	75	75	15	3	63	0·2	Coffee, cocoa	62	0·2	Palm oil
CONGO (KINSHASA)	337,522	316,078	32	42	10	4	1,865	0·5	Coffee, cocoa, bananas	2,001	0·5	
MADAGASCAR	82,079	127,439	61	82	3	2	1,770	2·2	Coffee, spices bananas	6,663	8·1	Sugar, rice, tobacco, meat

2. Others

REUNION	38,095	69,740	83	72	—	1	—	—		21,854	57·4	Sugar, rum, essential oil
ALGERIA (1961)	368,853	1,024,609	87	85	4	1	—	—				
MOROCCO (1962)	348,252	425,294	59	56	6	3	—	—		7,627 (c)	6·1	Wheat, fruit, olive oil
TUNISIA	125,996	221,810	70	66	4	3	—	—				
UAR (1962)	454,587	859,065	18	18	5	9	—	—		1,185	0·5	Cotton seed cake, dried vegetables, millet
LIBYA	373,896	238,778	64	43	28	18	—	—				
SUDAN	214,380	275,875	31	22	13	27	—	—				
ETHIOPIA (1962)	78,955	103,077	21	31	5	7	390	0·5	Coffee			
MOZAMBIQUE (1960)	73,007	126,800	8	20	8	14	—	—				
ANGOLA (1960)	124,000	127,639	26	19	15	11	1,153	0·9	Coffee	77	—	Vegetable oil
RHODESIA, ZAMBIA AND MALAWI	597,400	374,730	25	10	40	32	—	—		3,413	1·6	Tobacco, maize
SIERRA LEONE	71,295	83,617	5	18	71	41	69	0·1	Cocoa			
GAMBIA	8,297	11,759	72	9	27	42	—	—				
NIGERIA	513,926	576,786	37	22	40	34	1,887	0·4	Cocoa, pepper	821	0·2	Vegetable oil
GHANA	297,059	362,556	29	25	28	33	3,287	1·1	Cocoa	164	—	Cocoa-butter
KENYA (b)	121,853	267,985	28	17	25	31	1,870 (d)	1·5	Coffee, pine-apples, pyrethrum	335	0·3	
UGANDA (b)	143,100	50,631	16	19	19	32	175	0·1	Coffee			
TANGANYIKA (b)	176,678	84,561	21	18	33	36	676	0·4	Coffee	376	0·2	Meat, dried vegetables

SOURCES: Foreign Trade Statistics of appropriate country. ECA, Foreign Trade Statistics of Africa, Series B.
European Economic Community, Foreign Trade Statistics of Associated Overseas Areas, 1963.
(a) Trade between the members of the Equatorial Customs Union is excluded.
(b) Trade between the members of the East African Common Market is excluded.
(c) Excluding the duty on wine and on lead. Wine to the value of $22,812,000 was exported in 1963. Lead exports were valued at $2,117,000,
(d) Including tinned pineapple and juice.
(e) Cameroon imports bauxite from Guinea and exports processed aluminium.
'—' means nil or negligible.

F

source of imports, etc.) of any preferences which have to be offered to the Six as the price of an agreement, which is not taken into account in the calculation. All these considerations must be borne in mind in interpreting the table. Nevertheless, it seems certain that many countries benefit substantially, looking at present trade flows.

Apart from showing the present formal incidence of the preference arrangements, the table also gives estimates of the value of the preferences which might conceivably be negotiable in the future for 'sensitive products', that is to say, those exports of African countries which may compete with domestic products of the Community. Figures are also included showing the relative importance of trade by African countries with the United Kingdom. The size of this trade has a particular bearing on policy in former British countries which may wish to negotiate special association arrangements. So far, each of these countries has been requested to make some tariff concessions to the Six—partly as a quid pro quo and partly to make the agreements consistent with GATT. In general, however, they cannot afford to offer such concessions without weighing very carefully their possible effects on the preferences they presently enjoy in the British market.[25]

An interesting point brought out by the table is that the EEC trade preferences are not very equitable as a means of distributing aid. Some of the best endowed countries like Ivory Coast and Cameroon (both relatively wealthy and with a favourable trade balance) get most benefit, while the poorest countries receive little or nothing. Of course, most of the eighteen receive substantial direct financial assistance—mainly from France. It is mainly this which makes possible their large trade deficits (see columns 2 and 3). To most of these countries it is their connection with France and the direct financial aid they receive from her which are really important. The EEC trade preferences and the connection with the other European countries are by comparison insignificant at present.

As already indicated, the central economic issue in relation to association concerns the relative merits of the EEC link as compared with links with other African countries. The operative considerations can only be sketched in briefly here. For any country the answer would depend partly on the effects of the tariff preferences on the benefits from current trade and partly on the effects of association on the character and pace of industrial development in the participating countries as compared with the most favourable alternative under African integration. On balance, the trade preferences seem for many countries to offer the prospect of substantial short-term gain. As to the other considerations, the outcome is less clear. Preferential access to the EEC market for processed products might well stimulate industries that export to West Europe, such as oil crushing, cocoa processing, wood-working and aluminium smelting. In addition, light manufactures might be stimulated by the prospect of access to the European market. Both of these opportunities, if expected to be enduring, should stimulate an inflow of capital to the countries concerned, and so favour growth. It is evidently not possible to say how these gains might compare with those to be expected from alternative integration arrangements within Africa of unspecified extent and range.

But it is by no means certain that one should consider EEC and intra-African trade links as alternatives. The advantages of both may be obtainable for many African countries. Whether this is so or not turns partly on the compatibility of association with the creation of regional economic groupings in Africa which include both associates and non-associates.

On this point the provisions of the Convention are not clear. Article 7 calls for most favoured nation treatment for the Six with the exception of customs unions and free trade areas among associates which are explicitly permitted by Article 8. At the same time Article 9 permits associates to join customs unions and free trade areas that include non-associated countries 'in so far as they neither are nor prove to be incompatible with the principles and provisions of the said Convention'. If this criterion were interpreted ungenerously, it could provide a substantial hindrance to some otherwise feasible arrangements for economic groupings in Africa. Present indications are that, with the possible exception of France, the members of EEC are disposed to take a liberal approach to this question and that mixed unions will not be discouraged. Of late the possible adverse implications of the EEC link for integration arrangements within

Africa appear in any case to have diminished as a result of the willingness of the Six to offer trade agreements more widely to non-associates. Still, so long as some countries are unable to enjoy such preferences, and there continue to be important distinctions in trading terms between associates and non-associates, some hindrance to the formation of new regional integration arrangements in Africa may be anticipated from these arrangements. Partly this is because of uncertainty as to the light in which EEC may view groupings involving associates and non-associates; partly it is because of the possible difficulties which may be entailed by unbalanced export oriented industrial development stimulated by association confined to one group of African countries. Any adverse effect of the EEC link on African economic integration in the foreseeable future is probably likely to be small however, and it is certainly insignificant in relation to the obstacles which exist among the African countries themselves.

6 THE OPPORTUNITIES FOR GAIN FROM MARKET INTEGRATION IN AFRICA

Although there are certainly opportunities for gain from co-operation between African states in the monetary and fiscal fields, the basic gains from economic integration are bound up with the opportunities for specialization made possible by the integration of markets.

A general review of the African economy clearly cannot do more than put the opportunities and problems of market integration in Africa in the broadest perspective. A start can be made by analysing the dependence of different regions on imports from outside Africa from which an attempt can be made to estimate the possibilities of import substitution. This in itself is a difficult enough task because it really calls for detailed feasibility studies of different industries in terms of cost and demand. A proper assessment of the gains from integration would then require an assessment of the extent to which integration itself affects the scale of import substitution and the benefits from it. Short of such a detailed analysis one can only attempt to discern the broad outlines of the possibilities from an examination of existing import patterns and a knowledge of the production characteristics of industries which seem likely to be important in the next stages of industrial growth in Africa.

In the field of agriculture an examination of current trade flows suggests that major opportunities may exist of usefully expanding trade among African countries. In 1960 major African food imports from outside the Continent were wheat, maize and rice worth £55mn. (nine-tenths of its recorded import requirements), meat £10mn. (one-third of requirements), fish £20mn. (two-thirds of requirements), sugar £50mn. (nine-tenths), fruit £10mn. (two-thirds) and vegetables £15mn. (three-quarters). For a variety of reasons, statistics of aggregate import dependence obviously greatly exaggerate the possible opportunities of gains from integration in agriculture. It is neither possible, nor, on economic grounds, would it be desirable to replace much of these imports, but where supply can be readily expanded and the African product is a good substitute for the imported product, intercountry differences in the conditions of agricultural production may offer substantial gains from the abolition of trade barriers. Of course, high imports of agriculture produce in many African countries are often as much an indication of faulty national policies for agriculture as of possible gains from integration. Many African countries could profitably produce a much higher proportion of their own requirements of staple agricultural products without recourse to integration. Furthermore, non-market obstacles to integration in agriculture are widespread. For instance, among small scale producers in many African countries there exists a strong preference for a high degree of self-sufficiency in foodstuffs partly as a safeguard against market and climatic uncertainties. This operates to hinder specialization within countries as well as between them. In some cases these attitudes are reinforced by Government policies. In the Gezira scheme in Sudan for instance, tenants are obliged to devote a very substantial part of their plots to growing food crops for subsistence. Finally, transport difficulties and transport costs have to be taken into account. Making due allowance for all these factors, opportunities in Africa for short-run gains from increased specialization in food production are probably considerable. Moreover, since food production accounts for a high proportion of economic activity, even proportionately small gains may be very significant in terms of income gains. The gains from increased specialization *within* countries may, however, in some cases, be as great if not greater than those to be anticipated from expanded inter-country trade. In the longer run it can be expected that increased specialization will enable the continent to meet an increased proportion of its rising needs for agricultural produce efficiently from its own resources.

As we have seen, however, the general arguments for regional integration in less developed countries tend to place major weight not so much on possible gains within the existing framework of production as on the gains which integration may produce in the course of industrial development and structural transformation. In this connection table 3:5 showing the structure of imports into Africa in 1962 is of interest.

TABLE 3: 5

Commodity Structure of African Imports 1962

Food, beverages, tobacco	16.7
Crude materials	5.3
Fuels	7.9
Chemicals	7.4
Machinery	28.6
Other Manufactures	31.7
Misc.	2.4
Total (excluding gold) £2,675mn.	100.0

SOURCE: *UN Statistical Yearbook*, 1963, Table 160; World Trade by Commodity Classes and Regions.

Although, as we have seen, Africa imports very high proportions of a number of its foodstuffs from the outside world, Table 3:5 indicates that only a small part of aggregate African imports are made up of foodstuffs. Thus the opportunities for gain from integration-induced import replacement of manufactures and raw materials might be expected to be more considerable. Moreover, looking to the future it is relevant that the demand for manufactures can be expected to grow more rapidly than income whereas the reverse is to be expected for foodstuffs.

The dangers of using import dependence data as anything more than a first indication of possible areas of import substitution have already been stressed in the case of agriculture. If anything, these dangers are more acute for non-foodstuffs. Evidently, many imports of this kind depend upon sources of raw materials which have not so far been discovered in Africa. Others depend on complex technologies which will be out of reach of most African countries for some time to come. Another important reason for the limited usefulness of import dependence data from this point of view is that manufacturing products are very heterogeneous. Failure to take adequate account of this may lead to an exaggeration of the scope for import substitution, although, as noted below, it may also lead to an underestimate of the gains from integration.

From the standpoint of the opportunities for integration among less developed countries, a central question concerns the extent and size of potential economies of scale. Although opinions on their importance are numerous, meaningful and relevant facts are seldom available. Most analysis is based on data from more developed countries and is not necessarily apposite to less developed countries where factor proportions and operational and commercial problems may be quite different.

In the view of many economists, the potential importance of scale economies provides the chief economic justification for the formation of regional groupings in less developed countries. It is assumed that the technical and economic optima for many kinds of plants are necessarily large and that the extent of individual national markets is usually too small to sustain such plants.[26] This is certainly the case for a number of industries producing homogeneous products such as rayon, steel, polyethylene, fertilizers and petroleum. One documented example which may be cited as an illustration concerns the case of an oil refinery to serve the Equatorial African market. It was estimated in this case that if a single oil refinery were constructed at Libreville to serve the whole Equatorial African market, the rate of return would be of the order of 7.5 per cent. If, instead, two smaller refineries were to be established, one in Libreville and one in Pointe Noire, the estimated rate of return on the larger total investment would be only 1·1 per cent.[27] But although such cases may be important, industries of this kind are hardly likely to form the staple of industrial development in the less developed countries for some time to come.

Other economists argue that in many of the industries which are likely to be established in these countries, technical economies can be exhausted by firms of moderate size and that even relatively poor and small countries can have a number of plants of efficient size. But even if this is the case, it should not therefore be concluded that the potentialities for integration are limited. The question of scale economies is not disposed of by considerations of technical plant size. Economies of scale are also derived from specialization within plants on a limited range of a particular product, and from the vertical specialization of processes between plants. There are no doubt many industries where the output of a typical plant is not large in relation to the market of developing countries, if the market is broadly defined, but in many cases, the 'market' caters for a very heterogeneous end product. Textiles and clothing are cases in point. In these cases, substantial gain may be obtained from the specialization of different plants on a narrow range of output, but this is only possible if the market for such a narrow range is sufficiently large. This consideration suggests that attempts to estimate the gains from integration using census data on the size of plants in relation to a supposedly homogeneous demand may from this point of view greatly underestimate its potentialities.[28]

Economies of scale may of course be obtained, not only from manufacturing industry, but also from the large-scale operation of public utilities and public services in which indivisibilities are important. These factors may be managers of special abilities or the indivisibilities may, as in the case of manufacturing, be bound up with plant and equipment. In some services there may also be economies to be derived from operation over a wider geographical area. In the case of air and rail transport for instance, there is not only a strong case for operating on a large enough scale to make full use of specialized abilities and machines of large capacity; in addition, differences within a region in the seasonal pattern of traffic may make it possible to economize on vehicles if these can be shifted between the services of different countries. Power generation is another case in which similar economies may be exploited. Likewise, common organizations in money and banking often make economies possible by enabling resources to be shifted from one area to another in accordance with different seasonal needs for credit, thus providing a useful degree of elasticity in the credit structure. This was an important advantage in East Africa under the Currency Board System, and it continues to be important in West and Equatorial Africa, where monetary unions have been preserved. Research organizations are another case in which indivisibilities offer the prospect of potential economies. In Africa, indeed, one of the major reasons which disposed colonial governments to favour measures of economic integration was just this prospect of securing economies in the provision of public services.

An approach to the problem of estimating the gains from integration in different regions in Africa in quantitative terms may be based on the various attempts which have been made to explain the level and composition of manufacturing industry in different countries by reference to certain of their general economic characteristics. Two outstanding studies in this field have been made by Chenery[29] and by the United Nations,[30] following Chenery's methods. The basic tool employed is multiple regression analysis. The studies rely mainly on cross-section regressions which relate the value added data for total industry and for each one of thirteen sectors to the corresponding values of the explanatory variables in the same year. The data related to 42 countries in 1953 and 53 countries in 1958. The objective is to arrive at results which can be used to analyse the comparative experience of different countries and, it is hoped, for projection purposes. The outcome is a picture of the 'normal' level and pattern of a country's manufacturing industry, corresponding to the different explanatory variables, in terms of the average experience of the countries included in the sample.

So far as the level of manufacturing industry is concerned two main factors were found to explain variations in industrial output. These are income and size. By far the most important factor appears to be per capita income. The income elasticity of output for total manufacturing is about 1·37. In other words, assuming population to be constant, the value added of total manufacturing industry increases slightly over one third more than proportionately with *per capita* income. The second factor, which is of more direct interest for this chapter, concerns the effects of market size and economies of scale, which are reflected in the second elasticity, the population elasticity of manufacturing output. This was found to be 1·12. This means that as between countries having the same *per capita* income level total manufacturing value added varies approximately one eighth more than in proportion to the size of the population. To explain variations in the *structure* of manufacturing a third variable was introduced, namely the relative degree of industrialization which shows the effect on different sectors of a given deviation from the normal level of industrial output. Elasticity co-efficients are also calculated for this. They range from approximately unity for textiles to 1·91 for basic metals.

The regression equation for total manufacturing industry which resulted from the UN enquiry was as follows:

$$\log V_0 = -1 \cdot 637 + 1 \cdot 369 \log y + 1 \cdot 124 \log P$$

where V_0 = value added in manufacturing industry in millions, y is per capita income, both in terms of 1953 US dollars, and P is population in millions.

If this enquiry is applicable to Africa it has a clear bearing on an assessment of the opportunities for integration since it could be used to examine the degree and structure of industrialization in each of several countries separately and then jointly. The difference in the level of industrialization and the structure in the two alternative situations could then be attributed to market size and economies of scale—i.e. to integration.

For instance, application of the above regression equation to the three East African countries employing the projected per capita incomes contained in their development plans, and population forecasts, gives the following result for 1970.[31]

Industrial Output in 1970

'Normal' value added. Three East African countries separately	\$418·6mn.
ditto East Africa as a region	477·7mn.
Difference—reflecting the effects of integration	59·1mn.

The gain from integration shown here is about 14 per cent of forecasted value added in manufacturing in 1970. This would imply an improvement in the region's annual growth rate of GDP of 0·5 per cent over the period 1965–70. In other words, with integration, the rate would be 4½ per cent per annum. Without it, the rate would be 4 per cent. The structure of industrial production would also differ with integration, involving a greater emphasis on heavy industries with regional integration than with three separate national markets. A similar calculation for Equatorial Africa shows an improvement in the forecasted annual growth rate of about one half of one per cent for the same period.

But how relevant is this method to Africa? In the first place it must be borne in mind that the concept of normality here refers to what can be anticipated on average on the basis of the information in the sample of countries examined. In the list of countries included in the UN sample very poor countries form a minority, although most if not all African countries are in this category and European and Latin American countries predominate. Nonetheless a recent attempt[32] to apply the standard equations to East Africa indicates that their applicability in terms of deviations is not too bad from the structural standpoint, though the present level of industrialization in East Africa is only 50–60 per cent of what is observed in other countries with similar levels of *per capita* income and population.

Clearly, however, even if the sample were more representative of African conditions, this kind of analysis can only provide a complement, rather than a substitute for detailed analytical regional studies which would attempt to determine the opportunities for integration in terms of the needs, resources and policies of particular countries, and available technologies. The relationships derived in the studies outlined above are based on a very simplified model which comprises only a limited number of the supposedly most important explanatory variables. The specific economic, institutional and other pertinent characteristics of any particular region or country will be only partly reflected in these relationships.

In the last few years a more direct approach is being pursued to the problem of assessing the magnitude of possible gains from integration in manufacturing industry in Africa. It is exemplified in the many economic and technical 'pre-feasibility' investigations undertaken by the Economic Commission for Africa which now cover much of the continent.[33] These enquiries start from projections of gross domestic product in different countries (based on their development plans) and proceed on this basis to project their demands for individual commodities on the basis of income-elasticities of demand estimated from cross-country analysis. The estimated demands for the individual countries are then aggregated in terms of a suitable sub-region. The particular contribution of these studies is that they then go on to compare these demands on the basis of technical data, with estimated costs of production in various industries at different levels of output. Such investigations, embodying as they do technical production data, make it possible to form a more adequate estimate of the possibilities for import substitution with and without integration, and hence of the gains from integration.

Although many of these enquiries fall far short of providing an adequate basis for decision-making, in part because they fail to take adequate account of market differentiation and transport costs[34], they do suggest that a range of industries may be identified which, over the next years, would only be feasible in the context of sub-regional markets or in which, although national industries might be feasible, integration could result in substantial operating economies. In some cases indeed, the data suggest that local production for a regional market in Africa could result in products being produced at less than the present imported cost.[35] These opportunities for accelerating the establishment of industries and for reducing operating costs represent important potential gains.

It is hardly possible to summarize briefly the results of these diverse enquiries in terms of their implications for the gains from integration. But as an indication of the orders of magnitude involved, ECA investigations for Eastern Africa may be cited.[36] These suggest that between 1963 and 1974 the difference between the amount of industrialization that would be feasible in the sub-region with and without integration is of the order of 30 per cent. This would imply a primary income gain of some £200mn. in the forecasted income from manufacturing in the sub-region in 1975. In terms of rates of growth this gain may be expressed as an increase of about 0·5 per cent on the forecasted annual rates of growth of GDP that would otherwise be expected, that is, the rate of growth would be 4·5 per cent instead of 4 per cent. This would be a useful, but hardly a dramatic gain.

REFERENCES : CHAPTER 3

1 See UN *Industrial Growth in Africa*, N.Y., 1963, pp. 77–8 for some illuminating data on this point.

2 S. D. Neumark, *Foreign Trade and Economic Development in Africa*, Food Research Institute, Stanford University, 1964. This distinction is also employed in E. J. Berg, 'The Character and Prospects of African Economies', in (ed.) W. Goldschmidt, *The United States and Africa*, Praeger, New York, 1963.

3 See, on this whole question, S. H. Frankel, *Capital Development in Africa*, OUP London, 1938.

4 For some telling criticisms of the value of this statistic in measuring the relative position of backward economies, see Dan Usher, 'The Transport Bias in Comparison of National Income', *Economica*, May 1963, and references quoted therein. See also W. Beckerman, *International Comparisons of Real Incomes*, Development Centre, Organisation for European Economic Co-operation and Development, Paris, 1966.

5 See A. J. Brown, 'Should African Countries Form Economic Unions', in (ed.) E. F. Jackson, *Economic Development in Africa*, Basil Blackwell, Oxford, 1965, p. 180.

6 Because of the inadequacy of national income as a measure of development, many economists have tried to work with rankings based on a collection of real indicators. See for example M. K. Bennett, 'International Disparities in Consumption Levels', *American Economic Review*, Sept. 1951.

7 See *Economic Bulletin for Africa*, Vol. 6, No. 1, Jan. 1966. UN New York. See also *Proceedings of the United Nations Conference on Trade and Development*, Vol. VII, Part 2, 'Intra-African Trade', pp. 256–78. This section attempts an estimate of unrecorded trade, which in many countries is a considerable part of total trade.

8 *loc. cit.* pp. 259–60.

9 *loc. cit.* pp. 260–1. The note to Table 4, p. 261 indicates the composition of the sub-regions.

10 On this trade, see E. W. Bovill, *The Golden Trade of the Moors*, Oxford 1958, and Neumark, *op. cit.* Chapter 2.

11 A useful recent survey of the scope of bilateral trade and payments agreements in Africa will be found in *Bilateral Trade and Payments Agreements in Africa*, UNECA June 1965, ref. E/CN/STC/24/ Rev. 1.

12 *op. cit.* p. 54.

13 In some cases even when tariff preferences have been granted, competition with imports from outside Africa has been difficult. A case in point is the trade between Sudan and UAR.

14 At various times both Britain and France have given strong support for regional co-operation in Africa. The aid policies of these countries however do not appear to be directly related to the promotion of integration.

15 See UN *Trade and Development*, Volume VI, pp. 334–5, for a review of the past and present positions in this respect. After independence non-discrimination was abandoned by several countries in anticipation of association with EEC.

16 See *Trade and Development*, Vol. VI, Annex 1, 'Managed market arrangements in the franc zone'.

17 See 'The CFA Franc System', *IMF Staff Papers*, November 1963.

18 The *UN Yearbook of National Accounts, 1955*, contains data bearing on this point.

19 This case is discussed in Chapter 6 below.

20 On the size of the losses see *Trade and Development*, Vol. VI, pp. 342, 343.

21 Former President Nkrumah was one of the most vigorous exponents of the view that association will hinder the industrialization of African states and impoverish them or cause them to stagnate. See his *Africa Must Unite*, Heinemann, London, 1963, especially pp. 161 and 180–93.

22 See the *Convention of Association between the European Economic Community and the African and Malagasy States associated with that Community and Annexed Documents*, published by EEC, Brussels, 1963.

23 Duty-free entry for tropical products antedated the Yaoundé Convention of course and was provided for associates under the Treaty of Rome, Part IV.

24 Because raw materials enter duty free or at low rates, whereas materials in processed form pay import duty. For a discussion of 'effective' protection, with examples for Europe, see B. Balassa, 'Tariff Protection in Industrial Countries, An Evaluation', *Journal of Political Economy*, December 1965.

25 Some further discussion of this matter may be found in P. Robson, 'Africa and EEC; A Quantitative Note on Trade Benefits', *Bulletin of the Oxford Institute of Economics and Statistics*, No. 4, 1965, from which this table is reproduced.

26 See A. J. Brown, 'Customs Union versus Economic Separatism in Developing Countries', Part I, *Yorkshire Bulletin*, May 1961, for an attempt to identify industries which could be operated economically in the East African market. The analysis is based on British data.

27 See Chapter 5, Section 6.

28 Similarly the costs of breaking up existing common markets may be underestimated. The discussion in Chapter 4, Section 7, may be referred to with advantage.

29 See H. P. Chenery, Patterns of Industrial Growth, *American Economic Review*, September 1960. See also M. D. Steuer and C. Voivodas, Import Substitution and Chenery's Patterns of Industrial Growth—A Further Study, *Economia Internazionale*, Geneva, February 1965.

30 See United Nations, *A Study of Industrial Growth*, New York, 1963.

31 See *Normal Patterns of Industrialisation in East Africa*, unpublished memorandum by A. Stoutjesdijk, of East African Institute of Social Research, Kampala, 1966.

32 See Stoutjesdijk, *op. cit.*

33 See for example, *Report of the ECA Mission on Economic Co-operation in Central Africa* E/CN.14/L.320, 1966; *Industrial Co-ordination in East Africa;* E/CN.14/INR/102, 1965; *Proposals for Co-ordinated Industrial Development in West Africa; Suggestions for Further Action*, E/CN.14/INR/77, 1964.

34 In some cases it is recognized that a price equalization fund will be a prerequisite of expanded intra-regional trade in some products.

35 As an example, see the comparisons cited on p. 15 of *Industrial Co-ordination in East Africa*. This shows savings, for industries serving an Eastern African Market, on some steel products, basic chemicals and fertilisers and polyethylene.

36 See *Industrial Co-ordination in East Africa*, p. 2.

CHAPTER 4

ECONOMIC INTEGRATION IN EAST AFRICA

1 THE BACKGROUND

Of the extant examples of economic integration in Africa the most important is that of East Africa which consists of Kenya, Uganda and Tanzania.[1] Arrangements for integration in the region were developed during the colonial period and came to include not only a common market but also a monetary union and a high degree of fiscal integration. In addition a number of important services have been operated in common in the fields of transport and communications, administration, research and education. There was also a fair degree of labour mobility within the region. After independence the arrangements at first operated as before, but once the constraints of colonial government were removed, the arrangements progressively came under strain as each country independently evaluated the arrangements from their separate standpoints and as more active, and to some extent divergent, development policies came to be pursued. For a time, in 1965 there was a real danger that the structure of East African co-operation might collapse. This danger now seems to have been averted, and the arrangements laid down in the Treaty signed in 1967 should permit the region to continue to enjoy the major benefits from economic integration in relation to the common market and the common services. The recent experience of East Africa provides a case study of wide relevance of the stresses of integration between separate states and the kind of measures which may have to be considered if such arrangements between states at somewhat different stages of development are to be durable.

2 THE ECONOMIC STRUCTURE

A brief description of the economic structure of the countries is necessary to indicate the environment of the integration arrangements. East Africa covers 680,000 square miles, which is an area substantially larger than that of the European Economic Community and the British Isles together. Of the three countries, Tanganyika has the largest land area, though much of it is semi-desert, and Uganda has the smallest. The total population of the region in 1966 was about 28 million. The three countries are not very different in terms of population but Uganda's is somewhat smaller than the other two. Average population density is about 40 per square mile, and is highest in Uganda and lowest in Tanzania. Each country has sizeable minorities of immigrant Asians who dominate commerce and small scale industry. Kenya, and to a much smaller extent, Tanganyika, have also had European settler communities in the past.

In any common market the effectiveness of integration will depend greatly on the adequacy of transport facilities. Although East Africa's transport system is not highly developed by comparison with advanced countries it does enable goods to be shipped among the major population centres fairly cheaply. The basis of the goods transport system is the railway. The main line of the area runs from Mombasa, which is the principal port of the area, through Nairobi to Kampala and the north and west of Uganda. A second line links the port of Dar-es-Salaam with the interior of Tanzania. A third line connects the port of Tanga with the important agricultural areas of Moshi and Arusha, and with Mombasa, and, since 1963, also with the main line from Dar-es-Salaam. New road and rail links between Tanzania and Zambia are under active consideration. The road link is likely to terminate at the excellent deep water harbour at Mtwara in Southern Tanzania, thus making it possible to avoid the bottleneck of Dar-es-Salaam's extremely limited port capacity. These links may ultimately foster closer links between Zambia and the East African market. The railways are complemented by a road system which is very good in terms of the standards of tropical Africa. Uganda's system of main and secondary roads is very well developed. Kenya's road system in the main producing areas is also good though its link with the coast has been poor. Tanzania's main road system is poor but improving; its secondary road system is bad. Road

TABLE 4:1

The East African Common Market: Economic Structure 1966

Country	Population (millions)	Population density (inhabitants per sq. mile)	Rate of population growth	Gross Domestic Product			Proportion of GDP produced in the market sector
				Aggregate £mn.	Per cent of total	Per capita	
KENYA	9·6	43	3·0	318·8	38	33·0	76
UGANDA	7·7	85	2·5	242·6	29	31·3	71
TANGANYIKA	10·4	29	2·0	272·7	33	26·2	73
	27·8	41	2·5	834·1	100	29.9	74

SOURCES: *Economic and Statistical Review*, EACSO, March–June 1967; Kenya, *Economic Survey*, 1967; Uganda, *Background to the Budget*, 1967–8; Tanzania, *Background to the Budget*, 1967–8.

communications between Uganda and Kenya are good. Northern Tanzania, including the important agricultural area around Arusha and Moshi, is also fairly well linked to Kenya by roads, but Dar-es-Salaam, the southern part of Tanganyika, and the densely populated area around Lake Victoria all lack good road links with each other, and with the other two members of the common market.

In 1966 the aggregate Gross Domestic Product (GDP) for the region was about £834m. (£1 EA = £1 sterling). Kenya had the largest aggregate GDP, followed by Tanzania. In terms of income per head, the average for the three countries is about £30. Tanzania has the lowest income per head at £26 and Kenya the highest at £33. African incomes do not differ greatly amongst the three countries and are probably highest in Uganda.

For the area as a whole, the annual average rate of growth of GDP for the period 1960–66 (in current prices) was of the order of 6·8 per cent, the respective rates being for Kenya 5·9 per cent, for Uganda 8·2 per cent and for Tanzania 6·6 per cent.[2] In terms of constant prices, rates of growth for this period are estimated at 4·2 per cent for Kenya, 5·4 per cent for Uganda, and 4·8 per cent for Tanzania. In the period immediately prior to this however, from 1954–60 Kenya's rate of growth in current prices at 6 per cent was much higher than those of Uganda at 2·5 per cent and Tanzania at 4·6 per cent.[3] How far experienced differences in real growth rates within East Africa have been influenced by the operation of the common market is debatable,[4] but it is certainly felt widely that the pace and stability of Kenya's growth has been influenced favourably by its gains from the common market.

In economic structure the three East African countries are fairly typical of low income primary producing areas. Table 4:2 shows the relative importance of the different sectors of the economy. Except in Kenya, where industrialization and the provision of financial and commercial services to serve the whole of the common market has gone some way, the principal determinant of the level of economic activity is the production of primary products for export. Most of these primary products are produced on a small scale, partly for subsistence and partly

100

TABLE 4:2

Gross Domestic Product at Current Factor Cost by Major Sector 1966

	KENYA		UGANDA		TANZANIA		EAST AFRICA	
	£mn.	%	£mn.	%	£mn.	%	£mn.	%
Agriculture, forestry and fishing	126·2	40	148·2	61	145·9	54	420·3	51
Manufacturing	34·6	11	12·6	5	13·6	5	60·8	7
Trade	38·2	12	25·5	11	38·3	14	102·0	12
Other	119·8	37	56·3	23	74·9	27	251·0	30
Total	318·8(a)	100	242·6	100	272·7	100	834·1	100

SOURCE: Kenya, *Economic Survey*, 1967; Uganda, *Background to the Budget*, 1967–8; Tanzania, *Background to the Budget*, 1967–8.

(a) A new series of Gross Domestic Product figures is now being calculated for Kenya which gives a total for 1966 of £368·2mn. The figure given here is from the old series in order to facilitate comparison with earlier years.

for the market but there is a certain amount of large-scale commercial agriculture, which is confined to the former European areas of Kenya, and to the sugar, tea and sisal estates which exist in each country. These enterprises account for a high proportion of the value of marketed agricultural output.

In the region as a whole manufacturing industry is little developed. Its principal products are manufactured foods (particularly of sugar, coffee and wheat products), cigarettes, beer, metal products, cement, textiles and footwear and wood and paper products. Kenya is the most industrialized of the three countries and produces about 60 per cent of the region's total industrial output. Uganda has a small and growing industrial nucleus, mainly centred on Jinja, while Tanzania is the least industrialized of the three.

The area is heavily dependent on foreign trade, and in 1966 exports amounted to 24 per cent of GDP and imports to 27 per cent. As Table 4:3 shows, exports consist primarily of agricultural products. There is a high degree of concentration in exports and the four listed products made up 64 per cent of the value of total exports in 1966 even though export prices for coffee, and more particularly for sisal, were comparatively low.

TABLE 4:3

Exports from East Africa 1966

£000

Commodity	KENYA	UGANDA	TANGANYIKA	Total
Coffee	18,791	34,783	15,142	68,716
Tea	8,714	3,151	2,255	14,120
Cotton	869	15,345	17,496	33,710
Sisal	3,340	4	11,734	15,078
Total, all exports	58,073	65,936	79,106	203,115

SOURCE: *Annual Trade Report of Tanganyika, Uganda and Kenya for the year ended 31st December 1966.* Commissioner of Customs and Excise, East Africa, Mombasa, 1967.

Other major exports are copper (Uganda), diamonds (Tanganyika), pyrethrum (Kenya), meat (Kenya primarily) and oil seeds and cashew nuts (Tanganyika primarily). The United Kingdom takes about 25 per cent of the total exports, West Germany and the United States are the other two major customers, while the Far Eastern countries—Hong Kong, India, China and Japan— are an important market for the cotton crop.

The main imports consist of crude petroleum (before 1964 refined products were imported), fabrics, industrial machinery and motor vehicles. About half of the region's imports are supplied by three countries, UK, West Germany and USA.

The balance of visible trade of the three countries with the rest of the world is shown for 1966 in Table 4:4. In that year, Uganda and Tanganyika had favourable balances whereas Kenya had a debit balance. Kenya has had large visible deficits for a number of years, though that in 1966 was larger than for several years, partly because of capital imports on common market account mentioned below. Kenya's overall current account deficit with the rest of the world is normally partly offset by its favourable balance on visible trade within the common market and by its net earnings from the provision of financial, transport and other services to the other two countries which

TABLE 4:4

East African Foreign Trade 1966

£000

	Net Imports	Domestic Exports
KENYA	112,396*	58,073
UGANDA	42,947	65,936
TANGANYIKA	64,251	79,106
Total	219,594	203,115

SOURCE: *Annual Trade Report of Tanganyika, Uganda, and Kenya*, 1966. Commissioner of Customs and Excise, East Africa, Mombasa.

* Kenya's imports in 1966 were inflated by over £10mn. which was spent by East African Airways, East African Railways and Harbours, and Posts and Telecommunications on aircraft, railways, vehicles and telecommunications equipment. These are entered against Kenya since the headquarters offices are located there, but are properly attributable to all three countries.

results from their concentration in Kenya. In 1966, net capital inflow was large enough to offset Kenya's current account deficit and to produce an increase in foreign exchange reserves. In 1966 Tanganyika's favourable balance on visible trade was more than offset by a deficit on invisible and transfer payments but capital inflow also sufficed to produce an increase in monetary reserves. A similar outcome was recorded for Uganda.

3 THE DEVELOPMENT OF ECONOMIC CO-OPERATION IN EAST AFRICA

A high degree of economic co-operation has existed in East Africa for many years. Prior to independence the arrangements for co-operation reflected British Colonial policy, majority official opinion in the three countries, and the views of European settlers. After independence the new governments generally accepted the usefulness of the arrangements, and in particular of the common market, but their working has been the subject of unfavourable criticism on the part of Tanzania and to a lesser extent by Uganda. In an attempt to meet these criticisms, important structural changes are to be introduced at the end of 1967.

Of the steps towards regional economic integration the establishment of a customs union was one of the earliest. A customs union between Kenya and Uganda was established in 1917 and Tanganyika later became a part by successive stages. A common external tariff was accepted in 1922, tariffs between Tanganyika and the other two countries were eliminated in 1923, and the duty-free transfer of imported goods between the countries was established in 1927. The customs administration was operated jointly by Kenya and Uganda from 1917, but was not extended to Tanganyika until 1949.

Income taxation was introduced in Kenya in 1937 and in Uganda and Tanganyika in 1939. These countries adopted Kenya's rates and tax structures and for this part of the revenue system joint administration was practised from the outset (including Zanzibar).

A further important aspect of East Africa co-operation concerns the arrangements for joint operation of common services.

In addition to the joint administration of customs and excise and income tax, agricultural, medical and industrial research organizations have been operated in common as have civil aviation, meteorological services, and the newly established University of East Africa. Apart from these, major transport and communications services are jointly operated by East African para-statal agencies. These include East African Railways and Harbours, East African Airways, which provides foreign as well as domestic services, and East African Posts and Telecommunications. The latter are termed 'self contained'. They enjoy a substantial degree of autonomy and, except for development finance, are self financing on the basis of fees charged. Their operating experience has on the whole been very satisfactory.

Money and banking is another important area where co-operation has been close. From 1919, when the East African Currency Board was established, up to 1966, when Central Banks were established for each of the countries, a common currency was in use[5]. Although national currencies have now been established, the banking and exchange practices still imply a high degree of monetary integration amongst the three countries.

Other aspects of economic integration in East Africa may be summarized briefly. During the period of the monetary union, there were no restrictions on movements of capital between the three countries. With minor exceptions there have been no formal restrictions on the movement of labour and its employment, but intercountry migration was not significant though some occurred, particularly from Kenya into Uganda. Since independence the labour markets have become increasingly separate in practice and Kenya has recently introduced legislation requiring work permits for non-citizens, including those of African origin.

Although the customs union and other forms of functional economic co-operation thus have a long history in East Africa,[6] a common legislative body and an administrative organization were not established until the beginning of 1948. In that year an Order in Council established a permanent authority, termed the East Africa High Commission, which was made up of the

Governors of the three territories. Legislation was considered and enacted by a newly established Central Legislative Assembly (CLA), the members of which were partly appointed by the three Governors and partly elected by the unofficial members of the territorial legislatures.[7] The legislative powers of the CLA were somewhat limited and related chiefly to legislation on various aspects of the common services, including the structure (but not rates) of customs and excise and income taxation. The policy decisions of the High Commission were given effect through its Secretariat which was located in Nairobi.

Until 1961, the High Commission lacked any independent source of revenue. While the most important of the common services such as the railways, post office, etc. were self-financing, the other High Commission services were financed partly by annual appropriations from territorial revenues on the basis of a formula, and partly by grants from the British Government and from other outside sources. In 1961 the recommendations of the Raisman Commission led to the establishment of a Distributable Pool, one of whose purposes was to provide an independent source of revenue for the non self-contained common services.[8]

Important changes were made in the machinery of co-operation when Tanganyika attained independence in 1961. In that year the High Commission was transformed into the East African Common Services Organization (EACSO) with a supreme executive authority consisting of the chief executives of the three governments. At the same time the Central Legislative Assembly was enlarged and made to consist wholly of members elected by the legislatures of the three countries. The Authority itself operates through Committees each composed of three relevant ministers from each country, and which severally cover Finance, Communications, Commerce and Industry, Social and Research Services and Labour. The decisions of these Committees must be unanimous if they are to be implemented, which inevitably means that they are effective only in matters in which there are no major divergences of interest among the three countries.

The common market itself, however, still received no formal recognition in the 1961 enactment, and its operations continued to rest until 1967 on its *de facto* acceptance by the three countries. In that year following the protracted disputes of the last few years, a Treaty was signed by the heads of State of the three countries which provides a formal basis for an East African Community, and an East African Common Market. It will effect important changes in the basis on which the *de facto* market has hitherto operated.

4 THE CUSTOMS UNION AND THE INTEGRATION OF TAXATION

The basis of economic co-operation in East Africa is the customs union which manifests itself in a common external tariff. In addition there is a high degree of harmonization in respect of other major sources of public revenue.[9] Customs and excise are administered on behalf of the three governments by the East African Customs Department, which is a department of the Common Services Organization. The structure of the tariff is laid down by the Central Legislative Assembly[10] but the rates are enacted separately by each of the national legislatures. Income taxes are similarly administered by the East African Income Tax Department which is part of EACSO. The structure of the income tax is established by the Central Legislative Assembly[11] but the rates and allowances are enacted separately by each of the governments.

For both these groups of taxes, changes in rates are made only after negotiation among the three governments and they are announced simultaneously in the annual budget speeches. Tariff changes are first considered by a committee made up of the Permanent Secretaries of Finance and Commerce and Industry with advice from the Commissioner of Customs. Income tax changes are similarly considered by the Permanent Secretaries of Finance with technical advice from the Commissioner of Income Tax. The final agreements in both fields are reached by negotiation among the three Finance Ministers which have hitherto produced a high degree of uniformity, though latterly some differentiation has appeared and this may well increase.

The main revenue sources for which harmonization has not

been practised are the graduated personal taxes, which are a kind of local authority income tax levied at a low rate with a low maximum payment, and the export taxes which all three governments have employed to varying degrees in recent years. About three quarters of total central government tax revenue in the region is derived from sources for which harmonization is practised.

As far as customs duties are concerned, the present exceptions to complete uniformity are minor, and usually reflect a failure to reach agreement on changes which arises when one country seeks protection and the others do not. The differences are of three kinds. In the first place there are some outright differences in rates though these are insignificant. In the second place certain rates are suspended by legislation until proclaimed by the individual governments. Differences arise when such rates are applied in some countries and not in others. Thirdly, drawbacks of duty on imported materials used may be granted by each country in particular cases, after notification to the others. Such drawbacks make it possible for one country to provide additional protection for particular industries provided that it bears the direct revenue loss which is entailed. A number of drawbacks are in force, mainly in Kenya.

The basic excise duties were also virtually uniform for many years,[12] but latterly there have been some departures from uniformity as a result of the imposition of special 'consumption taxes'. Thus in 1964 Tanzania imposed a consumption tax on beer (collected by Customs and Excise), and Uganda did the same in 1966. In 1964 Tanzania also imposed a progressive registration tax on motor vehicles on first registration in Tanzania at 10–20 per cent of the imported price including import duty.

Further differences were created in 1966 when Uganda imposed a wide range of consumption taxes on certain goods produced locally but outside Uganda, such as bicycle tyres and tubes, corrugated sheets, distemper, paints and shoes.[13] This measure was justified as a means of compensating for the import duties which are lost when these goods are imported from inside the common market rather than from overseas. At the same time the customs tariff was adjusted upwards to

108

provide increased protection for the local producers. Other 'consumption' taxes for which differences exist among the three countries include hotel taxes, airport charges and motor vehicle taxation.

Personal income taxation and the taxation of company profits are virtually uniform. In the past from time to time small differences have existed[14] and at present some are found in relation to such matters as family allowances but they are insignificant. In the last two or three years, however, special development taxes have been introduced in Tanzania and Uganda which are in effect supplementary income taxes. Tanzania's development levy was introduced in 1965 and was imposed not only on all incomes over £10 a month but also on the sale of many primary products. In the 1966 budget the levies on production were mainly replaced by export taxes but the income levy continues.[15] Uganda's development contribution was introduced in 1966 and is a 'once for all' contribution of 5 per cent of chargeable income. These special taxes are not administered by the East African Income Tax Department.

From the standpoint of the operation of the common market the high degree of uniformity which has hitherto prevailed in the fiscal field has had many economic and administrative advantages, and it has certainly materially contributed to the smooth operation of the customs union. At the same time the price of uniformity is a high degree of budgetary inflexibility. Prior to independence the revenue 'strait jacket' was in practice a major restraint and expenditure in the three countries tended to keep in line with it. Latterly, while the administrative advantages of uniformity continue to be widely admitted, divergent paths of planned expenditure have caused greater weight to be placed on other objectives. Within limits this development need not cause too much concern in terms of the operation of the common market. The past emphasis on the need for complete fiscal uniformity for economic and administrative reasons was almost certainly misplaced. Uniformity of the tariff is certainly vital to the smooth operation of the common market. But it is difficult to believe that even quite substantial divergences in fields such as personal income tax need give rise to serious administrative or economic problems. The need for harmonization in the field of company taxation is no doubt greater in the interests of avoiding unwanted tax effects on location and also tax allocation problems. This need not rule out jointly agreed differentials in such matters as depreciation and investment allowances which could be a useful auxiliary technique for influencing the location of industry within East Africa for the purpose of offsetting any inequality in the operation of the common market. Unfortunately, in regional tax policy it is a much simpler task to agree on uniformity than upon differentials.

The Apportionment of Revenue between the Members of the Common Market

The basic rule for the allocation of customs and excise revenue is that both customs and excise revenue accrue to the country of final destination. In the few instances in which rates differ, for customs the rate of the country of destination applies, while for excise, the rate of the country of origin applies, even though the revenue accrues to the country of destination. An exception is sugar, where the excess of a higher rate is not transferred to the country of destination. Technically, however, excises are levied on production, not consumption.

When imported goods on which duty has been paid and allocated are subsequently transferred from one country to another a reallocation of customs duty is made, which is based on information contained in a transfer form which must be completed for any shipment of goods from one country to another. The same form is used for the allocation of excise duty. In the case of transfers which can be traced back to the import certificate of their original entry (known as 'referenced goods') the duty originally paid is reallocated. Of the goods imported through Mombasa and later re-exported, about half are dealt with in this way. For other goods, known as 'broken bulk goods', this cannot be done. The value the merchant enters on the transfer form is the value at which he will sell the goods, not the original c.i.f. value (which he may not know) on the basis of which the duty was originally levied. To allow for the difference in c.i.f. and transfer value, which represents value added in the distributive process, the c.i.f. value is assumed to be 70 per cent of the transfer value and duty is reallocated on this basis. This proportion is based on a weighted average of the ratio of c.i.f. to transfer value which was ascertained in a sample enquiry undertaken some years ago and which involved tracing transferred goods back to their original importation. Where imported goods are processed before being re-exported to other countries of the common market, the duty on the import content is reallocated in a precisely similar manner.

These arrangements for fiscal allocation have not been supported by frontier controls, and their reliability depends upon the accurate completion of the transfer forms by business firms. The major administrative control is the requirement that the transfer form be submitted before the rail, steamship, or air line will accept shipments. A very high percentage of all inter-territorial shipments is in fact made by rail. In most instances there is no financial incentive for the shipper to fail to execute the transfer form or to make erroneous statements. No additional tax liability is incurred by preparation of the form; it is merely the allocation of the tax revenue by the country which is affected. Nevertheless, when the country of destination has a higher customs duty or a higher special excise or other tax, there is an incentive to ignore the requirement. Although these instances are not numerous, rate differences have in the past given rise to illegal movements of paraffin by road. Some 'smuggling' of sugar has also occurred in the last few years.

For purposes of income tax, East African income is treated as a single sum, regardless of where it is earned within the area. Returns are filed on the basis of residence, and the tax due is normally allocated on the basis of the country in which it is earned. An exception is made for employees of EACSO. Although their income in theory is derived partly from each territory, the whole of their tax is allocated to the territory in which they are resident. Tax collected from corporations which have branches in more than one country is allocated on the basis of origin, that is, to the country where the revenue is earned. The Income Tax Department makes the allocation, almost entirely on the basis of reports made by the companies. There is no audit of the accuracy of the reported figures; it is assumed that the companies have no incentive to misreport, as their tax liability is not affected when rates are uniform. Although this may be so, somewhat conventional rules are used by companies in allocating their profit by countries. One anomaly of the present system is that sales made in one country by a firm located in another which has no establishment in the former, yield company tax only to the country where the firm is located.

The Distributable Pool

These basic arrangements for revenue distribution were modified as a result of the introduction of the Distributable Pool in 1961–2. The Pool was designed partly to provide an independent source of revenue for certain of the non self-contained common services; and partly to bring about a fiscal redistribution between the three countries so as to offset inequalities in the operation of the common market.

An independent source of revenue for certain of the non self-contained services was recommended by the Raisman Commission because it was felt that this would 'assist these services in their activities by providing them with greater certainty of funds and that it would also promote a more efficient use of funds between services by enabling the High Commission to function as a single authority, able . . . to administer its services from the point of view of the whole of East Africa rather than as an agency of territorial governments'.[16] The revenue was to be provided by allocating to the High Commission one half of the revenue of the Distributable Pool.

The main purpose underlying its establishment was, however, to redistribute tax revenue so as to provide some offsets to the alleged inequalities in the benefits derived from the Common Market. The extent of these inequalities is discussed in Section 7 below on the costs and benefits of the arrangements for co-operation. This section is confined to an outline of the distributable pool and an indication of the extent of the financial transfers it effects.

The pool works in the following way. From and including 1961–2 each territory was allocated only 94 per cent of the customs and excise revenue attributable to it according to the basic criteria outlined above and only 60 per cent of the revenue derived from income tax on companies' profits from manufacture and finance. Income tax revenue on all other income continued to be allocated as before. The proceeds from the revenues withheld from the three countries formed the Distributable Pool. After deducting the costs of its collection, one half was allocated to financing the relevant common services and the remainder was distributed equally amongst the three territories. The operations of the Distributable Pool are summarized for its first four years in Table 4:5.

TABLE 4 : 5

East Africa Distributable Pool

£000

Receipts from	1961–2	1962–3	1963–4	1964–5 (est)
KENYA	1,731	2,092	2,551	3,000
UGANDA	759	831	1,159	1,420
TANGANYIKA	791	1,028	1,164	1,300
TOTAL RECEIPTS	3,281	3,951	4,874	5,720
Payments to				
½ to GENERAL FUND	1,640	1,975	2,438	2,860
⅙ to KENYA	547	658	812	953
⅙ to UGANDA	547	658	812	953
⅙ to TANGANYIKA	547	658	812	953
TOTAL PAYMENTS	3,281	3,949	4,874	5,719
Net Receipts				
KENYA	−1,184	−1,434	−1,739	−2,047
UGANDA	−212	−173	−347	−467
TANGANYIKA	−244	−370	−352	−347

SOURCE : East African Common Services Organisation.
NOTE : The receipts of the Fund are net of its share of the costs of collection.

Since part of the receipts of the Pool finance the non self-contained common services no measure of the resulting fiscal redistribution can be arrived at without first making assumptions about the contribution which each country is conceived to be making through the Pool to the financing of those services. This is a problem which confronts all attempts to estimate the redistributive effects of public finance. The application to the Distributable Pool of the most plausible of the theoretical bases advocated in the literature entails assuming either that each country bears that part of the cost of the common services which is properly attributable to it, or alternatively that it bears a share of the costs which is proportional to the benefits it derives from their provision. The difficulty of using these bases lies in making an objective estimate of what these magnitudes are.

Short of attempting this, there are two assumptions which might reasonably be made. The first is that each country contributes to the financing of the common services in proportion to its present contribution to the Distributable Pool. This amounts to assuming that one half of each country's contribution goes to finance the common services, and the rest to provide the pool from which fiscal redistribution is made. An alternative assumption is that each country contributes equally to the financing of the common services, which for most services approximates to the position which prevailed before the Raisman recommendations came into effect.[17] Other possible assumptions might be that each country contributes in proportion to its national income or in proportion to its total public revenue. Table 4:6 indicates the fiscal redistribution brought about through the Distributable Pool on the first and second assumptions.[18]

TABLE 4 : 6

Territorial Redistribution through Distributable Pool

£000

		1961–2	1962–3	1963–4	1964–5
ASSUMPTION (i)	KENYA	−318	−388	−463	−547
	UGANDA	+168	+243	+233	+243
	TANGANYIKA	+152	+144	+230	+303
ASSUMPTION (ii)	KENYA	−637	−776	−927	−1,094
	UGANDA	+335	+485	+465	+486
	TANGANYIKA	+303	+288	+460	+606

5 MONETARY CO-OPERATION

From 1919 until 1966 the three East African countries used a single currency. During this period the monetary system of the area was what is known as a sterling exchange system. Under this system the external reserves are held in sterling securities, and the currency authority has the function of issuing and redeeming local currency in exchange for sterling at a fixed rate. If all local currency had to be backed by sterling to the extent of 100 per cent and if currency were the only form of money, such a system could be extremely restrictive since the local money supply would then be wholly determined by the balance of payments, and there would moreover be no possibility of providing any finance for governments. In practice the East African Currency Board system has operated more flexibly. In the first place, as in other parts of Africa where the system was employed, a large part of the local money supply consisted of the deposits of the expatriate commercial banks whose operations have ensured that the currency issue expanded to maintain an appropriate relationship to the total money supply as determined by their advances policy.[19] In addition, a fiduciary issue was permitted in East Africa from 1960. This provided an additional degree of monetary flexibility and permitted a degree of deficit financing to the three governments, which until recently has not been fully taken up.

Although the East African Currency Board has undoubtedly performed its purely monetary functions cheaply and efficiently, it was inevitable that, with the passage to independence, consideration should be given to the establishment of a Central Bank. Such a bank would itself determine credit policy, instead of leaving this to be determined largely by the commercial banks, and would also undertake other important functions, including the administration of the foreign reserves and exchange controls.

In the pre-independence discussions on central banking, a key issue which is also of central importance for integration, turned on the degree of centralisation to be built into a new system. Prior to independence there was an unwillingness on the part of Uganda and Tanganyika to give their support to the establishment of a unitary central banking system because of their fear that, since it would certainly be based on Nairobi, it would work to the advantage of Kenya. At the same time there was reluctance in all three countries to break up the single currency area by setting up three Central Banks. In the search for a generally acceptable compromise, some consideration was given at first to an arrangement which would have entailed the creation both of an East African Reserve Board, independent of the three governments, and of three territorial Central Banks. The intention was that the Reserve Board would have the task solely of determining monetary policy and controlling the currency issue, while the three Central Banks for their part would simply be responsible for implementing the Board's monetary policy and for performing banking functions. There would be common reserves but separately identifiable currencies would be issued on behalf of the State Banks.[20]

This proposal failed to find general favour, and discussions continued intermittently during the period when first Tanganyika and later, Uganda were moving towards independence. In 1962 the Tanganyika Government became impatient at the lack of progress towards new monetary institutions and commissioned a German banker, Mr Blumenthal, to report on 'whether Tanganyika's interests are adequately safeguarded under the present arrangements' and 'whether it is possible or desirable to establish a Central Bank—either on a territorial or on a regional basis'.[21] In examining this question Tanganyika's desire to maintain economic relations and to possess a common currency with her neighbours was to be taken into account.

In his report, Blumenthal strongly advised 'against all endeavours to establish an independent Tanganyika currency and a Central Bank'[22] and recommended instead the creation of a two-tier system with a Central Bank at the top and State Banks below. In his scheme the Central Bank would have had the sole right of currency issue and would determine the size of the fiduciary issue and its distribution among the three participating states.

The difference between Blumenthal's proposal and that which was considered prior to independence is not wholly clear

116

because the latter was not spelt out in detail. Despite appearances to the contrary the Blumenthal system seems to have implied a more centralized and, in fact, essentially a unitary system in which effective power would rest with the Central Bank. Among the points which support such an interpretation is the fact that Blumenthal did not contemplate the separate identification of notes by country except for an initial limited period.[23] But without such an identification it would be difficult to provide any substantial degree of autonomy for the state banks.

The publication of the Blumenthal report in 1963 was followed closely by the declaration by the Heads of the three East African States of their intention to federate.[24] If federation had come about it might have made the centralized system advocated by Blumenthal practicable. As it was, in the succeeding months, the prospects of East African federation rapidly receded and relations between the three countries deteriorated so much as to make even the continued existence of the common services and the common market doubtful.[25] By 1965, it had become clear that hopes of maintaining a common currency—strongly supported by Kenya—were doomed to failure, and in June of that year the three Ministers of Finance announced in their budget speeches the intention to establish three Central Banks.

From the standpoint of this chapter it is unnecessary to go into the constitutions and structure of the new Central Banks[26] in detail. What does require consideration are the implications which the transition from a single Currency Board to three Central Banks will have for East African economic co-operation. Important differences between the new and the old system are: the new Central Banks provide each government with an instrument for credit creation; the new banks have responsibility for converting currency and deposits into foreign exchange; they are responsible for administering exchange control; all intra-regional trade transactions will in future be settled in a foreign currency.

The implications of these changes for integration will depend on how the new banks operate. The arrangements originally envisaged entail (i) no exchange restrictions on current payments within East Africa; (ii) convertibility of the three currencies at par and (iii) par clearance by the commercial banks of the new notes. To the extent that these arrangements are maintained and are generally expected to be maintained, the existence of three separate currencies need have no significant adverse effects upon the East African Common Market. Neither trade nor foreign financed investment in the region should be subject to any additional hindrance. If, in addition, each Central Bank were to agree to accumulate short-term claims against the others up to an agreed limit, the economy of combined reserves in the face of different seasonal demands for credit, which was an important feature of the old system, could to a large extent be maintained. Such a system would have important similarities to the one in operation in Equatorial Africa discussed in Chapter 5. It would imply a high degree of *de facto* monetary integration even though, unlike the case of Equatorial Africa, there would be no formal institutional arrangements for monetary harmonization; indeed in these circumstances only in a limited sense could three separate currencies be said to exist.

But the important question is whether such conditions will be maintained. The creation of separate Central Banks has been undertaken because some East African countries feel that a monetary union unduly limits their discretion in relation to monetary policy. But, as pointed out in Chapter 2,[27] even where separate currencies exist, there are narrow limits to the extent to which any one country can pursue a more expansionary monetary policy than its neighbours, given free trade in goods and services in the common market and an absence of exchange control, without incurring a loss of foreign exchange reserves to its partners and possibly running the risk of capital flight. Once these limitations are fully recognized, the more expansionist countries in the region may be led to abandon some of the conditions just outlined and to introduce exchange control on current payments and perhaps even to contemplate changes in par values. The introduction of such restrictions or even an expectation of their introduction, could be highly disadvantageous for inter-country trade, regional investment and future exploitation of the gains from economic integration in the region.

6 inter-country trade in east africa

The extent to which a common market has developed in East Africa as a result of the integration arrangements outlined above can be indicated by the size, character and relative rate of growth of inter-country trade, though these characteristics cannot be attributed solely to the common market.[28]

Inter-country exports and imports and their origin and destination are shown for the period 1945 to 1966 in Table 4:7. Between 1946 and 1966 there occurred a twelvefold increase in inter-country exports for the region as a whole, the increases for Kenya, Uganda and Tanzania being 19, 7 and 9 times. Growth was fairly steady until 1966 when a slight contraction occurred, largely due to the imposition of quantitative restrictions by Tanzania, chiefly against Kenya.[29]

Table 4:8 relates inter-country trade to total exports and gross domestic product. It can be seen that over the period 1946 to 1966 inter-country exports have increased roughly 12 times in value by comparison with a 9 fold increase in domestic exports and by 1966 they had grown to nearly 20 per cent of total exports.

The importance of intra-regional trade in the economies of the East African countries could perhaps best be indicated by the share of the total product in each country which it generates. This information is not available, but the role of inter-country trade may be indicated less satisfactorily by the ratio of inter-country exports to money gross domestic product. Over the period 1956 to 1966 this ratio rose for Kenya from 5 per cent to 12 per cent. For the other two countries the importance of inter-country trade was in 1966 much lower than in Kenya and it showed no comparable rise over the previous decade. For Uganda the rise was only from 3 per cent in 1956 to 6 per cent in 1966. Indeed in 1966 the importance of inter-country trade was probably less for Uganda than it had been in the late 1940s, for despite a substantial absolute increase in her inter-country trade over the period, her export trade and gross domestic product grew even faster. For Tanzania the ratio appears to have fluctuated around 2 per cent since the 1950s with a slight tendency to increase of late. For East Africa as a whole the

TABLE 4:7

East Africa Inter-Country Trade

| | KENYA | | UGANDA | | TANGANYIKA | | Balance of inter-country trade | | | £000 Total inter-country exports |
	to Tanganyika	to Uganda	to Kenya	to Tanganyika	to Kenya	to Uganda	Kenya	Uganda	Tanganyika	
1945	577	494	878	327	555	113	−362	598	−236	2,944
1946	854	649	1,163	422	394	102	−54	834	−780	3,584
1947	832	723	1,387	411	437	110	−269	965	−696	3,900
1948	1,067	774	1,585	645	664	169	−408	1,287	−879	4,904
1949	2,033	1,084	1,271	645	779	140	1,067	692	−1,759	5,952
1950	2,355	1,211	1,553	847	727	170	1,286	1,019	−2,305	6,863
1951	1,959	1,740	1,541	901	895	246	1,263	456	−1,719	7,282
1952	2,261	1,963	2,418	1,182	678	256	1,128	1,381	−2,509	8,738
1953	2,419	2,686	2,621	1,948	819	401	1,665	1,482	−3,147	10,894
1954	2,630	2,889	3,175	1,972	810	233	1,534	2,025	−3,559	11,709
1955	2,365	3,360	3,112	1,642	1,202	475	1,411	919	−2,330	12,156
1956	3,678	3,706	1,725	975	1,490	567	4,169	−1,575	−2,596	12,141
1957	4,451	4,826	2,554	1,440	1,507	505	5,216	−1,336	−3,879	15,283
1958	5,644	5,101	3,361	1,465	1,516	1,076	5,868	−1,351	−4,517	18,163
1959	6,513	5,784	3,640	1,587	1,848	726	6,809	−1,282	−5,526	20,089
1960	7,608	6,163	5,120	1,574	1,875	450	6,776	81	−6,857	22,790
1961	8,901	7,047	5,152	1,704	1,844	390	8,952	−581	−8,371	25,038
1962	10,017	7,303	5,386	1,669	1,954	437	9,980	−685	−8,295	26,766
1963	10,365	9,425	6,248	1,993	2,915	508	10,627	−1,692	−8,935	31,454
1964	13,299	12,581	7,344	2,442	4,110	1,021	14,426	−3,816	−10,610	40,797
1965	14,087	15,339	7,135	2,592	4,569	1,346	17,722	−6,958	−10,764	45,068
1966	13,282	15,619	7,317	3,120	3,806	842	17,778	−6,024	−11,754	43,986

SOURCE: East African Statistical Department, *Economic and Statistical Review*.

NOTE: The figures exclude excise duty on excisable commodities and customs duty charged on imported raw materials used in local manufactures. Since 1959 these adjustments have been made by the East African Customs and Excise Department. The 1958 figures were adjusted by the East African Statistical Department. Figures for 1945–57 are estimates made by D. A. Lury in 'The Trade Statistics of the countries of East Africa 1945–64', *Economic and Statistical Review*, March 1965.

TABLE 4: 8

Significance of Inter-Country Trade in the Regional Economy

£ million

	KENYA			UGANDA			TANGANYIKA			EAST AFRICA		
	1946	1956	1966	1946	1956	1966	1946	1956	1966	1946	1956	1966
Inter-country exports (a)	1·5	7·4	28·9	1·6	2·7	10·4	0·5	2·0	4·6	3·6	12·1	44·0
Domestic exports (b)	6·2	29·0	58·1	8·9	40·4	65·9	8·5	44·9	79·1	23·6	114·3	203·1
Total exports (c)	7·7	36·4	87·0	10·5	43·1	76·1	9·0	46·9	83·7	27·2	126·4	247·1
(a) as % of (c)	19	20	33	15	6	14	2	4	6	13	10	18
Gross monetary domestic product (d)	n.a.	145·2	243·5	n.a.	102·8	172·8	n.a.	89·3	197·9	n.a.	337·3	614·2
(a) as % of (d)	n.a.	5	12	n.a.	3	6	n.a.	2	2	n.a.	4	7

SOURCE: *Statistical Abstracts for Kenya, Uganda and Tanganyika*, and *Economic and Statistical Review*, EACSO.

121

TABLE 4 : 9

Composition and Shares of Inter-Country Trade

	1959 Exports	Imports	%	1963 Exports	Imports	%	1966 £000 Exports	Imports	%
Unprocessed food and raw materials									
KENYA	1,419	2,168		1,846	2,338		3,150	2,620	
UGANDA	1,133	1,232		1,443	787		1,790	2,425	
TANGANYIKA	1,477	629		1,430	1,594		1,436	1,331	
TOTAL	4,029	4,029	20	4,719	4,719	15	6,376	6,376	14
Processed food									
KENYA	2,863	942		3,272	2,567		3,418	1,490	
UGANDA	933	1,467		2,189	1,857		1,357	1,541	
TANGANYIKA	381	1,768		519	1,556		321	2,065	
TOTAL	4,177	4,177	21	5,980	5,980	19	5,096	5,096	12
Drink & Tobacco manufactures									
KENYA	2,347	357		2,893	695		1,125	252	
UGANDA	1,102	1,059		969	1,129		238	458	
TANGANYIKA	15	2,048		12	2,050		46	699	
TOTAL	3,464	3,464	17	3,874	3,874	12	1,409	1,409	3
Other manufactures									
KENYA	5,668	2,021		11,779	3,563		21,208	6,761	
UGANDA	2,059	2,752		3,640	6,160		7,052	12,037	
TANGANYIKA	701	3,655		1,462	7,155		2,845	12,307	
TOTAL	8,428	8,428	42	16,881	16,881	54	31,105	31,105	71
All Items									
KENYA	12,297	5,488		19,790	9,163		28,901	11,123	
UGANDA	5,227	6,510		8,241	9,933		10,437	16,461	
TANGANYIKA	2,574	8,100		3,423	12,358		4,648	16,402	
GRAND TOTAL	20,098	20,098	100	31,454	31,454	100	43,986	43,986	100

SOURCE: *Annual Trade Report of Tanganyika, Uganda and Kenya*, 1959, 1963 and 1966, Commissioner of Customs and Excise, Mombasa.

ratio increased from 4 per cent in 1956 to 7 per cent in 1966. Thus while in the region as a whole inter-country trade has assumed a substantially more important role over the period, only in Kenya has its relative importance increased. For the other two countries, while the absolute increase is substantial, this has merely kept pace with the growth of domestic product.

Table 4:9 shows for the years 1959, 1963 and 1966 the share of inter-country exports and imports accounted for by different classes of products. In the early post-war period, most inter-country trade consisted of locally produced foodstuffs. Manufactures of food, drink and tobacco were among the first industries to develop in East Africa and they are still important. Nevertheless, while trade in processed foodstuffs continued to grow over most of the post-war period there has in the last few years been some reversal of the trend, for example, through the establishment of flour mills in Uganda and Tanzania, so that Kenya now exports unmilled wheat instead of flour. In drink and tobacco the move towards self sufficiency has gone farther and there has actually been a considerable absolute fall in this trade. The striking feature of the inter-country trade patterns of the last decade is the marked increase in the importance of trade in manufactures other than food which has occurred as a wide variety of industries producing substitutes for imports has grown up in response to tariff protection and the growth of incomes. As can be seen, non-food manufactures increased from 42 per cent in 1959 to 71 per cent in 1966. Excluding petrol, the share of manufactures in the latter year was about 60 per cent.

Further light is shed on the composition of inter-country trade by Table 4:10 which shows the position by commodity class for 1966, and notes the major products (items in excess of £350,000) which entered into this trade.

Several salient features of the inter-country trade in East Africa are shown up by Tables 4:10 and 4:7. The first is that Kenya has become the principal exporter of manufactures in the region. In 1966 she accounted for 68 per cent of total exports of manufactures. The share of Uganda and Tanzania were respectively 23 and 9 per cent. Kenya's dominant share evidently

TABLE 4 : 10

East Africa: Inter-Country Trade 1966

£000

S.I.T.C. Section	KENYA		UGANDA		TANGANYIKA	
	to Uganda	to Tanganyika	to Kenya	to Tanganyika	to Kenya	to Uganda
0. Food & live animals	3,405	2,518	1,567	375	842	182
1. Beverages & tobacco	532	850	615	198	397	14
2. Crude materials, inedible	283	160	194	58	427	29
3. Mineral fuels, lubricants etc.	2,445	2,187	442	7	5	—
4. Animal & vegetable oils and fats	79	54	679	51	353	122
5. Chemicals	1,857	1,930	774	78	91	5
6. Manufactured goods etc.	3,919	3,861	2,846	2,194	1,248	412
7. Machinery & transport equipment	222	181	13	11	63	42
8. Miscellaneous manufactured articles (inc. clothing etc.)	2,820	1,487	182	146	370	35
9. Commodities & transactions n.e.s.	57	54	5	2	10	1
Total	15,619	13,282	7,317	3,120	3,806	842

NOTE: Principal items (in excess of £350,000) included above were:

Kenya to Uganda, Fresh milk and cream, butter, wheat (unmilled), cigarettes, petroleum products, soap, paper bags and boxes, synthetic fabrics, clothing, footwear

Kenya to Tanganyika, Margarine, beer, petroleum products, cosmetics and dentifrices, soap, paper products, cement, footwear

Uganda to Kenya, Margarine, unmanufactured tobacco, vegetable oils, cotton fabric, electricity

Uganda to Tanganyika, Cotton fabric

Tanganyika to Kenya, Unmanufactured tobacco

Tanganyika to Uganda, None

SOURCE: *Annual Trade Report of Tanganyika, Uganda and Kenya* for the year 1966. Commissioner of Customs and Excise, Mombasa.

reflects the fact that a very large part of the growth in manu-facturing industry which has taken place in East Africa during the last twenty years has been located in Kenya.

The second feature is the growing imbalance in inter-country trade. This has been closely bound up with the growing importance of manufactures in inter-country trade, and the concentration of manufactures in Kenya. Agricultural exports from Uganda and Tanzania have not grown *pari passu* with their imports of manufactures. Lately indeed, the substantial increase in the deficits of Tanzania and Uganda is attributable almost entirely to their growing net importation of manu-factured goods from Kenya. At present Tanzania's agricultural trade is approximately in balance. Uganda's deficit is also mainly due to net imports of manufactures although she is also a substantial net importer of agricultural produce from Kenya, of which the chief categories are meat, wheat and fresh milk.

The pattern with respect to the country balances of trade has not in fact remained unchanged over the period, but exhibits several fairly well-marked phases. From 1945 to 1948, both Kenya and Tanzania were in deficit. From 1949 to 1955 Kenya enjoyed a growing surplus while Uganda remained in surplus. In 1956 Uganda incurred a substantial deficit for the first time and Kenya's surplus correspondingly increased. This change is attributable to the transfer of a large part of cigarette pro-duction from Uganda to Kenya. Since 1956, Kenya's surplus has increased fourfold while both her partners have enjoyed growing deficits, though in 1960 Uganda achieved a small positive balance. Until 1963 Uganda's deficit was fairly small and the main deficit country was Tanzania. Latterly the deficits of both Tanzania and Uganda have increased sub-stantially.

The third feature concerns the geographical pattern of inter-country trade. It can be seen from Table 4:7 that whereas Kenya's exports are divided roughly evenly between Tanzania and Uganda, those two countries send their exports largely to Kenya. The smallness of the trade between Uganda and Tan-zania is of course partly attributable to the cost and difficulty of communications between these two countries, but it is mainly due to the relative retardation of industrial development in Tanzania and Uganda which now acccounts for the bulk of inter-country trade.

The differences among the countries in the character, balance and the absolute increases in inter-country trade provide the background to the evaluations of the costs and benefits of the East African Common Market which forms the subject of the following section.

7 THE BENEFITS AND COSTS OF ECONOMIC INTEGRATION IN EAST AFRICA

The arrangements for economic co-operation in East Africa are generally thought to have been beneficial to the region as a whole. The common market in particular is widely believed to have increased the rate of growth of the region and is expected to afford even greater benefits in the future as development proceeds.

The Raisman Commission which was appointed in 1960 to study the operation of the common market and of the common services, summed up the matter in the following way.[30]

'191. On the effects of the Common Market upon national incomes, we have reached the following conclusions:

(i) The Common Market has enabled East Africa to become a substantially unified market in the sense that a considerable proportion of all home-produced goods and high proportions of some of them (especially tobacco, dairy produce, and manufactures) are traded between the Territories, while more than a fifth of imported goods also are consumed in a Territory other than that to which they were first consigned.

(ii) It has been an important factor in the establishment of manufacturing industry in East Africa, in that the size of the East Africa market is critical in relation to the minimum efficient scale of many kinds of manufacturing production.

(iii) By virtue of these effects, it has played an important part in enabling East Africa as a whole to maintain in recent years a rate of growth in its total volume of output which is comparable with that shown by most of the advanced countries. This has occurred in spite of adverse world market conditions which have caused part of this growth to be offset by a deterioration in the East African terms of trade.

(iv) Rates of growth in the separate Territories have shown disparity, Kenya's growth being much more rapid than that of either of the other two Territories. Uganda, moreover, suffered an especially adverse change in her terms of trade with the outside world, which largely offset the expansion of her physical volume of output. The largest part of the new capital and skill have gone to Kenya. Nevertheless, it is very doubtful whether Uganda or Tanganyika could, by setting up barriers within the Common Market, have gained more than they would have lost by the certain impoverishment of East Africa as a whole.

(v) As development tends to bring increased specialization and increased reliance upon activities in which the minimum scale of operations is large, the contributions which the Common Market arrangements can make to economic growth are likely to be greater in the future than in the past.'

Broadly similar conclusions on the effects of the common market on the region as a whole were reached by the missions of the International Bank for Reconstruction and Development to the three countries, and by B. F. Massell.[31]

According to these views, the primary advantage of integration arises out of the larger potential market, which permits manufacturers to attain greater economies of scale, and generates external economies for industrial development generally, through such factors as availability of a skilled labour pool, development of subsidiary industries, and the like. While each of the three countries is larger than many of the other less developed countries in Africa, their separate potential markets for manufactured goods are nevertheless very small by comparison with developed countries. Because of indivisibilities, it is impossible to manufacture most commodities efficiently with an output less than an amount fairly substantial in terms of the potential purchases in any one East African country; the common market therefore increases the potential number of industries that can be developed successfully.

In addition, it is probable that by creating more opportunities for industrial development the existence of the common market has stimulated a net inflow of capital and skills to East Africa. It is unlikely that capital made available for industrial development would otherwise have been supplied for investment in the public sector or in agriculture due to a lack of institutional arrangements or for reasons of profitability. Thus to the extent that there existed co-operating factors which would have otherwise been unemployed, integration should have contributed to an expansion of income and employment. Indirectly also, by increasing the opportunities for industrialization, integration will have increased the external economies provided by industry, and have contributed to the structural transformation of these economies which is a basic objective of policy.[32]

The other source of gain from the common market arises from specialization on the basis of comparative advantage; each country comes to specialize in the products in which it has greatest relative advantage—the trade creation of customs union theory. How great these economies are in manufacturing in East Africa is problematical, since the countries are basically very similar in resource endowments. However, there are certainly differences in comparative advantage in various lines of agriculture, though restrictions on inter-territorial trade in agricultural products and special marketing arrangements hinder their full exploitation.

Although the advantages of the common market from these and other sources have been widely accepted, it is generally believed that the gains have been unevenly distributed among the participants. This is thought to be a consequence of the fact that industry attracted to East Africa by the size of the common market has tended to locate in Kenya. The favourable effect of this in generating a higher rate of industrial development in Kenya and the adverse effect on the public revenue of the other two countries as imports from Kenya came to be substituted for imports from the rest of the world, eventually generated such strains and a threat of potential instability that the Raisman Commission was set up to consider the advantages and disadvantages of the common market generally and whether the arrangements were fair to the interests of each country.

The Raisman Commission was clear that the common market arrangements were in the long term interests of the three countries. It also thought it likely that the *spread effect* was sufficient to compensate Tanzania and Uganda for their purchasing from Kenya at more than world prices.[33] Nevertheless, the Commission concluded that some of the criticisms of the working of the common market had substance which consisted 'of the fact that the benefits derived by the territories have been unequal rather than that any one of them has suffered actual loss'.[34] Furthermore, 'while there might be short term advantages to some of the territories (from the disruption of the Market) . . . on any long term appraisal, no Territory would be likely to gain by withdrawing from it'. Nevertheless it took the view that the common market was so important to the economic future of the countries and the internal strains so great, that an interterritorial redistribution of income to offset in some degree the inequalities of the benefits derived was urgently called for to preserve the common market. Its recommended adjustment was, as we have seen, introduced.

In point of fact, both the advantages of the common market and the distribution of its benefits have been limited and influenced not only by the natural forces of polarization, but also by the policies and practices of the three governments which have to some extent prevented economic forces from determining the location, level, and the costs and prices of economic activity. The operations of statutory Marketing Boards, particularly those of Kenya, which control the internal marketing of the country's basic agricultural products may, with respect to their price and purchasing policies, in particular, have been disadvantageous to Uganda.[35] The operations of the public development corporations and the unilateral determination by territorial governments of drawbacks on duties negotiated in common also exert an influence. More recently the unilateral conclusion by particular East African countries of trade agreements with communist-bloc countries, by resulting in the sale of imports at less than world prices, may have reduced the effective tariff protection for comparable local products. Finally, different practices with respect to quantitative import restrictions against foreign countries have also affected the common market. To deal with the former difficulties and to remove impediments to trade imposed by unilateral action on the part of particular countries, the Raisman Commission suggested the introduction of a code of principles for inter-country trade which would exclude the unilateral prohibition or limitation of inter-country trade and the charging of unduly high prices on inter-country exports, but this recommendation was not implemented.

The fiscal adjustment recommended by the Raisman Commission was a fairly small one. Although it succeeded in abating the muted strains under the colonial régime, with independence the constraints on their expression lessened, and the obstacles to reflecting the strains in policy changes were removed, increasing the potential for instability. Even before independence, the IBRD Mission to Uganda had tartly commented that the Raisman Commission's conclusion on the favourable spread effect was 'a deduction from general principles rather than a proposition demonstrated by evidence'.[36] Over the succeeding years, controversy has continued, and it was both stimulated by, and has itself stimulated, efforts to measure the gains and losses of the East African Common Market.

Quantifying the Gains and Losses of the East African Common Market

The problem of measuring the distribution of the gains and losses of common markets is of widespread interest. Several notable attempts have been made to provide measures of the gains and losses generated by the East African Common Market. In order to evaluate these attempts, it is necessary first to make clear the questions which might be asked about the common market. There are three possible questions which might be analysed.

The first question is whether some countries would have gained by not belonging to the East African Common Market in the past. This involves an assessment of how the gains and losses of the common market have been distributed over its life.

An answer to this question is virtually impossible to provide. To do so we should need to compare how the members would have developed in the absence of the market with their actual progress. This would involve not only assessing the forces which emerge as a result of the customs union and their quantitative importance, but also the alternative paths and the alternative opportunities for each country outside the union. Even if economic analysis were able to provide an answer to such a historical exercise it would of course provide no guide to policy in the future for the participants in the common market.

The second question would be to ask what gains and losses would be involved for the members of the union if it were to be broken up, on comparative static assumptions. To arrive at an answer to this more manageable question, the actual situation in the common market as it is now, may be taken and compared with a hypothetical alternative position which differs from it in the existence of three separate national markets.

A third question which might be asked is what would be the long term gains or losses entailed for each member of the common market by its break up. This is really the crucial question from the standpoint of policy, but any attempt to answer it is open to not only the kinds of difficulties which confront an attempt at an historical assessment, but others as well. It would involve taking into account the problems of adjustment which are passed over in a comparative static analysis. Apart from this, an answer would entail comparing hypothetical development paths for the countries within the common market with alternative hypothetical paths if instead separate national markets are established. Any attempt to answer this question is bound to rely heavily on somewhat general presumptions as to the factors at work and their likely quantitative importance.

The quantitative analyses of the distribution of the costs and benefits of the East African Common Market to be discussed in this section refer essentially to the second question, and apply the methods of comparative static partial equilibrium analysis to its elucidation, though their authors normally recognize that they do not necessarily provide an answer to the vital policy question. The first attempt to provide a quantitative appraisal of the gains and losses of the East African Common Market was that of A. J. Brown in 1961.[37] A second attempt was made by D. P. Ghai in 1964.[38] In 1965 W. T. Newlyn published estimates of gains and losses.[39] In 1966 important comments were made on Ghai and Newlyn by A. Hazlewood.[40] Unpublished estimates have also been made by R. H. Green,[41] on similar lines to Newlyn.

Economic Separatism Versus a Common Market

Shortly after the publication of the Raisman Report, A. J. Brown, one of the members of the Raisman Commission, wrote an article in which he developed a model to analyse the effects of a development of manufacturing in one part of a free trade area, and went on to apply it to East Africa on the basis of plausible guesses at the magnitudes involved. The analysis is essentially concerned with the operation of the spread effect, and the circumstances under which this will offset the higher cost of imports for the members of a free trade area which import the manufactures of other members.

The analysis is essentially a 'Keynesian' multiplier analysis, which assumes that there are unused reserves of all factors of production. The model is set out in terms of country A and country B which share a common market with a common protective tariff. There is then supposed some development of manufacturing industry in A, which draws upon resources not previously employed, and whose products are sold in substitution for goods previously imported, at prices equal to the import price plus customs duty. A brief summary of the analysis follows.

Let the value of extra production of manufactures in A, displacing imports, be P. The tax-free value of the imports they displace will be $P(1-t)$, where t is the ad valorem rate of customs duty on these imports. Let a fraction x of P be consumed in country A, the remaining fraction, $1-x$, being sold in country B; it is assumed that none is sold outside the free trade area. Let the marginal propensities to import in the two countries be m_a and m_b, made up of m_{a_r} and m_{a_f}, and m_{b_r} and m_{b_f} respectively—the former component in each case being the marginal propensity to import from the rest of the free trade area and the latter that to import from foreign countries. s is the marginal propensity to save. Given domestic investment in both countries, and ignoring direct taxation and excises[42] it follows that:

$$\Delta y_a = \frac{m_{b_r}y_b + P(1-xt)}{s_a + m_a}$$

The numerator of this expression indicates the primary increases in income in A. Its second term is equal to the value of the increase in exports to B plus the value free of tax of the reduction in A's imports from the rest of the world. To this is added the term $m_{b_r}y_b$ which represents the *spread effect*, namely, the change in A's exports due to the change in B's income. To arrive at the total change in income the numerator then has to be divided by $s+m$ which is the multiplier.

Similar considerations apply for B, except that there is in its case no additional export, other than that induced by A's rise in income, and that imports, besides being increased by B's rise in income, are not only not reduced by internal production but are enlarged by an amount $t(1-x)P$ which represents the amount of import duty formerly collected on the foreign goods now replaced by imports from A, which is now not kept in the country but paid out to A as part of the price of the goods.

The change in income in B is given by:

$$\Delta y_b = \frac{m_{a_r}y_a - tP(1-x)}{s_b + m_b}$$

In the numerator the first term represents the *spread effect*. It is the change in B's exports which results from the rise in income in A. The second term represents the loss imposed on B because it purchases some part of its imports from A at higher than world prices.

The implications of this model are then worked out, on the basis of plausible guesses of the relevant magnitudes for East Africa, and with A denoting Kenya and B representing Tanzania and Uganda combined. The conclusion is that 'with these values the country in which manufacturing arises to displace imports into the free trade area experiences a rise in income equal to twice the new manufactured output, the rest of the area experiences a rise in income of about a tenth of the new manufacturing output'. It is clearly possible in this model for *B* to lose income, but on Brown's assumptions as to the value of the other coefficients, only if *A*'s marginal propensity to import from *B* is less than 0·024. This is a good deal less than the 0·05 he thought to be plausible for Kenya's marginal propensity to import from Tanganyika and Uganda combined.

At first sight the conclusion of this analysis appears to be consonant with those of the Raisman Commission. The conclusion it supports, however, is that, *given the common market*, the income generated by Kenya's extra imports from the rest of the common market compensates Tanzania and Uganda for their purchases from Kenya at more than world prices. The conclusion is not warranted that Tanzania and Uganda gain rather than lose from the common market in the sense that they would lose by withdrawal. This is because it may not only be the case that the common market gives rise to additional industries in Kenya which would not come to East Africa at all without the common market; in addition, some industries which do not need the common market may come to Kenya whereas in its absence they might come to Uganda or Tanzania. This potential loss is not dealt with in Brown's formulation and its omission debars us from concluding that Tanzania or Uganda would be better off in than out. Brown is well aware of this possibility, but he treats it separately, as a distant possibility, not presently relevant to Uganda (and presumably less so to Tanganyika) because of the small size of their local markets. 'Uganda is too small a market to support a plant of economic size in most industries'.[43]

Tariff Protection and the Distribution of Gains and Losses

A second attempt to estimate the benefits and costs of the East African Common Market was made by D. P. Ghai in 1965. In contrast to the judgement of the Raisman Commission, which was that the distribution of gains had been unequal but that no territory had suffered a loss, Ghai's conclusion was that 'it appears that Kenya has been the greatest net beneficiary, that Uganda has on balance gained rather than lost, and that Tanganyika has suffered a substantial net loss'. This conclusion was reached on the basis of an entirely different approach from that of Raisman and Brown.

The method employed is akin to one which has been widely applied to the problem of assessing the costs and benefits of integration in developed countries[44] and involves employing margins of protection as an indicator of gains and losses. Specifically, gains are indicated by weighting each country's categories of inter-territorial exports by the relevant nominal degree of protection, while the losses are measured by each country's imports similarly weighted.

The logic of this approach is presumably that gain is the difference between the terms on which factors could be used and exports sold within the common market, and what these could otherwise have earned if the resources had instead been used to produce for the domestic or the world market. This magnitude is impossible to measure globally, but a maximum figure can be given by the loss which would be incurred if the prices of exports to other members of the common market had to be lowered sufficiently to offset fully import duties at the height of the common external tariff. Likewise, with respect to losses, the analysis assumes that all local products enjoying protection could be obtained more cheaply from abroad, and that the extra cost of local products is measured by the tariff protection given to East African industry.

On this approach, net gain or loss is closely related to the balance of inter-territorial trade which, as we have seen, is strongly in favour of Kenya. Indeed, on this basis if all items entering into trade within the common market were subject to protection at a uniform rate, a surplus country would gain in proportion to its favourable trade balance, and a deficit country would lose in proportion to its unfavourable balance. If rates of protection differ on items traded, the direct connection between trade balances and gains and losses is removed. It would then be conceivable for a deficit country to enjoy a net gain if the margin of protection on the products it exports to its partners were higher than the margin of protection on the products exported to it.[45] As can be seen from Table 4:7, in 1962, the year to which Ghai's analysis relates, Uganda's trade balance was in fact negative, whereas on his assessment she enjoyed a slight gain. One important implication of this approach is that there can be no net gains from integration to East Africa as a whole. Gains must exactly equal losses because net surpluses on inter-territorial trade exactly equal net deficits, and the rates of tariff employed for measuring gains and losses are identical. The possibility of net gains from the operation of the common market is ruled out.

Although the model underlying this analysis is not made explicit, it seems clear that the situation which Ghai presupposes is very different from that envisaged by the Raisman Commission and by Brown. The Raisman Commission were at pains to point out that 'the growth of industry under protection, displacing imports both in Kenya and the other territories, does not simply divert resources from one productive use to another, equally (or perhaps less) productive, as may happen when protection is applied in a highly developed country. It draws into employment labour which would otherwise be largely unproductive'.[46] Ghai's analysis on the other hand seems implicitly to assume a situation in which there is a given level of inputs of factors of production so that the alternative product of the factors has to be taken into account when assessing gain. Moreover, the alternative considered to importation from the rest of the common market is importation from the rest of the world, so that inter-territorial trade must, where industries receive protection, merely involve trade diversion.

Even if this approach is accepted, it is open to criticism on the ground that it assumes nominal rates of protection to be identical with the effective degree of protection.[47] But some part of trade within the common market may be 'independent' of the tariff protection in the sense that it is 'competitive' with imports. The extent to which this is the case has some bearing both on the distribution of the gains from the common market, and on the extent to which they may be attributable to the tariff preferences.

The Dependence of Inter-territorial Trade on the Common Market

Several reasons may be suggested for supposing that part of inter-territorial trade is not dependent on the preferences. In the first place, part of this trade is in commodities which are not dutiable if imported from outside East Africa. In the second place, some products which are important in inter-territorial trade such as milk, beer, and cigarettes appear to be competitive in price and quality with imports. In the third place, some protected commodities are able to compete in third countries. To the extent that this ability to compete does not reflect price discrimination, there is a presumption that inter-country trade in such products may be independent of the tariff protection. Allowing for these factors Hazlewood has suggested that more than one half of inter-country trade for the region as a whole could be regarded as independent of the tariff preference in 1962,[48] the proportions for Kenya, Uganda and Tanzania being respectively 50, 60, and 58 per cent.

Taking account of these factors provides an important improvement on the assessment of gains based on nominal protection. Nevertheless the international competitiveness of a country's common market exports is still not wholly satisfactory, either as a measure of their dependence or independence upon the preferences provided by the common market, or as an indicator of potential gains or losses. Hazlewood's analysis, like that of Ghai, relates the distribution of gains in the common market to the international competitiveness or lack of it, of the commodities which enter into trade amongst the common market countries. Both analyses involve comparisons of the situation of the countries inside the common market with what they might be if instead, sales were to the rest of the world, or requirements were purchased from the outside world. But the realistic alternative to a common market is not free trade, but three separately protected national markets. In such an alternative situation, some products now bought from Kenya may not be purchased from the rest of the world, but may instead be produced domestically. Some of these may be products in which Kenya is 'competitive' for the reasons which make Kenya competitive may also favour production in other East African countries. The relevant question then appears to be how the position of each country with three protected national markets would compare with its position in a common market. In this context, a relevant calculation of gains and losses should be related not to the extent to which Kenya's products are competitive in price and quality with imports from the rest of the world, but rather to the extent to which any differences in interterritorial export prices and local costs of production in the three countries would be outweighed by a tariff against their neighbours when tariff-induced changes in relative costs and demands have taken place.

Gains and Losses from Break-Up of the East African Common Market

The latest attempts[49] to measure the gains and losses of the common market do in fact proceed by assuming the alternative to be three separated national markets. Newlyn's analysis approaches the problem by taking the actual situation and comparing it with a hypothetical situation which would obtain with separate markets protected by a tariff at the level of the common market tariff. He is thus concerned in the first instance with the second question distinguished on page 131 above. He considers the problem from the standpoint of Tanzania and Uganda and does not consider the outcome for Kenya, nor for the market as a whole. His procedure is to ask: (i) which industries could be developed in Tanganyika and Uganda in substitution for imports at present obtained from Kenya; and (ii) what would be the (primary) change in the national products of these two countries which would result from such a development of industry. The latter is used as the measure of gain or loss. The analysis explicitly deals with two categories of industry; the first is industry which would be viable in Tanzania and Uganda, given protection; the second is common market-based industrial output. This is single-plant industry dependent on exports to the other countries and which would only be viable on the basis of the whole common market. The former is assumed to shift under protection, whereas the latter is assumed

138

to disappear. The increased national product resulting from shiftable industry is taken to be the value added in respect of the shiftable industrial output after deducting the offsetting loss arising from the complete loss of manufactured exports from Tanzania and Uganda to Kenya, which is assumed to follow, plus the loss involved in the closing down of common market-based industries in Tanzania and Uganda.

Evidently a crucial problem is to identify the different kinds of industry. Newlyn deals with this problem by regarding a Kenya industry as shiftable if the average of output per plant in Kenya as shown by the 1961 Kenya Census of Manufactures was less than the value of exports to Tanzania and Uganda. On this basis, some 54 per cent of Kenya's exports of manufactures to Tanzania, totalling £4mn. was designated as shiftable, and about £3·4mn. of exports to Uganda representing about 60 per cent of Kenya's exports to that country. Only two common market-based plants were identified; one in Tanzania (Bata), and one in Uganda (Nytil). Allowing for the closing down of these, and assuming that three separate national markets would entail a complete exclusion from Kenya of manufactured exports from Tanzania and Uganda, and after correcting also for the (small) spread effect[50], the following estimate was arrived at:

1961 Gain from Separate Markets

TANGANYIKA	+£1,563,000
UGANDA	−£ 49,000

Thus Newlyn concludes: 'On the basis of the criteria used and in respect of the 1961 figures, there would be a clear gain to Tanganyika and an insignificant loss to Uganda from leaving the common market.[51] It would not be correct of course, as Newlyn recognises, to conclude that withdrawal could be expected at once to produce a gain for a country equal to its calculated gain. Shiftable industries would not immediately spring up in the countries concerned. Nevertheless there would be a presumption that the location of industry would adjust itself gradually on the lines indicated, if the conditions for their viability are satisfied.

Several objections may be offered to the criteria employed in this calculation of gains and losses. The first centres on the identification of shiftable industries. The validity of the procedure employed in this analysis depends in the first instance on the output of an industry being homogeneous. In fact, the categories of the Kenya Census of Manufactures include such a diversity of products that the average output per plant obtained by dividing the total output of the industry group by the number of establishments is a largely meaningless statistic.[52] But even if this difficulty is ignored, the criterion is in itself a purely technical one. Merely because it may be possible for production to be carried on in a plant of given size does not imply that it is economical to do so. Newlyn deals with this by making the arbitrary assumption that, if the technical criterion of shiftability is satisfied, protection against Kenya to the extent of a tariff no higher than that of the existing common market will be enough to offset the economies of industrial concentration in Kenya and to ensure viability[53]. He admits that there is no evidence for this assumption but claims it to be plausible. Closer examination of its implications make it appear rather less so.

Given inter-country tariffs at the height of the common tariff, technically shiftable industries will only be viable in Tanzania and Uganda in the following cases: (i) where the technically shiftable Kenyan industries need the full protection of the tariff but the Tanzanian and Ugandan industries can produce as efficiently as in Kenya (even though at a higher cost than imports from the rest of the world); (ii) where the technically shiftable industries of Kenya do not need the full protection of the tariff, and where any higher cost of production in Tanzania and Uganda still leaves the local price below that of comparable products imported from outside East Africa. In other words, except where Tanzania and Uganda can produce at the same cost as Kenya (or more cheaply), only Kenya industry which is *both shiftable and not fully dependent on the tariff* would be viable in Tanzania and Uganda, unless increased protection is provided in the shape of a higher tariff or import restrictions. No doubt part of Kenya's technically shiftable industry would concern products for which the protection enjoyed by Kenya is not fully required. Beer and cigarettes are cases in point. But there is likely to be a number of industries which satisfy the technical criterion of shiftability but which are dependent on the tariff. To this extent, the size of this viable component will be overstated unless industries can produce at the same costs as in Kenya.

A second difficulty is that the analysis concentrates on the cost side, and implicitly assumes that changes in the relative prices of East African and imported products would leave the demand for local products unchanged, subject to the price of the local product being below that of comparable imports. But even if the local product continues to be cheaper, a significant narrowing of the price difference between the local product and the imported product would in many cases result in a diversion of demand to the imported product.

Thirdly, following on the previous point, the analysis takes no account of the repercussions of the imposition of the tariffs on the inter-territorial trade of industries which are neither shiftable nor common-market based. If inter-country tariffs were imposed, some of these products are likely to be imported instead from the outside world. This would entail a reduction of cost to Uganda and Tanzania which is a form of gain which ought not to be disregarded. Moreover, some of the products of such industries would continue to be sold to Tanzania and Uganda over the tariff though possibly in smaller quantities. Changes in their prices net of tariffs would also have to be taken into account. If they fall, perhaps because inter-territorial tariffs succeed in eroding unduly high profit margins, there would be a further gain to Tanzania and Uganda.

Fourthly, the value added of the Census of Manufactures is not an appropriate concept to employ for calculating the increase in national product unless all factors are local and in surplus. If all factors were in surplus (and local) the problem of development would be simplified indeed. A mere rise in the tariff rate, or deficit financed public expenditure would be sufficient to bring it about. Under East African conditions, a part of value added will accrue to foreign capital and expatriate labour. Only the tax on these incomes should be included for the purpose of arriving at *national* value added which is the concept relevant for calculations of national product. Although data are lacking to indicate what adjustment is necessary on this account, it is likely to be considerable for capital intensive industries which are foreign owned, and which employ a large expatriate staff.

It is also an extreme assumption to take the whole of national value added in the new manufacturing industries as a measure of the increment in national product unless the calculation is designed to show an upper limit to the potential gain, for this procedure disregards the possibility that some alternative national product may be foregone as a result of the increased industrial output in the indicated industries. Even if unskilled labour is not scarce in East Africa, many varieties of skilled and semi-skilled labour certainly are, to say nothing of organizing ability. Moreover, to the extent that the capital employed is Tanzanian or Ugandan, its employment can hardly be regarded as without an opportunity cost. Taking into account these considerations would provide additional reasons for reducing the gain to a good deal less than the value added in the shiftable industries. Moreover, unless all factors are in surplus, productivity losses due to a changed locational pattern of industry and decreased specialization within the region would also have to be taken into account. The offset on this account may be quite important.

Finally, it needs emphasis that the whole calculation is based on the assumption that the alternative to the common market is three separated national markets protected by a tariff at the level of the common market tariff. This is a convenient and justifiable analytical simplification, but it needs to be said that present tariffs are by no means necessarily optimal from the standpoint of Tanzania and Uganda. Controversies on its level and structure certainly suggest that in the past somewhat different views have been held in the three countries as to the content as of an appropriate tariff.

These considerations suggest the need for a broader concept of static gain than that employed by Newlyn, as well as the need to qualify that component of it which relates to the income generated in industrial expansion. A more appropriate measure of gain would have to take into account the following factors:

(i) the additional industrial output made possible by protection. In this connection it should be borne in mind that if there is a preference for industry, as described in Chapter 1, industrial output may be valued even if it generates no additional real product; (ii) the net increment in national product generated by the additional industrial output; (iii) any gains resulting from the opportunity to purchase some imports more cheaply from outside the common market together with any gains from the changes in the prices of goods which continue to be traded inter-territorially, over the tariff; (iv) a fourth source of gain, not so far mentioned, is derived from the additional revenue from the imposition of tariffs on inter-country trade. As already pointed out, except to the extent that the prices of Kenya's products fall, this revenue would merely represent a transfer from the private sector in Tanzania and Uganda to the exchequer. Nevertheless, if there are real costs involved in raising revenue by other means, as is likely to be the case in East Africa, the ability to impose such import duties will represent a real benefit to Tanzania and Uganda.

It does not seem to the writer that employing this broader concept of gain would alter the conclusion that substantial short term potential gains could be made by Tanzania from leaving the common market though the potential gain would be made up of several components. Moreover, the potential industrial expansion in Tanzania would be smaller than Newlyn suggests, and the national product so generated would be a great deal smaller. The likely outcome for Uganda is less certain, but on balance, broadening the concept of gain is likely to mean that she too could anticipate potential gains. For Kenya, losses would certainly be entailed. There would also be losses for East Africa as a whole in the sense that industrial output would be lowered; if factors are surplus this reduction in industrial output would also entail a lower regional product than would otherwise be the case. It does not seem justifiable to go beyond these broad generalizations on static gains and losses in the absence of much more information about costs and demand—at least, unless one is prepared to make so many arbitrary assumptions that one might as well assume one's conclusions.

It was pointed out (see page 131 above), that the crucial

question about the common market is whether some members would be better off in the long run if they withdrew. Newlyn of course recognises that this is so, and having completed the static analysis goes on to conclude that Tanganyika (or Uganda) would not obtain a longer term gain from leaving the common market. In reaching this conclusion, he follows the previous judgements of the Raisman Commission and of Brown. This conclusion is reached apparently in contradiction to the implications of the quantitative and largely comparative static analysis on the basis of the hypothesis that 'statistical observations repeated through time, showing loss from a common market arrangement on the criterion used . . . are not inconsistent with continuous gain from the common market over time'. This hypothesis is based on two considerations. First, in less developed countries there needs to be a prospective market of considerably greater size than the plant optimum to induce an industry to set up, although once established it will be willing to continue to operate with a market smaller than the optimum. But this clearly diminishes the relevance of the shiftability criterion. Secondly, at any point in time, such an analysis will always show a number of industries to be viable in the separate markets which would not have been so at the time they were established, when the markets were smaller. In the absence of a common market any gains from this accelerated industrial development will be lost.[54]

But although these qualifications are valid and important, they merely indicate that statistical calculations of loss are not inconsistent with long run gain; they do not guarantee it. Ultimately, Newlyn's conclusion rests on his judgement which necessarily goes beyond the facts, that the gain from the spread effect which accompanies the earlier establishment of certain industries will outweigh the importance of that aspect of backwash, which leads industries to continue to locate in Kenya even when the market is large enough for them to establish themselves in one of the other two countries. The writer would be more pessimistic than Newlyn or Brown about this outcome in the absence of measures to influence the location of industry in the common market in favour of Tanzania and Uganda.

The Costs and Benefits of other Aspects of East African Economic Co-operation

Before leaving this discussion, it is necessary to take account of the fact that the benefits and costs of the arrangements for East African economic co-operation as a whole depend not only on the operation of the common market, but also on the operation of the distributable pool, which is discussed in section 4 above, as well as on the operation of the common services. Before any conclusions could be reached about the benefits and costs of East African economic co-operation and their implications for policy, an evaluation would have to be made of their effects as a whole.

As to the distributable pool set up as a result of the Raisman Commission's recommendations, it is clear that this has the effect of redistributing revenue from Kenya to the other two countries. In 1961–2 Tanganyika derived £152,000 and Uganda £168,000 from this source which is an offset to any loss derived by those countries from the operation of the common market.[55] Since this redistribution must be assumed to disappear with separated national markets, this would reduce any potential gain from withdrawal for Tanzania and Uganda.

The position with respect to the common services is less clear. It is, of course, conceivable that the common market could be abandoned without necessarily entailing the break up of the common services. In other parts of Africa it has proved possible to continue to operate common services in the field of transport, communications and education despite the break up of arrangements for market integration. If it is assumed that the common services would continue, their operations can be disregarded in the analysis of benefits and costs. If on the other hand it is assumed perhaps with more realism that the common services could not survive a break up of the common market in their present form, the costs and benefits involved in any hypothetical alternative would also have to be estimated in order to arrive at an overall view of the effects of East African co-operation. Some attempts have been made recently to estimate the territorial incidence of the costs and benefits of the tax-financed common services, several of whose headquarters are located in Kenya.[56] In addition guesses may be made about the costs and benefits of the services such as railways, posts and telecommunications and airways, although the lack of accounting data on a country basis (except for harbours) and conceptual problems render any accurate evaluation difficult.

Any attempt to evaluate the effects of the common services on the distribution of benefits and costs would have to take into account three main aspects of their operation. In the first place, it would be necessary to take account of any fiscal redistribution brought about through the offsetting of losses and profits on the operation of the commercial services. From this point of view it seems probable that income transfers are made from Kenya and Uganda to Tanzania as a result of their absorption of substantial losses incurred by railways and harbours, and domestic airways in Tanzania. For 1963 on railways and harbours alone, Tanzania may have benefited to the extent of £1·4mn., but re-routing with break up would reduce this to £1mn. In the second place, to the extent that common services represent 'shiftable' industries, it would be necessary to estimate the effects on each country's product of an appropriate decentralization of office staffs and workshop operations. If the non self-contained services including tax administration and research services were broken up, more incomes would be generated in Tanzania and Uganda at the expense of Kenya, where most headquarters are located. Decentralization of workshops as in railways and airways would also operate to the advantage of Tanzania and Uganda from the standpoint of industrial product and income generation. In the third place, however, it would be necessary to take account of losses of operating economies in the event of break up. From such a loss of the economies of scale, each country might suffer considerably. The outcome of these considerations for the three countries is difficult to judge, but the writer would guess that Tanzania would be shown on balance to gain considerably from the common services, partly as a result of internal subsidies and partly due to economies of operation. Uganda on the other hand might be shown to gain little on balance and might even lose. Kenya, however, certainly benefits substantially on balance from the operation of the

146

common services, mainly as a result of their concentration in Kenya.

Conclusion

No satisfactory estimates of the benefits and costs of the East African Common Market have yet been made, mainly because although in a static framework the factors on which these values depend are clear enough, the cost and demand data necessary for adequate quantification are not available. Nevertheless, on the criteria of gain set out on page 143, there appears to the writer to be a strong presumption that, on static assumptions, gain could be derived by Tanzania from withdrawal, considering the common market alone. This gain would take the form partly of additional industrial development, which would to some extent generate additional income, and partly of lower cost imports and revenue gains which would accompany the diversion of import demand from Kenya to the outside world. The writer would also rate the potential loss from backwash highly, so that in the absence of measures to bring about a more equitable distribution of benefits, potential long term gain from withdrawal might also be anticipated. Certainly, relatively greater expenditure on infrastructure might diminish the importance of backwash but so long as the bulk of the market for many products continues to be in or near Nairobi, its importance is likely to be considerable. It is also likely that to some degree, which at the moment may be considerable, any gain from withdrawal would be offset by the loss of the distributable pool revenue, and also losses from the operation of the common services. The position for Uganda is much less clear, but some short term gains from a withdrawal from the common market also seem inherently likely on the interpretation of gain employed here, and in this case although there would also be a loss of revenue from the distributable pool as a result of withdrawal, a significant offsetting benefit is unlikely to be derived from the operation of the common services. For Kenya, there can be little doubt that she enjoys substantial benefits from the operation of the common market and that these are reinforced by the operation of the common services.

Uncertainty of course is a factor which has to be taken into account in any evaluation of alternatives. Unless gains from a prospective withdrawal are likely to be large, the weight of inertia is thrown in favour of the *status quo*. Moreover, it must not be overlooked that the effects of break up on the expectations of business men, and therefore on investment, may be an important consideration in any final assessment of the prospects although it is difficult to anticipate what effects break up might have on these factors. Just as business men may exaggerate the importance of the common market in their investment decisions at the present time, so the adverse effects of break up may also be exaggerated. This could well affect the prospects of industrial development adversely for a number of years in all member countries, and upset any presumption of gain from withdrawal for any member.

But even if it cannot, in the nature of the case, be demonstrated that any country would gain from leaving the common market in the long run, there seems little reason to doubt that its major benefits accrue to Kenya. Not one of the several independent economic evaluations of the operation of the common market has suggested the contrary. To the extent that this is so and is felt to be so, the preservation of the common market and its opportunities for expanded foreign investment, the exploitation of scale economies and specialization seems likely to demand measures to ensure a more equitable distribution of its benefits than has hitherto been the case. There are two main means by which this might be done. One is by more generous fiscal redistribution. The other is for the member countries to agree on measures to influence the location of industry so as to ensure that any danger of backwash is overcome, and a net benefit is perceived to be received by each member, as compared with the alternatives open to it outside the common market. But divergent views on the distribution of benefits and costs, differing concepts of gain and finally costs of redistribution may in combination render a feasible and stable solution difficult to find.

8 THE KAMPALA AGREEMENT

After this review of attempts to quantify the distribution of the costs and benefits of the East African Common Market, events leading up to the signing of the new Treaty are related briefly. Dissatisfaction with the disparate rates and character of development in the three East African countries which were attributed to the operation of the common market continued to be expressed in Tanzania and to a lesser extent in Uganda, after the Raisman Commission whose main contribution was to bring about a degree of fiscal redistribution. For a time inter-territorial discussions continued against the background of the federation initiatives which had resulted in the declaration of June 1963, but in the early months of 1964 it became clear that federation was not immediately practicable. At this juncture, Tanzania, which had viewed federation partly as a means of resolving intra-regional economic difficulties, threatened to withdraw from the common market. It was only after extensive negotiations that this was averted. The outcome was the Kampala Agreement of April 1964, which laid down an agreed basis for dealing with the inequalities of the common market and provided a framework for continuing economic co-operation. A slightly modified version was later approved at a meeting of Heads of State in Mbale in January 1965.[57]

The central feature of the Kampala Agreement is that it sought the solution to the problem of inequalities in the operation of the common market through the elimination of trade imbalances between the three countries. The chosen means were industrial location and relocation agreements and trade restrictions. But although, as the previous section has shown, trade balances and the distribution of benefits are related, they are not the same thing. Attempts to balance trade even at a higher level, and *à fortiori* if they result in a reduction of intra-regional trade, could entail a substantial reduction of the benefits from regional integration[58] if the trade is controlled in such a way as to frustrate comparative advantage.

In the Agreement five approaches to the rectification of imbalances were listed in the order in which it was thought they could be applied.

149

1 In certain existing industries in which the firms operate plants in more than one country, the firms were to be requested to increase the relative share of output in Tanzania.

2 Several new industries about to be established, of such a nature that there could, initially, be only one plant in East Africa, were to be allocated by agreement among the three territories. Most were assigned to Tanzania which was to receive radio assembly and manufacture, the manufacture of motor vehicles, tyres and tubes, and the manufacture of aluminium foil, circles and plain sheets. Uganda was to receive a bicycle assembly plant and a fertilizer plant, and Kenya a light-bulb factory. The allocation was to be made effective by each government agreeing to schedule these industries under the Industrial Licensing Acts and then arranging that licences issued by the East African Industrial Council (over which the three Governments have ultimate control) would be issued in accordance with the decisions reached under the Kampala Agreement.

3 A system of quotas was to be introduced on exports from the surplus countries to facilitate the building up of productive capacity in the deficit countries.

4 The 'surplus' countries agreed to attempt to increase their purchases from 'deficit' countries.

5 A committee of industrial experts was to be appointed to survey the long-range problem of allocation of industry among the three countries and the provision of a system of differential incentives to attract manufacturing industry to the less developed countries.

An early start was made on the first of the five measures and in the course of 1965 arrangements were made to expand the production of cigarettes, shoes, cement and beer in Tanzania, for which plans had already been made by the firms in question. It was estimated that these shifts would reduce the intercountry trade imbalance between Kenya and Tanzania by £1·8mn. or about a quarter of the 1963 net imbalance.

It does not seem to have been intended that the introduction of the third measure, quotas, was to be the precursor of a general reduction in inter-country trade and a move towards territorial self-sufficiency. On the contrary it was stated that quotas were not to be a permanent part of the East African

Common Market. It seems to have been envisaged that they would be applied only to a limited range of products, presumably carefully selected in the light of cost considerations, and would be a means of facilitating, by a degree of initial protection, the development of industries in Tanzania and Uganda, which could in the long run be viable within the common market. An inter-country quota committee was set up to implement this part of the agreement. Finally, and most importantly from the standpoint of the gains from the market, quotas were not to apply to the products of regional industries allocated in accordance with the Agreement. Thus these industries would enjoy the benefit of continued free access to the East African market as a whole.

If the Kampala Agreement had been fully implemented and operated in a liberal way, it could well have made it possible for the benefits of integration in East Africa to continue to be exploited, though admittedly at the cost of some loss in its benefits. By the middle of 1965, however, it had become clear that the agreement was inoperative, and indeed that the whole of the common services and the common market was in doubt. The first overt indication of difficulty came in mid-1965 when Tanzania unilaterally made provision for a wide range of import restrictions on the products of Kenya and Uganda as well as on goods originating from outside East Africa, and introduced quotas for many others.[59] These restrictions, which were further extended in 1966, were not only unilateral but also well outside what was contemplated in the Kampala Agreement.

Tanzania's actions were evoked by a complex of factors, which combined to produce a serious deterioration of economic relations between the three countries and a progressive loosening of the arrangements for integration. One operative factor is that Kenya's somewhat cool assent to the Kampala Agreement had been given on the understanding that the common currency would continue, in addition to the common services and the common market. When, in 1965, Tanzania decided to establish its own central bank and currency, Kenya seems to have felt no longer committed to the Kampala Agreement and this reacted primarily on the industrial location agreements. Soon after the initial Kampala Agreement indeed, Kenya had gone back on its support for the allocation of a Land-Rover Assembly plant to Tanzania and an agreed reallocation was made in the revised Agreement. During 1965, when confronted with offers from investors to establish in Kenya industries which were allocated to other countries under the Agreement, her response apparently was to fail to take steps to schedule allocated industries as had been envisaged under the Agreement. This inaction had the effect of rendering these provisions inoperative and postponing the commencement of these industries in Tanzania.

The failure of the industry sharing agreements gave rise to much bitterness in Tanzania and seems to have been the factor above all responsible for her resort to large scale import restrictions against Kenya. In their turn these must ultimately have had repercussions on policy in Kenya if only because Kenya could not be expected to continue to be willing to pay fiscal compensation in the face of such measures.

Had Tanzania's restrictions been made fully effective they would have resulted in the first instance in a replacement of many of Tanzania's imports from the rest of East Africa by imports from the rest of the world, rather than in the replacement of Kenya products by Tanzania products, for in many cases the additional productive capacity in Tanzania did not exist and was not immediately in prospect. In some cases indeed, diversion did occur. On the whole, however, the evidence suggests that the Tanzania system of import restriction was applied flexibly during 1966. Only a few major Kenyan exports were seriously affected by the restrictions in 1966. These included clothing and footwear (exports of which were cut by more than 50 per cent) and cigarettes. Exports of beer also fell by a third, and aluminium ware, paint and varnish and soap fell substantially. On the other hand, exports actually increased of a number of products which were subject to the new restrictions. Despite the increase in some categories of trade, the total value of exports to Tanzania declined by about £800,000 or 6 per cent compared with 1965. But there was an offsetting reduction of imports from Tanzania into Kenya of about £750,000, so that the trade imbalance in Kenya's favour was reduced by only £50,000. One reason for this is that Tanzania's trade restrictions increased competition in Kenya's own market for the affected products and so reduced Tanzania's ability to sell her competing products there. Thus an important effect of the Tanzanian controls has been to reduce trade in both directions. The balance of trade remained much the same, and any gain to Tanzania is likely to have been small. Apart from its failure to reduce the imbalance, the process of imposing import restrictions seems to have been essentially *ad hoc* and likely to have given rise to increased costs and inefficiency. An unselective use of quotas and prohibitions is a very blunt instrument to use as a means of redressing regional imbalances for they drastically limit the possibilities of taking advantage of any opportunities for regional specialization which may exist, and, could indeed lead to a complete loss of the benefits of the common market if the products of 'regional' industries were also scheduled.

This was the discouraging background which led in late 1965 to the establishment of the three country Ministerial Commission, under the chairmanship of Professor Kjeld Philip of Denmark. Its terms of reference were as follows:

'To examine existing arrangements in East Africa for co-operation between Kenya, Tanzania and Uganda on matters of mutual interest, and having due regard to the views of the respective Governments, to make agreed recommendations on the following matters:

(a) How the East African Common Market can be maintained and strengthened and the principles on which, and the manner in which, the Common Market can in future be controlled and regulated.

(b) The arrangements necessary for effective operation of the Common Market consequential upon the establishment of separate currencies.

(c) The extent to which services at present maintained in common between the three countries can be continued, and the form which such services should take.

(d) The extent to which (if at all) new services can be provided in common between the three countries, and the form which such services should take.

(e) The manner in which the common services should be financed.

(f) The extent to which the management of different services can be located in different parts of East Africa.

(g) The legal, administrative and constitutional arrangements most likely to promote effective co-operation between the East African countries in the light of the recommendations made under paragraphs (a) (b) (c) (d) (e) (f).'

9 THE TREATY FOR EAST AFRICAN CO-OPERATION

Early in 1967 the Philip Commission finally reached agreed recommendations on the matters referred to it, and in June the three Heads of State met in Kampala and agreed and signed a Treaty for East African Co-operation.[60] The Treaty establishes an East African Economic Community and as an integral part of this, an East African Common Market. Thus for the first time the common market will have a legal basis. While the aims of the community are broad, its central concern is to preserve the contribution to development of the common market and the common services while ensuring the equitable distribution of their benefits, and in particular of industrial growth. The Treaty is an impressive witness of its sponsors' dedication to East African unity, and there can be little doubt that if it is made fully effective and proves durable, it should enable East Africa to continue to enjoy the benefits of economic integration. With the increased emphasis on industrialization, these promise to be much greater in the future than they have been in the past. In many respects the Treaty largely confirms the already well established foundations of East African Co-operation, although there are a number of important innovations on both the administrative side and the purely economic side, together with many smaller changes.

From the standpoint of the machinery of co-operation, the principal executive authority for co-operation in the new Community remains as it was before, namely the three heads of state who now constitute the East African Authority. An important innovation is that the Authority is to be assisted by East

African ministers who will be appointed by each country, be of cabinet rank and who will have no other portfolio. The Authority will also be assisted by a number of Councils, namely the Common Market Council, the Communications Council, the Finance Council, the Economic Consultative and Planning Council, and the Research and Social Council. Of these, the first three are purely ministerial. This system replaces the existing system of Ministerial triumvirates. The East African Legislative Assembly is also reconstituted. In future it will consist of nine members appointed by each country, together with the East African Ministers and certain other members. It will pass Bills but all measures have to be assented to by the Heads of State before they are enacted. Other important changes include the constitution of all the major 'commercial' common services of East Africa as public corporations, explicitly charged with the duty of operating on a commercial basis. Hitherto only the East African Airways Corporation has been organized this way. Corporations will henceforward exist for railways, for harbours, which is to be separated from railways, for airways, and for posts and telecommunications. Each will have a board of directors.

On the financial side, much of the Treaty confirms existing practice with minor changes. This is the case in relation to the operation of the common external tariff which is regarded as a vital aspect of the common market, and for the harmonization of excises, the joint administration of the principal sources of revenue and the basic rules for apportioning customs and excise amongst the members of the common market. In the monetary field the Treaty largely prescribes a return to the *de facto* position which existed before the imposition of the Tanzanian exchange restrictions of February last though formal provision is made for consultation and for harmonization of monetary policies and for a limited degree of reciprocal credit in the case of balance of payments difficulties.

The Re-shaped Common Market

From an economic standpoint, the main interest of the Treaty for East African Co-operation centres on those provisions which have to do with the operation of the common market and common services. To what extent are these likely to enable the region to enjoy the advantages of integration, while at the same time facilitating an equitable distribution of its benefits? These two aspects are intimately related. The major benefits of integration will only be secured if the stability of the market can be relied upon; long-term stability is unlikely, however, unless all partners are satisfied that their long run interests are best served by remaining within the Community.

From the standpoint of obtaining the gains from integration, the important features of the treaty are those dealing with the reorganization of the common services and common market. One important change is the decentralization of the headquarters of the common services. Each country is allocated two headquarters: Railways remain in Nairobi; Harbours and the Headquarters of the Community itself go to Tanzania; and Posts and Telegraphs and the new East African Development Bank will be set up in Uganda. There will also be some decentralization on the operational side, with a bias in favour of Tanzania and Uganda in relation to new development. Although these changes may result in some loss of administrative economies, they seem likely to preserve the main operating economies which are the justification for co-ordinated activities.

The gains from the common market itself derive largely from free trade and the stimulating effect this has on economic activity and development. The treaty provides that all trade between the three East African countries in goods of East African origin[61] is to be free of restrictions. There are exceptions, however; quantitative restrictions may be imposed on basic staple foods or major export crops subject to special marketing arrangements. Nevertheless the long term aim is to extend the common market to agriculture and trade in agricultural products, though no immediate changes in the present managed marketing system are proposed. Clearly the gains from integration in East Africa are largely bound up with industrial development. The bulk of present trade is in manufactured products, and it is here that the opportunities for potential expansion are greatest.

From this vantage point, the important aspect of the treaty

156

is the one which permits the imposition of the so-called transfer tax. The transfer tax is a euphemistic term for the imposition of limited inter-country tariffs. Precisely how it is to be administered is not specified in the treaty. It appears, however, that the tax will be collected from the importer on the basis of the transfer form which must be completed for any shipment of goods from one country to another. Hitherto shippers have had little financial incentive to fail to execute the transfer form or to make erroneous statements. This will no longer be the case with the imposition of transfer taxes. Presumably it will then become necessary to institute border checks in order to ensure that all imports are correctly documented.

A transfer tax may be imposed by a country which is in deficit in its total inter-country trade in manufactures on imports from a partner state on an amount of trade not exceeding its deficit in manufactures with that country. Once a country comes into 80 per cent balance in its total trade on manufactured goods in East Africa, however, it loses the right to impose new transfer taxes. Certain limitations are prescribed which are partly designed to prevent local products from being replaced by cheaper goods from outside the common market, and partly to prevent protected competition with the industries of partners. The rate of transfer tax cannot exceed 50 per cent of the common external tariff; it is levied on the market price at the frontier, including transport but excluding any tax already levied. Assuming a common external tariff of 30 per cent it would be possible for selected actual or prospective industries of a deficit country to receive a protective tariff of 15 per cent plus 15 per cent of the costs of transporting a Kenya product to the border. The transfer tax system is intended to be temporary. Under the Treaty, no individual tax may continue for longer than eight years; the working of the system is to be reviewed after five years, and is to come to an end after fifteen years.

On the basis of the 1966 patterns of trade, and the definition of manufacture contained in Annex IV of the treaty, these provisions would mean that Tanzania may impose transfer taxes against Kenya's goods to a maximum extent of trade valued at £9·8mn. and against Uganda's goods to the extent of £2·1mn. Uganda may impose transfer taxes against Kenya-produced articles to the extent of £7·4mn., but may not impose taxes against Tanzania. Kenya of course may not impose transfer taxes at all. The actual extent of trade so protected would be very much smaller than these amounts because of the condition that transfer taxes may only be imposed where the product is being produced in the deficit country or is expected to be produced within three months of the imposition to a value of £100,000 or 15 per cent of the deficit country's consumption of the product in question.

It is reasonable to anticipate that the transfer tax mechanism will lead to an expansion in the deficit countries of those industries for which the maximum permitted degree of protection is sufficient to offset Kenya's cost advantages from lower production costs, including external economies. Although the transfer tax does in fact represent some retreat from a full common market, it certainly represents an advance on the quota system prescribed in the Kampala Agreement; it will allow comparative advantage to determine trade—even if to a slightly restricted extent. Such a device is likely to be most useful to Tanzania and Uganda in encouraging completely new product lines. Where some reciprocal trade exists, the initial effect is likely to be a reduction of trade in both directions which is likely to be mutually unprofitable. If, for example, Kenya's clothing and textile exports to Tanzania are curtailed by the imposition of a transfer tax, competition for Kenya's domestic market will become more acute, and this may inhibit existing Tanzanian exports from coming into Kenya. This seems to have happened to some extent in 1966 as a result of the quantitative restrictions imposed by Tanzania against Kenya. Compared with 1965, Kenya's exports in paints, corrugated sheets, cotton fabrics, clothing and footwear fell by £0·8mn. and inward trade in these items fell by £0·4mn. Clearly the transfer tax system is to be applied only to those industries where additional plants can profitably operate within the confines of the national markets of the deficit countries and where protection against the rest of East Africa will not be needed for more than a temporary period. Transfer taxes, however, cannot be imposed in the case of industries where only one plant can operate profitably at present levels of tariff protection. Consequently, their imposition should offer no hindrance to the continued establishment of these industries which necessarily depend upon the whole of the East African market. Such industries may eventually find themselves facing protected competition from a second plant when the national market of a deficit country can support at least 70 per cent of its output. But when a second plant becomes profitable, it will presumably be set up in any case. In short, although the treaty permits a moderate interference with the common market in relation to small scale industries, and although these interferences are likely to result in some increases in production costs within the region, the framework of the treaty does appear to provide a good basis for the continued exploitation of many of the gains from integration.

The second standpoint from which the treaty may be assessed is the extent to which its provisions seem likely to produce an equitable distribution of benefits. The three main determinants of the distribution of the benefits of the present arrangements for economic co-operation in East Africa are the common services themselves, the system of fiscal redistribution which was established in 1961 following the report of the Raisman Commission and the gains and losses which arise from the operation of the common market which are related to the character and extent of inter-country trade. How does the Treaty affect these factors?

As to the common services, the Treaty provides for a decentralization of headquarters from Nairobi, for the establishment of territorial organizations and for some redistribution of actual and potential operations. These changes will result in some redistribution of income away from Kenya towards Tanzania and Uganda. It is not clear whether the fact that the new corporations are henceforward enjoined to operate on a commercial basis will entail any changes in tariffs or services. Probably it is safe to assume that within the requirement of overall profitability, room will continue to be found for concealed subsidies which hitherto have benefited Tanzania and, to a limited extent, Uganda.

The relative contribution of each country to the financing of the General Fund Services, which are operated by the Community itself, is determined much as at present. Each country is to contribute in proportion to the revenue it derives from customs and excise and from the income tax on companies engaged in finance and manufacturing. However, contributions will be limited to what is required to finance approved expenditures, so that, unlike the case of EACSO, it will not be possible for the Community to build up unexpended balances.

Fiscal redistribution, through the distributable pool, the second determinant of the distribution of benefits, is to continue for a transitional period, though on a reduced scale. However, by June 1969, the pool should disappear entirely. From this change, considered in isolation, Kenya may gain as much as £0·55mn., Tanzania may lose about £0·3mn. and Uganda £0·25mn.

The third and perhaps major determinant of the gains and losses of the common market is the character and extent of the industrial development which it promotes in each country and the inter-country trade which is associated with this development.There are two main provisions in the Treaty relevant to this, namely the transfer tax and the operations of the newly established East African Development Bank.

As noted already, the transfer tax should have a favourable effect on industrial development in Tanzania and Uganda. It is difficult to assess the extent of its impact; nevertheless since the maximum additional protection is limited to about 15 per cent its effect is not likely to be large. The imposition of the tax may also make it possible to increase tax revenues in the less developed partner states. Of course, if the prices of the taxed products do not fall, the additional revenues will merely involve a transfer from their consumers to the exchequer, but given the difficulty of raising the money in other ways, this is still an advantage. It may even be that the imposition of the transfer tax will cause price reductions in some Kenya products imported by the other countries. In this event there would be a real income gain to the less industrialized partners as they could import goods from Kenya more cheaply. Any such price reductions would render the manufacture of competing products in the less developed partners more difficult.

But any gains derived in these ways are solely gains in relation to the working of the existing common market. If the deficit

160

countries withdrew from the common market they might expect to establish even more industries which are viable within the confines of the national market; in addition they would be able to buy some of the products now imported from Kenya more cheaply from the outside world. Looking at the common market aspect of the new community alone, Tanzania and Uganda can only be said to benefit in a relevant sense if they attract more capital and industry than if they were outside the common market. This is partly bound up with the possibility of their attracting a share of large scale industry made possible by the existence of the common market.

It may be argued that the immunity of industry from the imposition of a transfer tax in deficit countries will in fact provide an incentive for some new large scale industry to locate in these areas. This conclusion must be regarded as very doubtful. To be sure, where such an industry is set up in Tanzania, it is virtually assured that no transfer tax will be imposed on its product in Kenya or Uganda. But as soon as market growth makes a second plant profitable, a competing plant will most probably be put into operation in Kenya, and on a scale to serve the Kenya market. Should the industry be located in Kenya in the first place (where a large part of the East African market for manufactures is), it will still be assured of freedom from the transfer tax, at least until such time as a second plant becomes viable in a deficit country as a consequence of the protection afforded by the transfer tax. If these are the alternatives, it is difficult to argue that the transfer tax will significantly affect the location choice for new large scale industries in East Africa.

There is one remaining institution provided for in the treaty whose operations might conceivably affect the balance of industrial location within the region: the East African Development Bank. The Development Bank has been set up to promote industrial development in the partner states through financial and technical assistance. Industry is defined to include manufacturing, assembling and processing (including food) but not building, transport or tourism. Initially its subscribed capital is to be £10mn. Of this, £6mn. will be subscribed in equal shares by the three countries. Provision is made for subscription by approved institutions as long as the total holding of the three partner states does not fall below 51 per cent, and presumably the negotiators of the Treaty hoped that £4mn. would be so subscribed.

From the standpoints of balance and equity in the common market three important aspects of the Bank's operations may be mentioned. (i) It is to give priority to industrial development in the relatively less industrially developed partner states, thereby endeavouring to reduce the substantial industrial imbalances between them. (ii) Wherever possible it is to finance projects designed to make the economies of the partner states increasingly complementary in the industrial field. (iii) Of its total loans, guarantees and investments, Tanzania and Uganda are each to get 38·75 per cent and Kenya the remaining 22·5 per cent.

What role can the Bank be expected to play in bringing about the growth and equitable distribution of industry? Its contribution will depend on two main factors: the extent to which the establishment of the Bank results in the provision of *additional* finance for the region and not merely the diversion of funds which would otherwise be available through direct aid or capital raised by the three countries acting separately; and the extent to which the availability of finance acts as a major constraint on establishment of industry in East Africa. It will not be possible to form a judgement on the first aspect for some time, for the Bank's ability to attract additional funds will be bound up with the reputation it earns. Initially its impact is not likely to be large in this area.

Its contribution therefore must be assessed primarily in terms of the constraint of finance and the contribution to balanced development which results from its investment policies. The extent to which finance is a constraint on industrial development varies in the three East African countries. It is probably least important in Kenya and most important in Tanzania. Finance for large scale industries has hitherto come mainly from outside East Africa, and it has been readily available for viable industries. This situation seems likely to continue, so that the contribution of the Development Bank to balanced development will be limited if, as is laid down in its charter, the Bank finances only economically sound and technically feasible projects. On the other hand, private capital may not flow as freely into some parts of East Africa as in the past. For instance, the nationalisation measures adopted by Tanzania can hardly have been without effect from this point of view. Thus scope exists for the backward members to derive gains from the operations of the Bank. Initially, however, any gain to the lagging members will be limited to the difference between their contributions (one third) and their shares (38·75 per cent). This amounts to £0·325 mn. plus, in the longer run, a gain from whatever effect the Bank's operations may have in attracting additional capital to the region. Of the hoped-for £4mn. from institutions, Tanzania and Uganda would be entitled to £1·55mn. each, and Kenya to £0·9mn. By no means all of this would be additional capital, however.

The Treaty on East African Co-operation is an impressive measure. If it is fully implemented and proves to be durable, it will provide a basis for the continued exploitation of the economic gains from integration, though it does admittedly entail some modest initial departure from a full common market in manufactures. By preserving the main structure of economic co-operation in East Africa, and in some ways extending it, the agreement provides a springboard from which an even closer unit may be fashioned, involving perhaps a full common market and possibly political integration. Moreover the treaty may become the basis of a wider East African Community, perhaps including Zambia.

But all these possibilities depend on an assurance of stability in relation to the market's operation and a determination to make it work on the part of its members. Ultimately this must depend on the extent to which each member is satisfied. Obviously the mere fact that the treaty has been signed at all is an indication that the three member countries are in earnest about the common market. However, possible dissatisfaction on the part of one or more members may emerge in the future. And should doubts arise about the cohesiveness of the present arrangements, the main gain from integration—any additional capital inflow—may be likely to fall away.

Naturally it is very difficult to assess the equity of arrangements such as this, but it is arguable that the outcome is a shortsightedly hard bargain for certain partners. It is true that Tanzania and Uganda will continue to derive benefits from the redistributive effects of the common services—as well as benefits from their operating economies, and will enjoy new benefits from their decentralization. It is also clear that Tanzania and Uganda will get some differential benefit from the operations of the Development Bank, but this seems small compared with the annual fiscal transfers hitherto received by those countries. In relation to the operation of the common market itself, however, Tanzania and Uganda seem to get little out of the new arrangements that they might not have enjoyed independently. Not only does fiscal compensation disappear, but the kind of industrialisation which will be fostered by the transfer tax does not need the common market to make it viable. And once such protected industries compete substantially in the markets of the other countries, the protection afforded by the tax may be withdrawn.

The problem of ensuring that the lagging countries get a share of the *additional* industry made possible by the existence of the common market, which takes the form mainly of industries requiring the whole of the market for profitable operation, has not been tackled. It is, of course, not necessarily the best economic sense to try to push industries which need the East African market to the more backward members, because such industries often require advanced technologies and might, in some cases, be at a particular disadvantage in those areas. However, if the lagging countries are not to get any 'regional' industries it can be argued that they deserve more than their fair share of the other smaller-scale industries.

It seems that the basic problem which has confronted the common market ever since industrialization got under way has not been resolved. This might conceivably happen in two ways. In the first place, within the framework of the Treaty, fiscal incentives might be worked out to attract more industry to Tanzania and Uganda; nevertheless, the chances of doing this satisfactorily *after* the Treaty has been signed and the bargaining has been done are surely minimal. In the second place, there is a possibility that bargaining will still take place over the location of industries. This possibility arises basically because the common external tariff is not static; even Kenya is likely to wish to institute changes in order to facilitate industrial development, and part of the price for agreement on adjustments may conceivably be a deal on industry. In other words, bargaining for industry may find a focus in the tariff which to some extent has always been the case. In the course of these negotiations additional incentives may be provided for Tanzania and Uganda. These incentives may improve the long run prospects of cohesion for the common market.

Finally, although this discussion has focused on economic considerations, it cannot be too strongly stressed that East African Co-operation is a matter of politics as well. But, idealism and defence considerations apart, politics is very much concerned with who gets what. The less equitable are the economic aspects of co-operation, the more strain will be placed on the purely political motive which is undoubtedly a factor of continuing importance in relation to East African Co-operation.

REFERENCES: CHAPTER 4

1 Although it was technically united with Tanganyika in April 1964 Zanzibar did not form part of the common market until June 1967 when by Presidential decree, the East African Customs and Excise Management Act was extended to Zanzibar. Prior to this Zanzibar maintained its own customs tariff (in general much lower than that of the mainland) and its own customs administration, although it did participate in the common income tax administration and in the monetary union. In this chapter, the name Tanzania will be used to refer to the country as a whole, but all statistics relate to Tanganyika alone, and the tables are so headed.

2 See *East African Statistical Review*, March 1967, pp. 74–5, and footnotes to Table 4:2.

3 Quoted in C. P. Haddon-Cave, 'Real Growth of the East African Territories 1954–60', in *East African Economics Review*, June 1961, p. 37.

4 For an attempt to relate the importance of inter-territorial trade to monetary GDP in East Africa see P. Ndegwa, *The Common Market and Development in East Africa*, East African Publishing House, Nairobi, 1965. pp. 110–11.

5 The operations of the Currency Board have at various times included Ethiopia, Somaliland and Aden.

6 On the growth of economic co-operation in East Africa see in particular, *East Africa, Report of the Economic and Fiscal Commission* (The Raisman Report), HMSO London, CMD 1279, 1961.

7 See Jane Banfield, 'The Structure and Administration of the East African Common Services Organisation', in (ed.) C. Leys and P. Robson, *Federation in East Africa; Opportunities and Problems*, Oxford University Press, 1965.

8 The purposes and operation of the distributable pool are discussed below in Section 4.

9 For a detailed account of the fiscal arrangements up to 1964, see J. F. Due, and P. Robson, Tax Harmonisation in the East African Common Market, in *Fiscal Harmonisation in Common Markets* (ed. C. S. Shoup), Vol. 2. Columbia University Press, 1967.

10 See the Customs Management Act 1952, amended to 1966.

11 The current legislation is to be found in the Income Tax Management Act of 1958, amended to 1966.

12 There have been one or two minor differences—see Due and Robson, *op. cit.*

13 See *Uganda Government, Budget Speech*, June 15, 1966.

14 A review of past differences will be found in Due and Robson, *op. cit.*

15 See Tanzania, Budget Speech by the Minister of Finance, June 1966.

16 See Raisman Report, para. 205.

17 See Raisman Report, para. 37.

18 See A. Hazlewood, Economic Integration in East Africa, Nairobi, 1965. Unpublished Seminar paper, p. 14.

19 For a very good account of the structure and operation of the monetary system of East Africa, see W. T. Newlyn, *Money in an African Context*, Oxford University Press, Nairobi, 1967.

20 See W. T. Newlyn, *Economic Policy in Uganda*, Entebbe, 1965, Chapter 7. The authority for the last sentence is a personal statement by W. T. Newlyn to me.

21 See *The Present Monetary System and its Future*. Report to the Government of Tanganyika by Erwin Blumenthal, Government Printer, Dar es Salaam, 1963, p. 1.

22 *op. cit.*, para. 75, p. 32.

23 See *op. cit.* para. (d) page 38.

24 The Declaration is reprinted in Leys and Robson, *op. cit.*

25 These developments are discussed on pp. 151-3.

26 They are discussed in detail in Newlyn, *op. cit.* (1967), Chapter 9.

27 See p. 51.

28 For a review of attempts to establish empirically the effects of integration on trade flows in EEC and elsewhere, see the interesting article by B.

Balassa, Trade Creation and Trade Diversion in the European Common Market, *The Economic Journal*, March 1967 and the various works cited therein.

29 These are discussed in section 8 below.

30 *op. cit.* pp. 61–2.

31 See International Bank for Reconstruction and Development, *The Economic Development of Tanganyika* (1961); *The Economic Development of Uganda* (1961); and *The Economic Development of Kenya* (1963), all published by Johns Hopkins University Press. Also B. F. Massell, *East African Economic Union: An Evaluation and Some Implications for Policy*, Santa Monica: RAND, 1963, p. 84.

32 See for instance Raisman Report, p. 24, para. 81.

33 *op. cit.* p. 25, para. 83.

34 *op. cit.* p. 62, para. 193.

35 For a discussion see D. Belshaw, 'Agricultural Production and Trade in the East African Common Market', in Leys and Robson, *op. cit.*

36 *op. cit.* p. 74, para. 101.

37 See A. J. Brown, 'Customs Union Versus Economic Separatism in Developing Countries', Part I and II, *Yorkshire Bulletin of Economic and Social Research*, May and November 1961.

38 See D. P. Ghai, 'Territorial Distribution of the Benefits and Costs of the East African Common Market', in Leys and Robson, *op. cit.*

39 W. T. Newlyn, 'Gains and Losses in the East African Common Market', *Yorkshire Bulletin*, November 1965.

40 See A. Hazlewood, 'The East African Common Market: Importance and Effects', *Bulletin of the Oxford University Institute of Economics and Statistics*, February 1966. Also 'The Shiftability of Industry and the Measurement of Gains and Losses in the East African Common Market', *Bulletin*, May 1966.

41 See R. H. Green, 'East African Economic Union—An approximate Balance Sheet', *EDRP Paper* 93, Makerere University College.

42 Brown's model in fact takes these into account.

43 *op. cit.* p. 94.

44 See for example, H. G. Johnson, 'The Gains from Free Trade in Europe; an Estimate', *Manchester School*, September 1958.

45 It is one of Ghai's contentions that the average degree of protection on Kenya's inter country exports is higher than that on those of the other two countries. Compare however, Hazlewood, *Bulletin*, February 1966.

46 Raisman Report, p. 24, para. 80.

47 Ghai does recognize (p. 38) that it is, strictly, effective protection which

is relevant to this exercise and hence that the tariff rate provides an estimate of the maximum protection afforded. Nevertheless he suggests that the rate of customs duty imposed on competing imports 'is a close approximation of the effective protection enjoyed'. On the concept of effective protection, see the important article by W. M. Corden, 'The Structure of a Tariff System and the Effective Protection Rate', *Journal of Political Economy*, June 1966. B. Balassa has attempted an empirical analysis of effective protection in a number of industrial countries in his article entitled, 'Tariff Protection in Industrial countries: an Evaluation', *Journal of Political Economy*, December 1965. See also M. J. Flanders, 'Measuring Protectionism and Predicting Trade Diversion', *Journal of Political Economy*, April 1965.

48 See Hazlewood, February *Bulletin*, page 6. Hazlewood does in fact suggest two alternative definitions of independence, namely where 'the products Kenya sells inter-territorially would still be competitive with imports from outside East Africa *if there were no external tariff* (my italics) or, alternatively, if the tariff were applied to inter-territorial trade (p. 3). Nevertheless, the demonstration on p. 4 *et seq.*, on which the estimates are based, rests on the proposition that for category (1) 'the local products would still be cheaper than the imported products if they enjoyed no preference', and for category (3) that they are competitive with imports. But of course, if these conditions apply, it does not follow that the products would necessarily continue to be traded in the presence of inter-country tariffs.

49 By Newlyn and Green. See footnotes 39 and 41 above.

50 Newlyn terms his spread effect *net spillover ratio*. It is made up of the loss Tanganyika and Uganda incur by buying Kenya's products at a higher price than from the rest of the world, offset by their gain from Kenya's higher imports from Tanganyika and Uganda. If this ratio is positive, there will be an offset to the income gain from any industry which is shiftable to Tanganyika and Uganda. Newlyn puts this ratio at 0·1 for Uganda and zero for Tanganyika.

51 *loc. cit.* p. 135.

52 See Hazlewood, *Bulletin*, May 1966, for comments on this.

53 *op. cit.* p. 133.

54 *op. cit.* p. 137.

55 Employing assumption 1. See Table 4:6 above.

56 See Hazlewood, 'The Territorial Incidence of the East African Common Services', *Bulletin*, August 1965.

57 The revised version was reprinted unofficially in the *East Africa Journal* of April 1965.

58 See for instance Appendix 1 to the Kampala Agreement, *Operation of the Quota System*, para. 6, which seems to have very restrictive implications.

59 The position at December 12, 1965 is summarized in *Inter-territorial Trade Restrictions by Tanzania through Import Licensing*, EACSO Economic Advisory Unit, Paper 97. Papers 98 and 99 list restrictions by Kenya and Uganda. Only one item is listed for Kenya (onions), and two for Uganda (ale, beer and stout; cement).

60 See *Treaty for East African Co-operation*, June 6, 1967, Government Printer, Nairobi, Kenya, on behalf of the East African Common Services Organization.

61 Goods of East African origin are those of which the value of materials imported does not exceed 70 per cent of its ex-factory value. See *Treaty*, Article 11, para. 3.

CHAPTER 5

ECONOMIC INTEGRATION IN EQUATORIAL AFRICA

1 THE BACKGROUND

THE second important example of economic integration in Africa is that of French-speaking Equatorial Africa, which consists of Congo (Brazzaville), Gabon, the Central African Republic and Chad, together with the Federal Republic of Cameroon. A substantial measure of integration between the first four of these countries has existed since 1910 when the federation of French Equatorial Africa (AEF) was established with a Governor-General and a High Commission located in Brazzaville. At the time of its formation, it seems to have been envisaged that the Federation's four constituent territories, then known as Moyen Congo, Gabon, Oubangui-Chari and Chad, should retain a substantial amount of economic and administrative autonomy. The government-general was to undertake a limited range of common services, including defence, transport, posts and telegraphs, and the collection and distribution of customs duties which provided the main source of revenue. Apart from undertaking these activities, its functions were to be limited to guiding and giving coherence to territorial policies. As things turned out, however, the government-general developed strong centralizing tendencies. Although some decentralization took place soon after the second world war, up to the period immediately before independence the administration of the area retained many of the characteristics of a fairly strong federation.

During the early fifties the structure and the operation of AEF was increasingly criticized by the elected members of its Federal Grand Council. A main ground of complaint was that the federal government was spending a disproportionate amount of the resources of the individual territories. It was claimed that the federal administration was overstaffed and that its administration of the financial services was inefficient. The representatives of the individual territories demanded that a greater proportion of territorial revenues should be available for territorial purposes. A further source of dissension was that Gabon, the wealthiest of the four, increasingly objected to subsidising the poorer members through the federal fiscal system.[1] Although it was not apparent at the time, 1956 marked the beginning of the end for the federal system and during the next four years the absence of any widespread sentiment in favour of attaining independence within a federation coupled with the territorial dissatisfactions with the operations of the old one were enough to produce dissolution. Following the *loi cadre* of 1956, elected territorial governments were established, and in 1957 most of the responsibilities of the federation were transferred to them. By 1958 these territorial governments had become separate autonomous republics within the French Community and by 1960 all were fully independent.

Despite their ultimately expressed wish to attain independence separately, it was hardly possible during their gradual movement towards this objective for the territorial governments to be unaware of the very real economic limitations to which they were subject by virtue of their small size, lack of skilled manpower and the difficulties of controlling the movements of goods and factors of production across their borders. Thus, despite their lack of support for federation, all four, including Gabon, were ready to agree to maintain the former federal economic links though part of the price for Gabon's co-operation was a change in her favour of the method of revenue distribution.

A convention of June 1959[2] was the instrument through which provision was made for the preservation of the customs union and the operation of certain common services. Apart from providing for the establishment of an Equatorial Customs Union, the Union Douanière Équatoriale (UDE), and for co-ordination of the internal taxes of the four countries, the convention also made provision for the establishment of certain central organizations to replace former high commission administrative services and for the continued common operation

172

of rail and river transport services, posts and telegraphs, the customs administration and certain other services. Provision was also made somewhat later in a separate measure for the continuance of the monetary union. Thus, on July 1, 1959, when the Federation was formally terminated there existed a framework which offered the possibility of a high degree of continued economic co-operation among its four former members.

The fifth member of this area is the Federal Republic of Cameroon, which was created in October 1961 out of the former French Cameroon (which attained independence in January 1960) and the former British Southern Cameroons.[3] The major partner in the new Federation, the former French Cameroon, had already enjoyed close market links with the other countries of Equatorial Africa for a number of years, and also shared a common currency and these arrangements were continued after independence. In 1961 co-operation between Cameroon and UDE was taken a stage further by a new convention[4] which provided for the progressive integration of the Cameroon market into UDE, and for other forms of co-operation comparable to those existing between its four original members. The framework of economic co-operation in Equatorial Africa has since been further strengthened by the treaty of December, 1964, which established the Union Douanière et Économique de l'Afrique Centrale (UDEAC).[5]

2 THE ECONOMIC STRUCTURE OF THE UDEAC COUNTRIES

The salient features of the area in terms of physical conditions are its vast size, sparse population and underdeveloped transport facilities. The five UDEAC countries have a total area of nearly 1,200,000 square miles, which is roughly equivalent to the whole of Western Europe or India. For the area as a whole, population in 1964 was probably of the order of 11 mn, and the rates of growth are for Africa relatively low. Average population density is about 9 per square mile and the range is from 24 in Cameroon to 5 in the Central African Republic and Gabon. The population density of the four equatorial states is thus among the lowest in Africa.

This vast area is on the whole poorly provided with transport facilities. Railways are few. The road system, both within the countries and between them is bad. The so called *voie federale* or federal road, which consists of the Congo–Océan railway (CFCO) from Pointe Noire via Dolisie to Brazzaville and the Congo river from Brazzaville to Bangui, has up to now been the main commercial artery of the four UDE countries, and the chief means of access to the sea for its two land-locked members. The route is slow and involves many handling operations. Much of the Upper Oubangui is very distant from the Bangui terminal. Fort Lamy itself is 625 miles from the Bangui terminal of the *voie federale* and thus 1,850 miles from the sea at Pointe Noire. From Dolisie a branch of the Congo–Océan railway runs north to Mbinda just south of the Gabon border and links with an industrial line serving Gabon's manganese ore deposits at Moanda. A common organization, the Agence Transéquatoriale des Communications (ATEC) with headquarters at Pointe Noire is responsible for the operation of this system. There is a separate directorate for the river services (*voies navigables*) at Bangui. In 1965 a separate directorate for roads was created within ATEC which operates from Fort Archambault. It has the function of maintaining the two inter-state roads which link with the system, namely that from Bangui via Fort Archambault to Fort Lamy, and that from Dolisie (Congo) to N'Dende in Gabon.

The only other railways of the area are in Cameroon. The main line links the port of Douala with the federal capital at Yaoundé and with Mbalmayo a little to the south of the capital. Douala is also connected by rail to Nkongsamba to the north-east. A branch from this line is in course of construction from Mbanga to Kumba, in West Cameroon. The line from Douala to Yaoundé and the northward road provides for Chad an alternative all-UDEAC outlet to the sea. It is about 1,250 miles, which is approximately the distance involved in the two routes which link Fort Lamy with the sea through Nigeria. One of these employs the road to Maidaguri (150 miles) and the railway from there to Lagos. The other, which is usable for only two months of the year, goes to Garoua and from there by way of the Benoue and Niger rivers to Burutu.

The main line to Yaoundé is now being extended northward to Ngaoundéré. This extension is the start of the Trans-

Cameroon railway which is a strategic element of Cameroon's Development Plan. There is a project which is supported by the Governments of Chad and Cameroon to extend the Trans-Cameroon railway beyond Ngaoundéré through Moundou to Fort Archambault. This would traverse the major part of Chad's cotton zone and would offer Chad the prospect of substantial economies in transport costs. Another project, which is supported by the Central African Republic, envisages the construction of a railway from Bangui eastward to Ébaka in Cameroon. This would link up with the Northern extension of the railway from Yaoundé, and provide a direct route from the Central African Republic to the sea at Douala, which would be cheaper than the *voie federale*. This railway would also open up the CAR's high potential regions of Lobaye and Haute Sangha. In addition to these developments, the Gabon government is seeking to finance a 560 km. railway estimated to cost 160mn. dollars from the coast at Owendo to Mekambo in the east to exploit the Mekambo iron ore deposit.

If the planned links of Chad and CAR with the Trans-Cameroon railway should materialize, they will have important implications for the future pattern of industrial economic activity in the common market. Hitherto this has been centred on the Brazzaville-Pointe Noire axis for the UDE countries. The *Transcamerounais* and its extensions are likely to bring about a marked transformation of the traditional pattern of distribution and industrial development and will enhance the importance of Douala which is already the primary industrial centre of the larger five-country UDEAC grouping.

In terms of basic economic structure, the area as a whole is heavily concentrated on the production of agricultural and forest products. More than half the total product is accounted for by this sector, whose relative importance ranges from 70 per cent in Chad, which is a largely traditional, pastoral agricultural economy, to 30 per cent in Gabon. The agricultural industry has a large subsistence sector. Indeed, except in Chad which produces animals on a large scale, and to a smaller extent in CAR, and Cameroon, peasant agriculture produces a very small marketable surplus. Modern large scale agriculture is at present confined mainly to the Congo where sugar is produced, and to banana plantations in Cameroon. However, the important forest product industry, chiefly in Gabon and Congo, is mainly modern and commercialized.

Except in Gabon, where petrol, uranium, and manganese are exploited and iron will shortly be mined, known mineral resources are few. Petrol is exploited on a small scale in Congo, and there is a diamond industry in Central African Republic. Industry, (including mining) generates only a small fraction of GDP. In the early 1960's its contribution was about 14 per cent of the total regional product, and its importance in the several countries ranged from 10 per cent in Cameroon, Chad and CAR to 20 per cent in Congo and 30 per cent in Gabon. Virtually the whole of the produce of Gabon's industrial sector consists of mineral products which are exported, though forest products are also important. Saw milling is also found in Cameroon and Congo. Apart from industries which process mineral and forest products, much of the industry of the area is concerned with the processing on a small scale of agricultural products, such as cotton ginneries, coffee hulleries, oil and soap mills and the like. Apart from these there are also establishments which produce beer, cigarettes and sugar on a large scale for the area as a whole. In addition, both Cameroon and Congo have a small range of light manufacturing industries, those in the Congo having been set up to serve the UDE area as a whole. Estimates (Table 5:1) based on the most recent national accounts adjusted for changes in the major determinants of national income suggest that for 1963 the total gross domestic product (GDP) of the area (at factor prices) was of the order of 280 th.mn. francs or about £405mn. at the official conversion rate. In terms of aggregate GDP, Cameroon is by far the most important of the five countries and in 1963 it produced more than 40 per cent of the total product of the area, or nearly 50 per cent including West Cameroon.

Expressed in terms of product per head, the average for the five countries is estimated at 26,000 francs (£38). Gabon's *per capita* product is the highest at 73,000 fr. (£106), followed by Congo and CAR with 31,000 fr. (£45). Chad's *per capita* product is the lowest at 15,000 fr. (£22).

TABLE 5:1

UDEAC: Economic Structure 1963

Country	Population Millions[1]	Population Density Inhabitants Per Sq. Mile	Rate of Population Growth	Gross Domestic Product[2]					Proportion of GDP Produced in the Market Sector
				Aggregate 000 mn. Fr. CFA	£mn.	Per cent of Total	Per capita 000 Fr. CFA	£mn.	
CAMEROON	4·4	24	1·9	109[3]	158	42	25	36	69
CENTRAL AFRICAN REPUBLIC	1·3	5	1·9	40	58	15	31	45	72
CHAD	2·8	6	1·1	42	61	16	15	22	60
CONGO (BRAZZAVILLE)	1·0	8	1·3	31	45	12	31	45	84
GABON	0·5	5	2·1	37	54	14	73	106	88
UDEAC	10·0	9	1·6	259	375	100	26	38	73

NOTES: 1 *U.N. Statistical Yearbook* 1963, Table 2.

2 Author's estimates based on accounts mentioned below, adjusted. GDP is '*Produit Interieur Brut*' less Indirect Taxes plus subsidies. This has been employed to facilitate comparison with East Africa. For the French system of accounts, see Leroux and Allier, *Presentation Normalisée des Comptes Économiques*, Ministère de la Co-opération, 1963.

3 East Cameroon only. West Cameroon accounts for a further 20,000 mn. francs. See also Table 3, page 17, Vol. 1 in *Étude Monographique de Trente-et-Un Pays Africains*, Cogeraf, Paris, 1964.

SOURCES: *Comptes Économiques*, République Fédérale du Cameroun 1951/1959.
Comptes Économiques, République du Tchad, 1958
Comptes Économiques, République Centrafricaine 1961
Comptes Économiques, République du Congo 1958
Comptes Économiques, République du Gabon 1960
(Ministère de la Co-opération, Paris.)

See also *Comptes Économiques*, Cameroun Fédérale, CIDEP, which estimates PIB for the Federation in 1962–63 at 128·2 bn. fr.

In comparing these product figures with similar estimates for other parts of Africa the usual qualifications have to be borne in mind. In particular, at the official exchange rate the general level of prices in the UDEAC area is a good deal higher than that in many other parts of Africa. Also, because of high transport costs and distributive margins, prices in CAR and Chad are higher than in the coastal states so that their relative real product is overstated in comparison with those of Congo, Gabon and Cameroon. Finally, in comparing relative *per capita* GDP figures within the area it should also be borne in mind that the population estimates on which they rest are subject to a wide margin of error since reliable censuses have never been undertaken.

As far as concerns rates of growth of national income, reliable data are sparse. The indications are, however, that over the decade to 1963, Gabon has enjoyed a consistently high annual growth rate of GDP of about 10 per cent in current prices while on the same basis Congo and Cameroon appear to have been growing at about 4 per cent or perhaps a little more. Chad's growth rate has been rather lower than 4 per cent and has been showing some tendency to fall. As to the Central African Republic, until recently its growth rate was as low as or lower than that of Chad, but the recent growth of its diamond industry has boosted its income and latterly CAR's growth rate may have been as high or even higher than in Gabon. The foregoing rates of growth must of course be corrected for price changes which, over the last decade, may have averaged 2·5 per cent per annum.

A brief review of the extent, structure and orientation of the foreign trade of the area may usefully conclude this section. Like most other less developed areas, UDEAC is heavily dependent upon foreign trade. In 1963, exports to countries outside the area amounted to 64,000 mn. francs or about 25 per cent of GDP at factor cost. Imports were rather higher at 68,000 mn. fr. giving a trade deficit which has been a normal state of affairs for a number of years. Not all of the countries are in deficit. Gabon and Cameroon normally enjoy an external trade surplus. Congo, however, has a trade deficit, which is large both absolutely and in relation to its imports, but it is to some extent

178

1961 did not exist, but by the area's close cultural and administrative links with France which have been reinforced by the procedures for obtaining foreign exchange and trade agreements and other factors. As to exports, a concentration of sales on France has been encouraged chiefly by favourable price arrangements and guaranteed markets. Although the *surprix* arrangements are to disappear, as associates of EEC, the UDEAC countries now enjoy trade preferences in France and the other countries of EEC.[6] On the import side the links with the area's traditional suppliers will have been reinforced since 1962 by the introduction of the common external tariff of UDE and Cameroon, which provides a substantial margin of preference for France and other EEC countries.[7] This preference is likely to maintain and may extend the concentration of trade upon EEC, but it may in due course be accompanied by some change of emphasis in favour of France's EEC partners when, as required by the arrangements for association, each African country institutes global import quotas for EEC as a whole.

The salient features of the economy of the UDEAC area from the standpoint of integration may thus be summed up as: a vast geographical area where links within each country and between them are poor; a commercial production concentrated mainly on primary products for exports; very low cash incomes and correspondingly small internal markets for manufactures. Scope clearly exists for expanded trade in traditional agricultural products for internal consumption, but this must rest on the creation of expanded market surpluses which at present are small, particularly in Gabon and Congo. While the possibilities of industrial development for the home market are restricted by its very small size, the three coastal states, by virtue of resource base, historical development and strategic positions in relation to existing or planned transport systems are well placed to get a good share of whatever development occurs. The two inland states on the other hand have a rather poor resource base for the development of manufacturing industry based on domestic raw materials, except for cotton, and their relatively low incomes and distance from the sea places them at a marked disadvantage in relation to the development of manufactures based on imported raw materials.

3 THE WORKING OF THE COMMON MARKET

The Machinery

Except in relation to the monetary union, the supreme policy making body for the various forms of economic co-operation which existed before 1966 between the UDE countries was the Conference of Heads of State which (on a basis of unanimity) approved acts and decisions which had legal effect in all four countries so long as they were consistent with the basic inter-state conventions.[8]

A Secretariat (under the Secretary General) and certain common administrative services provided the machinery through which economic co-operation was effected. The Secretariat included an economic and financial office and a statistical service. Certain other common services of an administrative nature, such as the common customs service, were also under the authority of the Secretary General. Of these administrative services, the Secretariat was financed in principle by equal contributions from each state, while the common customs service was financed by a 3 per cent levy on customs revenues. On the other hand the major common services such as posts and telegraphs and railways were not responsible to the Secretary General and were self-financing.

Although the Conference of Heads of State had ultimate jurisdiction, in practice the real business of the customs union was handled under the authority of the Conference by a Committee of Direction, except for matters concerning the self-financing common services. The Conference was referred to only when the Committee was unable to reach unanimous agreement. As far as can be ascertained this was rare. The Committee of Direction was made up of the Finance Ministers of each country, one other representative from each country and certain other persons (for instance the Chairman of the Central Bank) acting in an advisory capacity. Its Acts and Decisions had legal effect in the four states.

One of the most important functions of the Committee was to

182

decide upon the levels of import duties. Apart from this, the Committee had certain other executive functions which had a major bearing on the operation of the common market. Of these, the most important was the responsibility to determine the treatment to be given for purposes of indirect taxation to enterprises serving the common market as a whole. Any such enterprises of a manufacturing nature might be exempted from all import duties and all internal indirect taxes and be subjected instead to a single tax (the *taxe unique*) which generally represented a lower burden (and certainly a less complex system) than the combined indirect taxes to which the firm would otherwise have been subjected.[9] The Committee decided on the enterprises to be taxed in this way, and on the rates of tax to be applied. The rate of the *taxe unique* normally varied for different products. The levels of the tax might also be different for a single product according to the country in which it is produced. In the case of sugar, which was an important source of revenue, the rate varied with the country to which the product was consigned. Of the 30 firms which were subject to this form of taxation in January, 1965,[10] 18 were located in the Congo, 6 in CAR, and 6 in Chad. The products of such firms located in Congo included beer, sugar, tobacco, soap, aluminium ware; textiles and clothing, beer, shoes, cycles and aluminium were produced in the CAR; beer, sugar, cycles, soap and radio receivers were produced in Chad.

The problem of fixing the level of such a tax cannot be an easy one because it involves in effect the need to get inter-country agreement on the level of protection to be accorded to an industry which may be located only in one country. In such cases the interests of the country in which the enterprise is to be located will be to some extent opposed to those of the countries which will provide a market for its products. In part for budgetary reasons the latter are likely to seek high rates whereas the interest of the former will often lie in seeking a low rate to facilitate the industrial development, from which it can expect to derive indirect advantages which may offset its loss of revenue. Further problems arise if the rates are allowed to vary according to the country in which the product is produced for this provides a means of limiting inter-country competition in the products in question. In UDE, however, although this was permissible, the problem did not in practice arise, for the rates were uniform.

In addition to its executive functions, in relation to the matters outlined, the Committee of Direction also had advisory functions in relation to a number of other matters. Of these the most important were concerned with the harmonization of various taxes which were within the jurisdiction of the member states,[11] and the level and distribution of the Solidarity Fund whose purpose and operation are discussed in the next section.

The Apportionment of Tax Revenue between the Members of UDE

A basic matter in any customs union and one which often gives rise to controversy, concerns the principles on which to distribute the revenue from import duties and from tax revenues produced directly or indirectly from inter-country sales of local products. In UDE income and profits taxes accrued to the country in which the earning unit was located and no attempt was made to reallocate revenue from company tax among the countries even though in some cases part of the income was generated by inter-country sales. For both the basic UDE import duties and the indirect tax on enterprises serving the common market as a whole, however, the basic criterion was consumption, with some correction by means of a Solidarity Fund.

So far as import duties and taxes are concerned, these (after deducting a levy of 20 per cent for the Solidarity Fund and the levy for the cost of running the customs service) were paid to the budget of the state in which the goods were declared to be consumed at the time when they were released from bond. Thus, irrespective of whether imports arrived in a UDE country in bond, or were released from bond in another UDE country and thus arrived after payment of duty, the consuming country got the duty, so long as the declarations of consumption were correct. However, because of the concentration of wholesaling and import houses in Brazzaville, a substantial part of the imports which were declared for consumption in the Congo were transferred to other countries as a result of later commercial decisions. This was taken into account in the Solidarity Fund, whose operations are described below.

The proceeds from the indirect tax (*taxe unique*) imposed on inter-country trade in locally produced manufactures were also distributed to each state according to its consumption of the products in question. For this purpose records were kept by the producer of the places to which his products were consigned within the union. The gross revenue which each state received from customs duties was also affected by the Solidarity Fund, which was created mainly to take account of errors in the customs declarations but partly to compensate to some extent for the different economic positions of the various members of the union and also for differences in the benefits they derived from the union. As mentioned already, the fund received 20 per cent of all the common import duties levied by offices operated by the common customs service. Not all UDE imports passed through the offices operated by the Bureaux Communs. While there are several exceptions, the only one of any real importance concerned Gabon, which, since the formation of UDE, insisted on operating its own customs service. Consequently only that relatively small part of Gabon's imports which passed through the common office at Pointe Noire was subjected to the levy for the Solidarity Fund. Since the bulk of Gabon's imports entered through Libreville or Port Gentil which were under the jurisdiction of the Gabonese customs service, Gabon largely avoided this levy, though of course imports were subject to import duty at the rates prescribed in the UDE tariff. To the extent that the Solidarity Fund was designed mainly for correcting the attribution of duty this arrangement could be justified by the fact that none of Gabon's imports through its own ports are subsequently transferred to other UDE countries. However, the fund had a wider purpose, and the justification for excluding most of Gabon's imports from the levy must be evaluated in the light of the weight which was intended to be attached to these other objectives.

The principles of the Solidarity Fund and the basis for sharing of its revenues were agreed at a meeting of the Prime Ministers on June 23, 1959. Prior to this, customs duties in the AEF had been distributed on a percentage basis[12] for a number of years.

The newly adopted method of distribution of customs duties based on declarations of consumption and modified by the Solidarity Fund gave both Gabon and the Congo more than they would have received under the former AEF regime, while CAR on the other hand got about the same and Chad a good deal less. This adjustment in favour of the coastal states was made necessary by their dissatisfaction with the old system, which for a variety of reasons was difficult to resist. Nonetheless, both Chad and CAR continued to receive more customs revenue through the operation of the Solidarity Fund than they would have done if the distribution of the proceeds of a uniform customs tariff had been based on declarations of consumption alone, for in this event the inland states would have lost the revenue on goods released from bond in the Congo, and declared for consumption there, but subsequently transferred to Chad or CAR. If the assumption is made that the establishment of separate customs systems would not have made it possible wholly to tax such transfers, it could be said, as it was in fact in the persuasive arguments used to get the new system accepted, that Chad and CAR got more than they would have done under a 'balkanised' alternative.[13]

The proceeds of the Solidarity Fund were distributed to the four states in the following proportions (rounded) which remained unchanged from the inception of the Fund in 1960 until the establishment of UDEAC. CAR 35 per cent; Chad 62 per cent; Congo 3 per cent. Gabon's share was a small fraction of 1 per cent. The gross and net amounts received by each country from the Solidarity Fund since its establishment are set out in table 5:3. It can be seen that the main transfer was from the Congo to Chad, and, to a smaller extent, to the Central African Republic.

Expressed as a proportion of ordinary budgetary receipts in 1964, the net revenue from the Solidarity Fund amounted, in the case of Chad, the major beneficiary, to about 7·5 per cent of revenue. For the Central African Republic the corresponding proportion was about 2·5 per cent. As far as the contributors are concerned, the payments represented a negligible share of Gabon's total ordinary revenues, and 6·5 per cent of those of Congo. These payments were not, therefore, a major item in the budgets of either the beneficiaries or the donors.

TABLE 5 : 3

UDE Solidarity Fund (mn. francs CFA)

YEAR	CAR			CHAD			GABON			CONGO		
	(a)	(b)	(c)	(a)	(b)	(c)	(a)	(b)	(c)	(a)	(b)	(c)
1960	n.a.	310·3	n.a.	n.a.	548·3	n.a.	n.a.	1·3	n.a.	n.a.	26·6	n.a.
1961	210·7	368·6	+157·9	206·9	651·3	+444·4	26·6	1·6	−25·0	608·4	31·6	−576·8
1962	264·4	395·8	+131·4	207·6	699·5	+491·9	20·6	1·7	−18·9	613·3	34·0	−579·3
1963	293·5	424·0	+130·5	266·6	749·2	+482·6	43·4	1·8	−41·6	607·8	36·3	−571·5
1964	321·4	455·5	+134·1	315·9	804·9	+489·0	39·9	2·0	−37·9	624·1	39·0	−585·1

(a) = Levy (20 per cent of common import duties administered by Common Customs Service).
(b) = Gross receipts from Solidarity Fund.
(c) = Net fiscal redistribution through Solidarity Fund.

SOURCE : Unpublished data provided by Bureaux Communs des Douanes ;
Secrétariat-Général de la Conférence des Chefs d'État.

With respect to the distribution of the burdens and benefits of the union it would be of great interest to know how far the redistribution of revenue through the Solidarity Fund simply corrected the allocation of revenue in accordance with the basic principle of consumption, and to what extent these payments represented compensation for an imbalance in the burdens and benefits of the union. Available data are inadequate to enable such an estimate to be made, but from indications provided by an inter-country trade inquiry carried out in 1958,[14] and certain data submitted to the Prime Ministers' Conference mentioned above, it does seem likely, however, that the bulk of the Congo's original net payment to the two inland states represented compensation for errors in attributing the place of consumption. The justifiable conclusion seems to be that over the period 1960–64 Gabon certainly (because it had no inter-territorial exports) and Congo probably (to the extent that the 1958 relationship held good over the period) each made a true fiscal contribution to the position of the inland states over and above what was called for on grounds of attribution. But these contributions are unlikely to have been large, probably not more than 40 mn. francs CFA for Gabon in 1964, and perhaps 60 mn. francs CFA in the case of the Congo.

The Tariff of UDE and Cameroon

Until 1962, the four UDE countries on the one hand and Cameroon on the other, each applied their separate tariffs to trade outside the area, which differed somewhat in structure, but which shared the basic quality of non-discrimination. From July, 1962, as a result of a decision of the five heads of state, an additional import duty, termed the common external tariff, was introduced in both areas on top of existing duties, thus giving them a common element. The introduction of this duty was intended to be the prelude to further harmonisation of tariffs between UDE and Cameroon.

The common external tariff was introduced at fairly high rates. Its most important feature, however, was that the rate on a particular product might vary for different foreign countries. It therefore had the effect of giving both UDE and the Cameroon, for the first time, a two-column tariff. Imports from EEC, UAMCE and Algeria were exempted from the common external tariff. Certain exemptions were also provided for imports from Britain into West Cameroon with the object of easing the problems involved in adjusting its economic system to the very different one of its dominant partner. The introduction of the common external tariff thus produced in the five country area a dual tariff with a common element which discriminated very markedly in favour of the area's present major trading partners.

The tariff situation in the UDEAC area has in fact been more complicated than this outline would suggest, for within UDE itself there was not a strictly uniform tariff. From the outset certain duties were levied on a non-uniform basis, and in some cases these differences became larger. The non-uniformities in the UDE tariff resulted mainly from two groups of taxes:

1 Those levied by the customs services on behalf of and for the benefit of the countries concerned;

2 Those levied by the internal tax administrations of the various countries. These taxes appear to have originated in the desire of certain states to avoid in part the compulsory contribution to the Solidarity Fund.

Apart from this, in the case of all four countries, certain suspensions or exemptions from the general tariff also produced a number of minor differences.

Under the first head, CAR, Chad and Gabon levied specific consumption taxes on alcoholic drinks. In CAR a consumption tax was imposed upon imported cloth and clothes (15 per cent) and on cars, radio receivers and electric batteries (10 per cent). Chad imposed a consumption tax on imported cloth (12 per cent). In Gabon a tax of 15 per cent was imposed on radio receivers and certain other things including photographic equipment, the receipts from which were paid into a special fund for financing the radio and television service. Gabon also imposed a specific tax upon petrol which was oddly termed the 'solidarity tax'. In the case of all four countries, suspension or exemptions from the general tariff also produced a number of differences. There were two other taxes of a more general nature which were levied on imports by Gabon and Congo. In Gabon a tax of 3 per cent was levied upon a wide range of imports (and exports) to finance the extra budgetary road fund. In the Congo, a solidarity tax of 14 per cent was levied upon all imports.

Under the second head the position in mid 1965 was that Congo levied its own taxes on imported drinks, sugar and petrol; Chad levied its own petrol tax; CAR taxed selected imports and also imposed a fairly general tax on imported products (except inter-country imports). For 1964 this general tax on imports was estimated to produce over 60 mn. francs which represents a substantial proportion of CAR's revenue from import duties.

These differences in the taxes imposed on imports in the UDE countries resulted in a situation in which the total formal burden of import duties was rarely identical for any tariff position. However, according to calculations made by the Bureaux Communs[15] the differences in 1965 as between Congo, CAR and Chad were quite small except in a limited number of cases, which include cars, radios, cloth, clothing, beer, wines and spirits.

Although the inquiry did not cover Gabon the differences between it and its partners in this respect, are also believed to be minor. These differences do not appear to have impaired the working of the UDE common market by, for instance, providing an incentive to transfer imports from one country to another, but they have certainly increased the complexity of the system and have raised its administrative costs.

Of course, large differences have persisted between the effective tariff of the UDE countries on the one hand and Cameroon on the other. Before UDEAC can operate as a full common market these differences will have to be eliminated. In the meantime, trade between the two areas has been governed by special arrangements.

Inter-country Trade in UDE

With respect to a development of natural resource based trade, the UDEAC grouping is, in principle, well placed because of the diverse natural and agricultural conditions found in the different member countries. As to trade in manufactures, the very small size of the local market certainly makes co-operation particularly important if industries are to be developed in the region.[16] What are the main characteristics of the internal trade of the area and how has it developed in the last few years under the influence of market integration? This question will be examined first for trade within UDE and secondly for trade between UDE and Cameroon.

During the period 1958 to 1964, inter-country imports in UDE more than doubled (Table 5: 4) from 1,964 mn. fr. in 1958 to

TABLE 5:4

UDE Inter-country Trade in Local Products (Agricultural Products and Local Manufactures) 1958–1964
(mn. francs CFA)

Country	Imports			Exports			Balance		
	1958	1963	1964	1958	1963	1964	1958	1963	1964
CONGO	309	212	262	951	2,418	2,674	+642	+2,206	+2,412
GABON	245	342	395	56	—	—	−189	−342	−395
CENTRAL AFRICAN REPUBLIC	540	969	1,077	443	537	316	−97	−432	−761
CHAD	870	2,496	2,434	514	1,064	1,178	−356	−1,432	−1,256
All	1,964	4,019	4,168	1,964	4,019	4,168	—	—	—

SOURCE: (1) *Études Économiques*, No. 7, tables 1–2, Bureau Centrale de la Statistique et de la Mécanographie, Brazzaville, 1958.
(2) *Commerce Extérieur de l'UDE* 1960–64, Brazzaville, 1965.

NOTE: The original table for 1958 included smuggled goods as well as legitimate trade. This chiefly affects Chad in relation to Nigeria and Cameroon. In this table, the figures for Chad and the totals for 1958 have been adjusted to exclude smuggled goods on the basis of the estimates contained in Table 2:1, page 58 of the Comptes Économiques for Chad, 1958. The figures for later years have been similarly adjusted on the basis of information supplied by the Statistics office of UDE.

4,168 mn. fr. in 1964. This trade thus grew more rapidly than total imports to represent 9 per cent of total imports in 1964 (including inter-territorial and foreign imports) as compared with 6·5 per cent in the earlier year. Local agricultural produce, mainly steers, meat, cotton and fish, appears to have accounted for a roughly constant proportion of 30 per cent over the period, while the balance was accounted for by local manufactures. It should be borne in mind however, that while estimates of trade in manufactures are fairly reliable, those for movements in agricultural produce are notoriously inaccurate, and certainly understate its true importance.

TABLE 5:5

UDE Percentage Shares of Inter-country Trade in Manufactures

	CONGO			CAR			CHAD			GABON		
	1958	1963	1965	1958	1963	1965	1958	1963	1965	1958	1963	1965
Exports	74	82	90	26	18	10	—	—	0·1	—	—	—
Imports	8	—	0·4	20	10	25	59	80	63	13	10	11

SOURCE: 1958 *Études Économiques*, No. 7, Brazzaville. 1965 *Bulletin des Statistiques Générales de l'UDEAC*, April 1966.

Inter-country trade in UDE possessed a number of significant features. In the first place, as Table 5:4 shows, Congo enjoyed over the period a large and increasing net surplus with its neighbours, all of whom were in deficit to a varying extent. In the second place, as Table 5:5 shows, the trade in 'manufactures' was dominated by the Congo, which exported chiefly to Chad and to a lesser extent to the other two countries. CAR also had a small trade in manufactures, mainly to Chad. During the period, Congo increased its dominant position in exports of manufactures from three quarters in 1958 to nine tenths in 1965. Agricultural exports came mainly from Chad which produced meat, steers and fish, but to a limited extent CAR was also involved in this trade. A third feature of the trade is that, so far as manufactures were concerned, it was heavily concentrated on a very few commodities. As can be seen from Table 5:6, three categories alone, namely cigarettes, sugar, and cloth and clothing, accounted for 90 per cent of the total in 1958. By the beginning of 1965, sugar and cigarettes dominated the trade (nearly 85 per cent) while cloth and clothing declined in relative and absolute importance. Of the increase in trade which has occurred over the period, no less than three quarters is accounted for by sugar and cigarettes. Trade in other manufactures (bicycles, cartridges, and metal furniture) has been growing but it remains on an insignificant scale.

TABLE 5:6

UDE Percentage Composition of Inter-country Trade in Local Manufactures

Commodity	1958	1965
Cigarettes	44	36
Sugar	23	45
Cloth	17	6
Beer	6	2
Clothing	6	1
Soap	4	3
Cartridges	—	2
Miscellaneous	—	5

SOURCE: 1958, *Études Économiques* No. 7, Table 1–2 adjusted. 1965, *Bulletin des Statistiques Générales*, April 1966, pp. 22–9. This is based on declarations for the *taxe unique*.

Further light can be shed on the character and importance of inter-country trade in manufactures in UDE by examining the statistics for each country of the production of goods which are subject to the *taxe unique*, and their country of consumption. This information is set out in table 5:7 on pages 194–5 for 1965. In that year the Congo's major exports were of sugar and cigarettes. The Central African Republic's major exports were of cotton cloth and beer. Exports from Chad were insignificant and those of Gabon were nil. The column in the tables showing the percentage output of the establishments concerned which was consumed locally is also of interest as providing an indicator of the importance of the common market for the concerns in question.

Although trade diversion and trade creation constitute only one aspect of the operation of a common market and not necessarily always the most significant, an estimate of these magnitudes can provide an important basis for an appraisal of the costs and benefits of a common market. While an estimate of trade diversion and creation in manufactures in UDE cannot be made, a measure of what may be termed the 'primary' costs of the common market to the participants, can be obtained by comparing the prices of the local product before *taxe unique* with the price of a similar product if imported from outside the market. Both of these prices must be adjusted for transport costs to the primary distribution centres of Brazzaville, Libreville,

TABLE 5:7

Products Subject to Taxe Unique 1965 (000 francs CFA)

CONGO

Product	Produced & Consumed in Congo	Exported to:				Total Production	% Consumed Locally
		Gabon	Chad	CAR	Total		
Refined sugar	194,742	293	1,270,791	193,154	1,464,238	1,658,980	11·7
Lemonades etc.	78,400	314	240	2,060	2,614	81,014	96·7
Beer	410,439	448	—	—	448	410,887	99·9
Cigarettes	405,760	325,072	389,078	445,504	1,159,654	1,565,414	25·9
Soap	68,407	6,945	45,627	31,656	84,228	152,635	44·8
Cartridges	52,056	7,842	—	60,778	68,620	120,676	43·1
Others	226,937	28,706	32,274	79,236	140,216	367,153	61·8
Total	1,436,741	369,620	1,738,010	812,388	2,920,018	4,356,759	33·0

194

TABLE 5:7—contd.

Products Subject to Taxe Unique 1965 (000 francs CFA)

CAR

Product	Produced & Consumed in CAR	Exported to:				Total Production	% Consumed Locally
		Gabon	Chad	Congo	Total		
Lemonades, etc.	90,932	—	11,688	—	11,688	102,620	88·6
Beer	783,177	—	75,283	—	75,283	858,460	91·2
Cotton cloth	95,710	—	183,982	6,355	190,337	286,047	33·5
Clothing	183,675	947	15,202	4,231	20,380	204,055	90·0
Aluminium ware	54,383	—	4,364	—	4,364	58,747	92·6
Bicycles	53,775	—	12,720	—	12,720	66,495	80·9
Others	27,680	—	1,328	1,446	2,774	30,454	90·9
Total	1,289,332	947	304,567	12,032	317,546	1,606,878	80·2

CHAD

Product	Produced & Consumed in Chad	Exported to:				Total Production	% Consumed Locally
		Gabon	Congo	CAR	Total		
Refined sugar	461,956	—	—	—	—	461,956	100·0
Beer	218,690	—	—	—	—	218,690	100·0
Perfume (non alcoholic)	10,597	—	—	590	590	11,187	94·7
Perfume (alcoholic)	32,908	—	—	—	—	32,908	100·0
Radios	2,887	158	—	3,692	3,850	6,737	42·9
Others	22,385	—	—	—	—	22,385	100·0
Total	749,423	158	—	4,282	4,440	753,863	99·4

GABON—There are no establishments producing goods subject to *taxe unique*.

SOURCE : *Bulletin des Statistiques Générales de l'UDEAC*, April 1966

195

Bangui and Fort Lamy. Table 5:8 shows the result of such a calculation for 1965 for the main products traded, which in that year accounted for 94 per cent of inter-country trade in manufactures.

It can be seen that there are losses for all of the three countries listed in the table. These measure the additional real income which could be obtained if the countries in question purchased these quantities of the products in question from the outside world instead of from their partners, chiefly the Congo. As can be seen, the magnitude of the losses is much affected by the price assumed for imported sugar. The international market for sugar is controlled and its price fluctuates considerably from year to year. For the purpose of this analysis, two alternative prices were taken, namely 43 and 53 francs CFA per kilo c.i.f. which correspond to the range of prices at which sugar was imported into Apapa and Libreville in 1965. If the higher price is taken, the primary losses to the participants are substantially reduced, and as can be seen, for Chad and CAR local sugar would be cheaper.

The bulk of the country losses arose on sugar, the major component of inter-country trade, except for Gabon, which in 1965 imported the bulk of its requirements from outside the common market. A relevant factor here is that Gabon's import duty on sugar is much lower than that of her partners. Imported cigarettes cost about as much on average as the cigarettes made by SIAT in Congo. Local beer is more expensive than the imported product. Soap produced in UDE is much more expensive than the imported product which is also of superior quality in terms of fat content.

The table does not directly show the gains to the Congo and it is only under very restrictive assumption that these would necessarily be equal and opposite to the indicated losses of her partners. No attempt has been made to calculate figures of the revenue losses on the basis of the difference between the common external tariff and the *taxe unique*. In most cases such a calculation would be of little value for the imposition of the common external tariff on imports from the common market would generally result in much higher prices for the commodities concerned, which would affect the quantities purchased.

196

TABLE 5:8

Primary Cost and Benefit of Market Integration—UDE—1965
Amounts and losses as per cent of local trade in products concerned

	CHAD		GABON		CAR		UDE	
	000 fr.	%	000 fr.	%	000 fr.	%	000 fr.	%
Sugar (a)	−112,570	−12	−51	−26	−6,085	−5	−118,705	−11
(b)	+6,138	+1	−19	−10	+13,681	+10	+19,800	+2
Cigarettes	−6,500	−3	−22,273	−11	−10,141	4	−38,914	−5
Cloth	−21,291	−12	—		—		−21,291	−12
Beer	−17,041	−17	−91	−25	—		−17,132	−18
Soap	−12,719	−23	−3,802	−46	−5,618	−19	−22,139	−24
Cartridges	—		−1,374	−29	−4,858	−10	−6,232	−12
Total (a)	−170,121	−11	−27,591	−13	−26,702	−5	−224,413	−10
(b)	−51,413	−3	−27,559	−13	−6,936	−1	−85,908	−4

SOURCE: Derived from data presented in Études Statistiques, supplement to *Bulletin des Statistiques Générales de l'UDEAC*, No. 2, April 1967.

NOTE: (a) imported sugar taken at 43 fr. per kilo.
(b) imported sugar taken at 53 fr. per kilo.

If the UDE market is evaluated in terms of this measure of cost and benefits it seems clear that Congo was the major primary beneficiary of the market integration which has taken place in UDE, and if indirect effects and dynamic factors are also taken into account this conclusion could only be reinforced. Nevertheless, the primary losses involved for the other countries are not large. For the Central African Republic they were small even on the upper estimate, and taking into account its own opportunities to sell in Chad, CAR broke even, or may perhaps have derived a modest gain. The losses were largest for Chad which is the poorest of the countries in terms of per capita income, though the size of its loss is affected considerably by the assumed import price of sugar. If the higher of the two indicated prices is used as the basis of the calculation for sugar, Chad's aggregate loss becomes insignificant.

Thus it appears that a relatively small amount of trade diversion has taken place in UDE. This is probably a factor which has made for stability in the common market hitherto, despite the unequal distribution of industry serving the common market. How far this situation will continue to characterise the common market in the face of growing industrial development is necessarily conjectural. If future industrialization develops on the basis of industries which are high cost producers, and which can only be viable with a high degree of protection, as may increasingly be the case, a potentially greater uneven distribution of costs and benefits in the future may give rise to dissension in the absence of industry sharing arrangements, or greater emphasis on fiscal redistribution.

Although these calculations are suggestive, they are not, as suggested in Chapter 4, wholly relevant, if the alternative to the common market is assumed to be, not free trade but a non-discriminatory tariff at the present level. If this were the alternative and capital and labour were freely available, then it is unlikely that all of the products now being imported from UDEAC would instead be imported from the outside world. Importation from outside would not occur unless the import duty, less the *taxe unique* were insufficient to make production viable in the other countries, taking into account any transport protection which a locally produced product might enjoy. If such a degree of protection makes the goods viable they will tend to be produced. Where such products can be produced at the same costs as elsewhere in the Union and they are produced by resources which would otherwise be unemployed, there will be a primary gain equal to the value of the additional value added in the 'shifted' production. There would then be an increase in income for the country in question, relative to the position in the common market, but not necessarily in relation to the free trade alternative, which is, however, assumed to be irrelevant. Where the products can only be produced at a higher cost than elsewhere in the Union, such excess cost would have to be taken into account in calculating the net additional benefit; there must also be taken into account the possibility of retaliation by the partner states, and any loss of spill over effects, on the lines of the calculations in Chapter 4. Finally, any loss of fiscal redistribution through the Solidarity Fund would also have to be considered.

The information available for UDE is insufficient to make possible a precise estimate of the outcome, but it seems likely that some products such as sugar would certainly have been imported from outside,[17] whereas most of the remainder would have been produced locally, except in the case of Gabon, which would be likely to find it advantageous to import her requirements of most of these products. Thus the figures in Table 5:9 would probably understate the losses, except for Gabon, if the Solidarity Fund is ignored.

Trade between Cameroon and UDE

Although the Cameroon market was never fully integrated into UDE, preferential trade arrangements were in operation for some time before the establishment of UDEAC. During the War there was, effectively, free trade between Cameroon and AEF. After the War the Cameroon administration wished this to continue but the authorities in AEF resisted this, apparently because of fears that competition from the more advanced Cameroon would hinder its own industrial development. Eventually, in 1955, with some persuasion from the Minister of

199

Colonies in Paris, a trade convention between the two areas was established.[18] This provided for the customs-free exchange of certain products on the basis of annually agreed quotas. In 1961 these arrangements were revised and incorporated into a wider convention which was drawn up against the background of the decision of the five heads of state to adopt a common external tariff, to unify their investment regimes and codes and to promote fiscal harmonization.[19] The task of implementing this convention was given to a newly established Mixed Commission consisting of the Committee of Direction of UDE and two representatives of the Cameroon.

Under the terms of the Convention and subsequent Acts and Decisions most local agricultural products might be freely exchanged subject to a turnover tax (currently 12 per cent) on imports in the importing country. Quotas were applied, however, to animals, meat, sawn wood, rice, refined cotton oil, and kola nuts.

Most local manufactures might also be freely imported on payment of a tax (*droit unique*) in the importing country. This tax ranged from 4 to 20 per cent and was normally the same for trade in both directions.[20] Products freely traded included sugar, beer, cigarettes, soap, cloth, sandals, aluminium roofing and bicycles. Sugar had a zero rate and cloth was free of duty into the UDE, but subject to a rate of 15 per cent in the other direction. A certain number of other local manufactures were imported under annually agreed quotas. They included furniture, clothes, plastic shoes and metal hollow-ware. (To these the import turnover tax of 12 per cent was applied.)

Special provisions applied to exchanges of agricultural products in the vicinity of the frontiers, which were tax-free except for cotton, coffee, cocoa and groundnuts. Products imported from abroad for re-exportation to the other state or group of states were of course subject to normal import taxation.

Under the convention the quotas were fixed annually by the Mixed Commission for each of the five countries for the different commodities and for trade in both directions.[21] These quotas were non-transferable so that if, for instance, Cameroon did not export its full quota of clothes to the Congo it was not permitted to export in excess of the agreed quota to Gabon.

In the past many of the quotas have been unused or only partly used. From the inception of the convention Cameroon consistently urged that the separate product quotas for the different UDE countries should be amalgamated into one for each product but this was unacceptable to UDE except in the context of a wider integration agreement. This has now been effected in the UDEAC treaty, and quotas on trade between the former UDE countries and Cameroon no longer exist.

Despite these favourable trade arrangements, trade between the two areas has not hitherto been of much importance. In 1963, exports of UDE (excluding transit trade) to Cameroon amounted to only 175 mn. fr. CFA, or 4·1 per cent of total inter-country exports. Imports amounted to 461 mn. fr. or 10·3 per cent of total inter-country exports. UDE's major exports were of sawn timber, meat, and a variety of agricultural produce. From Cameroon UDE imported a large amount of meat (20 per cent of its total imports from Cameroon were of this item), various agricultural produce, beer, mineral water and a number of manufactured products including clothing, aluminium products, bicycles and metal furniture. Over the period 1961–63 the total level of inter-country trade remained roughly constant but UDE's adverse balance fell slightly. Imports of manufactures from Cameroon increased, however, mainly because of a large rise in imports of beer and mineral waters. With the ultimate removal of restrictions on trade between Cameroon and its UDE partners, and the improvement of transport links, a substantial increase in this trade can be anticipated in the future.

4 MONETARY INTEGRATION

The second major area in which the UDEAC countries enjoy a measure of economic integration is in monetary matters. As noted already, the five countries enjoyed close monetary links prior to independence. In effect, Equatorial Africa has enjoyed a common local monetary system since 1940. Before that time its monetary system—that of metropolitan France—was also common, but not locally based. An independent issuing institution dates only from 1955.[22] On independence the UDEAC countries and Cameroon entered into arrangements to preserve their monetary links. The issuing institution was in 1960 termed a Central Bank and its constitution was revised to make it appropriate to serve a monetary union of sovereign states.

The Banque Centrale des États de l'Afrique Équatoriale et du Cameroun rests on an agreement between the five states and France. In setting up the Bank, the member states gave it the sole right to issue currency. Among other things they agreed to centralize their external reserves in the Bank, and to guarantee freedom of movement of currency and transfers in the area. They also adopted common rules in relation to foreign exchange control; legislation concerning cheques and bills of exchange, the organization of banking and the distribution and control of credit. The currency of the area is the franc of the Communauté Financière Africaine (CFA) whose par value (at present 2 NF = 100 fr. CFA) cannot be changed without the agreement of all members.

The external reserves of the area are held exclusively in French francs. External payments and receipts are settled through an account termed the operations account which is maintained with the French Treasury. Free convertibility of the CFA franc into French francs is provided by an agreement with the French government whereby the French Treasury provides automatic overdraft facilities to the Central Bank in the event that the operations account should be in deficit.[23]

Apart from the issue of notes and coins and the management of the foreign exchange reserves, the most important functions of the Bank relate to the provision of credit. So far as governments are concerned, the statutes of the Bank provide that credit may be extended to them both directly and indirectly within specified limits. Although it is only recently that the Bank has been authorized to make direct short term advances to the governments against Treasury obligations, it has been possible since its establishment for indirect financial support to be provided for the Treasuries in various ways. Thus the Bank is authorized to rediscount Treasury obligations of the commercial banks which have less than six months to run. It may also discount medium term obligations issued to finance the purchase of equipment included in the public development plans which will generate revenue enabling the repayment of the credit. Advances may also be made against these obligations. It has also been permissible for the governments to discount promissory notes issued by importers to the order of the respective Treasuries in respect of customs duties (*crédits douaniers*). A ceiling is fixed for total direct and indirect financial support to governments which is expressed as a small fraction of the average level of bank deposits or budget revenues of the member countries,

In practice, neither Treasury Bills nor bonds are issued to the Central Bank by the Treasuries. Treasury Bills proper have not been issued at all, since the five governments have been able to obtain any needed short-term advances from the French Treasury at low rates of interest. On the other hand, medium-term obligations to finance the purchase of equipment have been issued to the commercial banks by the governments of Gabon, Chad and Cameroon, and these have provided the Central Bank with the instruments needed for providing indirect financial support. Actually the Central Bank has provided only an insignificant amount of credit against such obligations. Direct credit to the Treasuries by the Central Bank has so far taken the form solely of discounting *crédits douaniers*—again on a very modest scale. Thus the Central Bank has played a very limited role in the provision of finance to governments.

Its main function in the field of credit has in fact been to provide short and medium term credit to the private sector chiefly by rediscounting for the commercial banks commercial bills with less than six months to run. In the field of medium term credit (maximum five years), indirect support is also provided through rediscount provisions where the purpose of the operation is to finance the export of industrial products. The Central Bank also has a variety of other responsibilities of the usual kind including the supervision of the national credit institutions in accordance with the national regulations, managing the accounts of the national Treasuries, giving advice to the Treasuries, and maintaining deposits for the commercial banks.

The administration of the Central Bank is undertaken at two levels. Its ultimate authority consists of the Board of Directors of whom one half are representatives of France (including the managing director who has a casting vote) and the other half are representatives of the five member countries. Beneath this Board there are five National Monetary Committees, one for each of the five countries,[24] and a sixth which deals with questions common to the Congo, Central African Republic and Chad. The numbers of members of the five national Monetary Committees, as well as the importance of French representation on them, varies between the countries. The Cameroon committee consists of 8 members, 5 representing Cameroon and 3 representing France. In each of the other countries the Committee has 4 members, and there is equal representation of France and the African states. All of the members of the National Monetary Committees are members of the Board of Directors so that for practical purposes the former are committees of the Board.

Broadly speaking, the division of responsibilities between these two levels of administration is that the Board is responsible for fixing the overall supply of short term credit in the light of resources and needs, and for determining the ceilings to be granted by the local branches of the Bank to each economy in respect of rediscounts, advances, and so on. It is also responsible for fixing the discount rate. The National Monetary Committees in their turn, are responsible for advising the Board from time to time on the credit limits in the individual countries. When these have been fixed they are responsible for determining the ceilings for each Bank and for individual enterprises. The Bank has, however, delegated to the Monetary Committees the power to fix aggregate rediscount ceilings for their countries, and to act on its behalf in certain other matters.

Since the fiduciary issue is employed almost exclusively to support short term commercial credit (in particular crop finance) to which normal banking criteria apply, and not to provide finance for the government, the possibility of conflicts of interest between the five countries over the distribution of credit is minimized. Nonetheless the supply even of short term commercial credit may be insufficient to meet all the demands of a sound banking nature which may be made on it so that its territorial distribution may be a contentious issue. The problem has been resolved in the union by arrangements which allow each country a degree of flexibility in relation to credit creation in its own area, but which at the same time provide a fairly automatic discipline. In effect, the arrangements subject each member to much the same constraints as if each operated its own currency.

TABLE 5:9

UDEAC: Contribution to Changes in External Reserves,
1960–1966 (mn. fr. CFA)

	CAR	GABON	CHAD	CONGO	CAMEROON	AREA
1960	−200	+800	+300	+400	−700	+600
1961	−400	+300	−1,100	−600	−300	−2,100
1962	+400	+100	+600	+1,300	+1,700	+4,100
1963	+600	−1,400	+300	−2,700	+1,400	−1,800
1964	+1,000	−1,200	+300	−1,500	+3,800	+2,400
1965	−200	+2,500	+300	+2,200	−800	+4,000
1966	+300	+1,200	−1,300	−800	−2,800	−3,300

SOURCE: *Rapports d'Activité*, Banque Centrale des États de l'Afrique Équatoriale et du Cameroun, 1960–1965/66. Section, Avoirs Extérieurs.

This is achieved by operating monetary accounts for each country in the books of the Central Bank. This involves in the first instance identifying the note issue in each country separately though not in a way which entails any restriction upon the interchangeability of the notes within the Union. However, notes issued in one country are withdrawn from circulation when they reach commercial banks in another country and are returned to the (branch) Central Bank of the country of issue. Payments through banks between the member states and between any one of them and 'abroad' can be readily identified for the most part. It is thus possible to arrive from the monetary side at a balance of payments for each country which shows the net effect of the overseas commercial balance, of the inflow and outflow of capital, and of the balance of inter-country exchanges. It is then possible to ascribe to any country the responsibility for a change in the external assets whose level provides the ultimate limit to credit creation. Preparation of the separate accounts enables each country to appreciate the monetary effects of its own operations as well as those of its neighbours.[25] Table 5: 9 above shows the result of such a balance of payments calculation for each country for the period from 1960 to 1966.

The approach to credit policy in the UDEAC area requires that, in the long run, credit expansion for each country should be kept within the limits necessary to maintain balance in the individual monetary balance of payments accounts. So long as this is done, short term variations in each country's reserve position are permissible, and as the table shows, these have occurred on a substantial scale.[26]

A monetary system of the kind used in Equatorial Africa places narrow limits on the abilities of its members to pursue different monetary policies. Unless all members are content to keep in line with each other in all relevant respects—credit expansion, exchange control policies, etc., it would not be feasible. This does not of course mean that each country has to expand at the same pace in terms of rates of growth of national income. Such rates of growth will be influenced of course by capital inflows and local conditions of supply. As indicated already,[27] it has certainly not been the case that rates of growth of national income have been the same in the five countries of the region.

Despite its attractive simplicity one might on general grounds reasonably have doubts about the cohesiveness of a system of this kind because of the likely pressures which would be exerted upon it by active and possibly divergent development policies within the different member countries. As it happens, in the equatorial monetary situation, however, very strong stabilizing factors are present which are provided partly by French influence and partly by the basic monetary inflexibility of the system as it has developed up to the present time.

In the first place, despite the fact that these countries have become independent, France continues to assume the major responsibility for their development financing. Part of its price for this substantial benefit is the acceptance of a very conservative monetary policy by the members of the monetary union.

The French attitude is summed up in the following quotation from the Jeanneney Report.[28] 'France in effect renounces the possibility of refusing to finance initiatives taken unilaterally by African Governments, in return the States accept a certain monetary tutelage, particularly in the matter of deficit financing'. In effect, so long as these governments are prepared to pursue financial policies which France regards as sound, the French government has been willing to meet their development needs and so far the availability of capital finance for the public sector has not been a major constraint. Apart from making direct grants in aid of recurrent budgets, which practice has now come to an end, capital finance has been placed at the disposal of the UDEAC countries indirectly by grants for development projects and social services through the Fonds d'Assistance et de Co-opération (FAC), and by loans from the Caisse Centrale de Co-opération Économique (CCCE) to finance specific projects or to supply capital to national development banks. Assistance is also received from the European Development Fund (FED) to which France is a major contributor. In recent years the aggregate assistance received from these various sources has been very large. In 1962, for instance, about 13,500 mn. francs were disbursed,[29] a sum which exceeded the total external reserves of the Central Bank.

By comparison the possibilities of deficit financing would be insignificant even if France had not set its face against such a policy. Basically this is because of the very low ratio which the external reserves of the Central Bank bear to annual imports. For the three years 1962–64 the ratio was respectively 17, 23 and 21 per cent, or in other words less than what would be required to finance three months' imports. It is unlikely that these reserves could be permitted to fall lower in an autonomous system and indeed without the contingent support of the over-draft facilities provided by the French Treasury the need would probably be to build them up. The external reserve-import ratios do vary somewhat between the countries, but even the best off have no substantial margin of external reserves from which a major deficit financed expenditure programme could be undertaken.

These factors do not, of course, rule out the possibility of divisive factors ultimately developing on the monetary side, but if they are taken in conjunction with such factors as supply inelasticities, the restricted range of development alternatives, and the extreme scarcity of skilled manpower, they clearly represent stabilizing and cohesive factors of some importance.

5 FISCAL HARMONIZATION

Since factor and product movements and investment decisions in a common market may be affected by internal fiscal differences, some harmonization of fiscal policies amongst the members of a common market will be necessary if the market is to function effectively. This is the third important area of co-operation between the five UDEAC countries. The arrangements for economic co-operation in the UDEAC countries provide for fiscal harmonization without saying very explicitly what it is.[30] It appears, however, that the objective sought is an equalization of formal tax rates on products or factors irrespective of the country of production or consumption.[31]

Apart from the various kinds of import duties which have been discussed in earlier sections, the main sources of tax revenue in UDE and Cameroon are (1) income taxes which fall into three main categories: (a) a personal or poll tax (graduated in some cases) of a kind widely used in Africa; (b) income taxes (impôts cédulaires) levied proportionately at different standard rates on particular categories of the taxpayer's income such as dividends, profits, wages and salaries; (c) a general income tax based on the taxpayer's total income irrespective of sources and levied at progressive rates. (2) the internal turnover tax (TCAI); and (3) consumption taxes. Harmonization provisions exist for all of these except the personal tax and the 'consumption' taxes. There must be consultation before any changes are made in the 'harmonization' taxes, and if a majority of the Committee is opposed to any changes, they must be withdrawn, unless the issue is carried to the Heads of State and supported.

Prior to 1960, a uniform basis was laid down by the Federal Grand Council, for assessing liability to the various direct taxes throughout the Federation. The tax rates themselves, however, were fixed by each territory and their levels diverged somewhat according to their respective needs. Since 1960 each country has introduced its own code both for direct and indirect taxation. From the outset this resulted in some divergence in the rules of assessment and some differences in tax rates have also appeared. The current situation may be illustrated by a glance at three of the more important direct taxes, the proportional tax on wage income, the general progressive income tax and the company tax.

In 1965 the proportional tax on wage income varied from 2 per cent in Congo to 5·5 per cent in CAR and Gabon. With the general progressive income tax the basis of assessment is fairly similar in each country, although provision for family circumstances is made on a varying basis. In terms of rates, the picture which emerges is of a broadly similar level of progressive taxation on income except in the poorest state, Chad, where it tends to be rather more severe. In CAR too, the burden of this tax tends to be rather higher than in the coastal states.

From the standpoint of inter-country competition for industrial development, perhaps the most important direct tax is the proportional tax on company profits. Methods of determining taxable profits for this tax are broadly the same in each country. In 1965, the rates of charge were in the neighbourhood of 30 per cent and ranged from 26 per cent in Congo to 34 per cent in Gabon.

In the field of indirect taxation, apart from import duties, which have already been discussed, the only other important tax is the internal turnover tax, the incidence of which in part is likely to be on business profits. For this tax the rules of imposition are similar for all countries, though differences in coverage and stage of taxation exist. Within UDE, the level of this tax currently ranges from 11 to 13 per cent but it is substantially lower (6 per cent) in the Cameroon.[32]

Fiscal harmonization also extends to the reliefs from taxation which may be offered to intending investors. For all four UDE countries, concessions to new investment in manufacturing are defined on a uniform basis, by the Convention on Investment.[33] Between UDE and Cameroon, fiscal harmonization was provided for initially under the Convention of June 1961[34] in which the five countries agreed to harmonize their investment codes and fiscal regimes according to a timetable to be established by the Heads of State.[35]

In short, within UDE, though there are differences in wage and personal income taxation, they are probably not of much significance for the movement of labour whose mobility is in any event, significantly limited by non-economic factors. In relation to investment in industry, the differences in rates of company taxation are also of minor significance. But, of course, tax harmonization does not altogether rule out the possibility of competition for new investment for regional industry, since it is open to the different countries to compete in the extent of the relief from company tax which is offered.

6 INDUSTRIAL HARMONIZATION IN THE EQUATORIAL COMMON MARKET

In a common market or customs union a basic issue which arises in relation to the location of industry is whether this should be left to the free play of government and private initiatives subject to common rules about fiscal and other concessions, or whether the common market authorities should attempt to influence it, and if so, on what basis?

In the early years of UDE's operation, this problem was not directly considered. The individual members of the Committee of Direction must have had these issues in mind in their consideration of the scale of fiscal concessions to new industries, since it was impossible to overlook that the costs and benefits of any protection accorded would be influenced by location. Nonetheless in determining these fiscal concessions there appears to have been no attempt to consider whether the initially suggested location, which emerged from initiatives taken by a single country, necessarily represented the least cost location from the standpoint of the Union nor did the committee regard itself as competent to use the offer of concessions or their withholding to bring about an equitable distribution of industry. By 1963, however, it had become clear that the problem of co-ordinating industrial development within the region would have to be tackled. Given the procedures followed by the Committee of

Direction in considering claims for fiscal concessions, there was nothing in the situation so far reached to stop individual UDE countries from making plans for establishing regional industries to serve the common market even though these might be in conflict with the plans of some other countries. As between the Cameroon and UDE this was not the case because free trade between these two market areas was not automatic. Not surprisingly several bilateral co-ordination agreements were made between Cameroon on the one hand and individual UDE countries on the other for industries whose viability depended on unrestricted access to a market area wider than that provided by either. These agreements provided among other things for market sharing, co-ordination of production, and in some cases for joint governmental participation in the enterprises in question.

One of the earliest and most important examples of bilateral harmonization to be developed in the five country area concerned cement. In April 1963 Chad and Cameroon agreed on the establishment of a cement factory in north Cameroon which would serve the markets of Chad and Cameroon. Chad will participate in the ownership of the Cameroon enterprise. A bilateral agreement on cement was also made between Gabon and Cameroon. A factory to be established in Libreville will supply clinker to a grinding mill to be established by Cameroon to serve part of its local market. The Gabon product will enjoy preference in the Cameroon market. There will be participation by the two governments in the share capital of these two enterprises.

A second attempt at bilateral harmonization between Chad and Cameroon was made in the textile field, but it was less successful. Following a study made by the Syndicat Général de l'Industrie Cotonnière de Paris[36] which had recommended a harmonization and specialization of cotton manufacture among the three cotton producers of the area, an agreement was reached in April 1963 between Chad and Cameroon which provided for the establishment of a spinning and weaving factory in south east Chad and a bleaching and printing works in north Cameroon which would utilize the output of the former. From the outset this agreement seems to have encountered difficulties and each of these countries soon began to plan for the establishment of textile industries to undertake all these operations, although the available evidence suggests that while there might be room for two weaving factories in UDEAC there is not scope for more than one in the Chad-Cameroon area in addition to that already existing in Bangui.[37]

A further field for which harmonization has been suggested on a rather wider basis is sugar refining. A sugar plan for the whole area has been drawn up by la Société Industrielle et Agricole de Niari (SIAN) located at Jacob.[38] At present this company provides the bulk of the needs of UDE, from its plantations in the Niari Valley which is situated midway between Brazzaville and Pointe Noire. As we have seen, sugar was not only one of the largest categories of inter-country trade in UDE but also one of the fastest growing. The plan would involve a large expansion in the output of raw sugar, the bulk of which is to be produced in Congo although possibly Chad may be able to produce some in the future. The crude sugar from Niari would then be further processed in refineries to be set up in Fort Lamy, Bangui and in Cameroon.

Although the conclusion of bilateral agreements without reference to other UDE countries in the common market organization could perhaps be justified on the ground that the nature of the products or their effective market areas made it unlikely that the other countries would be affected, their use contained the seeds of latent conflict. Wide recourse to such agreements could obviously not be disregarded by the other UDE countries if only because in general it would be difficult to prevent goods received by one UDE country under such an agreement from being sent to another. In the long run therefore the extension of such agreements could affect the interests of all UDE members so that ultimately a consideration of industrial co-ordination could hardly have been avoided. The issue of co-ordination seems however to have been precipitated, not so much by the need to consider the wider implications of the bilateral agreements, though these were certainly a factor, as by the need for the five countries to take a decision on the choice of location for a projected oil refinery to be set up to serve the needs of the five country area as a whole. For such an issue a collective decision

212

was clearly called for and the matter was accordingly referred to the Mixed Commission in May of 1963. The Commission seems understandably to have taken the view that the proper solution to this matter raised issues which went beyond existing agreements and its own competence. Consequently it delegated the task of studying the oil refinery issue to an industrial commission and at the same time set up a committee of experts to consider the general problems involved in industrial co-ordination and to make recommendations. Simultaneously, as a result of other initiatives, a committee of experts from the Ministry of Co-operation in Paris was sent to the UDEAC area during May and June, 1963, to consider the possibilities of industrial co-ordination in the area.

These developments are important, partly because the oil refinery issue involved the first attempt to consider the location of a UDE industry on the basis of a detailed appraisal of costs in alternative locations, and partly because it was this issue and the related decision to set up the committee of experts that initiated the series of meetings and commissions which finally led to the signing of the UDEAC treaty eighteen months later.

When the Mixed Commission met in Bangui in January, 1964, it had before it the recommendations of the experts on the oil refinery issue and on the general problem of industrial co-ordination. With the help of the latter it was able to submit agreed general proposals to the Heads of State for interim measures on industrial co-ordination, but it was unable to reach agreement on the specific issue of the oil refinery.

The basic facts on the economics of the location alternatives for the oil refinery are fairly clear. Technical and economic studies indicated that a single refinery for the whole UDEAC area would be the most profitable solution. The least cost location indicated was in Gabon, at Port Gentil, near the main oil fields, although earlier studies showed that Pointe Noire would not be greatly inferior. The disadvantage of the latter stemming from its low output of oil would in part be offset by its better equipped port and by its more favourable position at the present coastal railhead for inland distribution. The studies also showed two refineries to be feasible—one at Pointe Noire and the other at Port Gentil, but in this case the anticipated overall rate of return on the total investment would have been very much lower,[39] because of the loss of economies of scale.

There seems little doubt that on purely economic grounds a single oil refinery was indicated, nor that the Gabonese location was better. Nonetheless, the Congolese government made a strong bid for the refinery, or failing that, for the construction of two smaller refineries, one of which would be in the Congo. Since a single oil refinery would not have been feasible without assured access to the whole market, the agreement of all members was vital. Thus the rather special case of the oil refinery highlighted the incompleteness of existing arrangements for economic co-operation in as much as they lacked any provisions to prevent two countries from establishing competing industries. It also foreshadowed the kind of controversy which could be expected to become increasingly common with the development of industries in which economies of scale were important.

Throughout the discussions Gabon made it clear that it would view the decision on the oil refinery as a test case for the common market of the possibility of developing what it regarded as a rational policy of industrial development for the area. Such a policy, in its view, would entail that industries should be established within the common market in their most profitable location, since all members would benefit from such a policy in the long run. Whatever the validity of this contention, which is certainly not supported by experience elsewhere, Gabon was in an extremely strong position to make its views effective in this particular instance. Gabon was, it is generally agreed, the most economic location for the refinery. Moreover at that time it had no manufacturing industries serving the common market and it could therefore argue with some justice that it had not benefited at all from its past operation. Finally its economy was quite viable in isolation from the common market and by virtue of its geographical position, it could easily meet its import requirements from outside the common market if its neighbours became awkward. The refinery itself had particular attractions for Gabon since it would not need a large labour force and unlike most countries in Africa, Gabon suffers from a chronic shortage of labour.

In February, 1964, the Heads of State met at Fort Lamy to consider industrial development and related problems. On the recommendation of the Mixed Commission, it was decided to insert a new provision in the Convention on industrial harmonization which provided that where new industries are dependent upon the market of more than one UDE country, the country initially interested in the project is to provide information to the Committee of Direction. Unless the committee unanimously agreed with the suggested location, the project must be referred to the Heads of State.[40]

At the same meeting the Heads of State took the first decision under this provision by deciding to locate the common oil refinery at Port Gentil. In abandoning Congo's claim, apparently against the views of his advisers, President Massemba-Débat was possibly motivated by the desire to improve political relations with Gabon which were then at a low ebb.[41] But it is at least as likely that longer term economic considerations were given weight, for a decision adverse to Gabon might have had serious consequences for the maintenance and the progress of the Union. The Gabonese market is not in itself of great importance to the Congo. But Gabon's withdrawal from the common market which could not altogether be ruled out in the event of a decision not to give it the oil refinery, could hardly have taken place without disruptive effects on the economic cohesion of the whole area from which the Congo would have been a principal loser. Whatever the reasons underlying the Congo's compliance, Gabon's effort to secure the oil refinery was successful. The Gabon government subsequently declared its desire to develop a number of other industries to serve the common market, including glass bottles, natural gas and steel, for the production of which it is relatively well placed. Apart from these, it has indicated a readiness to continue to rely on import competing industries which are capable of operating in the other countries of the Union,[42] with jointly agreed fiscal exemptions.

The new provision on industrial harmonization fell short of resolving the latent difficulties. In the first place, it did not apply to Cameroon, which was not part of UDE. In the second place, it did not specify the criteria by reference to which decisions on the location of regional industries were to be reached. From the standpoint of the development of economic co-operation in the area the important contribution of the Fort Lamy meeting lay not so much in decision on the harmonization provision itself as in the recognition by the Heads of State of the short-comings of the existing arrangements for economic co-ordination and of the need to strengthen existing economic links if in the long run, the customs union were to survive. Above all it was important for their decision to proceed as soon as possible to a full treaty of economic co-operation, incorporating Cameroon, so as to enable the difficulties to be overcome. These developments and the resulting UDEAC treaty are discussed in the following section.

7 THE UDEAC TREATY AND SUBSEQUENT DEVELOPMENTS

The decision of the Heads of State to attempt to conclude a five-country treaty of economic co-operation by the end of 1965 was followed by rapid progress towards this objective. In May 1964 at Brazzaville a committee of experts produced recommendations on institutional arrangements, on harmonization of industrial projects, development plans, infrastructure development and on the problems of harmonizing the investment codes. In the following November at Yaoundé a second committee met to consider in particular the problem of harmonizing the taxation of imports. Later in November the Mixed Commission commenced work on the basis of these reports. Finally the Heads of State met early in December in Brazzaville to resolve differences which could not be resolved in the Mixed Commission and agreed and signed the Treaty establishing the Union Douanière et Économique de l'Afrique Centrale. The Treaty came into effect on January 1, 1966.

The Institutions of the Union

The principal institutions of the Union are similar to those of UDE, although there are several important changes in their functions. The Council of Heads of State remains the supreme organ of the Union. It supervises the Committee of Direction and decides in the last resort all matters on which the Committee is unable to reach unanimous decision. The Committee itself (made up of two Ministers from each country) remains the body which is responsible for the day to day work of the Union within the framework of policy laid down by the Council. Apart from dealing with the wide range of matters which occupied its predecessor, its functions extend to decisions in respect of the harmonization of industrial projects, of development plans and transport policy. In addition it has consultative functions in relation to certain other matters which affect the operation of the common market, including wages and social policy.

A secretariat is provided to service the Council of Heads of State and the Committee of Management. It consists of two divisions; the Division of Foreign Trade, Fiscal Matters and Statistics; and the Division for Development and Industrialization. The headquarters of the expanded Union are transferred from Brazzaville to Bangui. Nominations to the key posts in the secretariat are initially shared between Cameroon, which nominates the Secretary General, Congo which nominates the Chief of the Foreign Trade Division and Chad, which nominates the Chief of the Development and Industrialization Division.

One important difference between the institutions of UDE and UDEAC is that the former Direction des Bureaux Communs des Douanes at Brazzaville disappears. It is replaced by national customs administrations, the officers of which are of course appointed by and responsible to their respective Finance Ministries. However, all customs offices concerned with transactions which affect more than one partner state are designated '*bureaux communs*'. In these offices separate accounts are kept for each member state for whose account collections have been made according to the customs declarations. The corresponding revenues are transferred at intervals among the respective Treasuries. In reflection of these changes the Committee of Direction is charged by the Treaty with establishing the procedures for verifying the accounts and for transferring customs revenue from one state to another. It is also responsible for such matters as tariff nomenclature and regulations.

The Customs Union and Fiscal Policy

Within the customs area there is in principle to be free movement of persons, goods, services and capital. To this end,

217

provision is made for the adoption of a common import tariff and the prohibition of all duties and charges when products are transferred among the members.

The Treaty provides for a tariff consisting of four elements. The first is the *droit de douane*, which in the form of the common external tariff has been common to the five states since July 1962. The second element is the *droit fiscal d'entrée*. The third is the *taxe commune sur le chiffre d'affaires à l'importation*. These three components have been taken over from the UDE tariff and are to be uniform for all states. A fourth tax, the *taxe complémentaire sur l'importation* may be imposed in addition, at a level which may vary from one state to another. The establishment of the complementary tax was a realistic way of allowing for the likely difficulty of initially establishing a completely uniform tariff among the members of the wider union and at the same time it allows for the emergence of possibly differing budgetary needs among the partners from time to time. If extensive use were to be made of the supplementary tax the customs union would become a free trade area. However, the supplementary tax is not to be a regular feature of the system and its level is to be limited. In effect it is a substitute for the diverse internal consumption taxes on imports in the various UDE states which grew up, partly as a means of overcoming the need to get agreement on tariff changes, and partly to avoid the compulsory contribution to the Solidarity Fund which was charged on customs duties proper.

The basic criterion for distributing import and export revenues remains as it was in UDE, but in order to make the attribution of import duties more precise, efforts are to be made to ensure that wherever possible, goods are released from bond in the country of final consumption. As a further safeguard, in the case of commercial transactions, statistical checks are to be made on the quantity and value of imports which are transferred from one country to another after having been declared for consumption in another state. For a period of three years from the coming into force of the Treaty, the country of first importation is to reimburse the country in which the goods are consumed for the duties and taxes attributable to the transactions recorded.

It will be recalled that in UDE the Solidarity Fund served

among other purposes, to provide financial compensation for such transfers, although this was done on a basis which, even if it may have been accurate at the time of its introduction, is hardly likely to have remained so throughout the period of its operation. Notwithstanding the provision just mentioned, the Treaty also provides for a Solidarity Fund: 'In a spirit of solidarity, and to take account of any errors indicating the state of consumption and of advantages deriving from transit activities, in particular for coastal States'.[43] During the initial period of three years the contributions and receipts from the fund will take account of the reimbursements mentioned above. Presumably it is envisaged that in due course the reimbursements will be abolished and that the payments and receipts of the Solidarity Fund will then be revised to take account of this.

With respect to products of local origin the Treaty provides that these are exempted from all import and export charges when transferred from one country to another. However, industries producing manufactured products which are sold in more than one member country are subjected to the *taxe unique*. This is levied in the country of manufacture, but the revenue is distributed to the countries of consumption on the basis of declarations of consumption in accordance with rules applicable to customs duties. For a period ending on January 1, 1972 the level of the *taxe unique* may differ for a given product according to the place of production. This provision may be of significance to those members of the union which do not provide attractive locations for manufacturing industries.

The Treaty also provides that attempts are to be made to harmonize the rules and rates of internal taxes, in particular those such as the tax on business profits and the internal turnover tax, which affect the operations of business enterprises. Also investment codes are to be made uniform within one year and once harmonized, they may not be unilaterally modified.

Other provisions of the Treaty which have relevance to the operation of the customs union are those concerned with safeguards. The imposition of quantitative restrictions against third countries could clearly affect the operation of the Union. The Treaty contains a clause which provides that if a member imposes restrictions for the purpose of meeting its development needs or industrialization requirements the Committee of Direction must be informed and shall decide on any measures necessary to prevent trade diversion. The Committee may also authorise any member state to take special measures to deal with disturbances in any economic sector.

Industrial Co-ordination and the Harmonization of Development Plans

With respect to the operation of the customs union itself, the UDEAC Treaty contains little novelty. Its innovation lies in those provisions which concern industrialization and development policy. In this connection the Treaty lays it down that industrialization policies, development plans and transport policies are to be harmonized with a view to promoting the balanced development of the economies of the members within a framework permitting growth and the development of the market. In pursuit of these objectives all members are to provide the Secretary General with detailed information on their plans and progress in these matters. The Secretariat has the task of studying these proposals, and presenting proposals aimed at correcting conflicts. The chief interest of the Treaty lies in the detailed measures proposed for dealing with these aspirations, in particular, those for balanced industrial development.

During the negotiations leading up to the Treaty two opposed views were expressed with respect to industrial development policy. On the one hand, the view of Cameroon, Gabon, and to some extent, Congo was that there should be free competition for industrial development within an agreed framework of investment concessions. On the other hand, Chad and CAR insisted that since they would be unlikely to be able to attract industry in such a framework, account should be taken of their unfavourable position by the introduction of measures to influence the location of industry in the common market. Neither the experts nor, in their turn, the Mixed Commission succeeded in reaching agreement on this issue and it was in the end referred to the Heads of State. The measure of agreement reached is reflected in the Treaty's provisions. They are designed to influence location of industry chiefly by providing a framework for negotiation rather than by the provision of agreed general incentives operating in favour of the two land-locked states.

Under the Treaty industrial projects are divided into five groups:

(a) export industries

(b) industries serving the market of only one country and for which no economic privileges are sought in the other UDEAC countries.

(c) industrial projects serving only one market but which will affect the interests of an established industry in another state or one which is to be created in another state.

(d) industrial projects for which the market is limited to two states and for which bilateral harmonization arrangements are sought.

(e) industrial projects concerning more than two states and for which harmonization at UDEAC level is sought.

Industries in categories (a) and (b) may be set up in any of the member states without reference to the Union, but those in category (b) are not permitted to market their products in other states in the absence of prior consent from the Committee of Direction. In the case of industrial products which reach the market of other member states but which have not been the subject of harmonization procedures, and are not subject to the *taxe unique*, those member states which consider their interests impaired may prohibit the importation of the commodities in question or temporarily impose a fiscal charge. For projects in category (d) a joint report is to be made by the states concerned to their partners through the Secretary General. For an industry in categories (c) and (e) full information must be sent to the Secretary General by the State in whose territory the industry is to be situated before any decision or understanding is reached on its establishment. All states have the right to ask the Secretary General to examine projects in these three categories from the standpoint of the objectives of industrial harmonization. The member states are then consulted and may object to proposals. In case of disagreement the project is submitted to the Committee of Direction for a decision. Among the factors the Committee is to take into account in reaching its decision on the location of projects in category (e) are: location of raw materials; the advantages which each state offers to its partners, and the possibility of compensating for the less developed situation of certain states in the Union. Another provision requests the Secretary General to prepare a plan for industrialization in the Union covering projects in category (e) in consultation with the Planning Ministers. This plan is to be approved by the Council of Heads of State on the advice of the Committee of Direction.

The Implementation of the Treaty

At their first meeting in Yaoundé in December 1965 the Heads of State of UDEAC took several important steps towards the implementation of the provisions of the Treaty. In the first place, the envisaged convention on investment was adopted.[44] It will be recalled that investment incentives had been harmonized among the UDE countries since 1960 but that practice differed between Cameroon and UDE. As a result of the new convention the hitherto different fiscal and customs regimes applicable to private investment in the UDEAC countries are fully harmonized. The new arrangements broadly follow those formerly in force in UDE. The provisions relating to the grant of concessions are related to the categories of industries distinguished in the section of the Treaty dealing with industrial co-operation. Concessions to industries in categories (a), (b), and (c) are in the hands of the individual states, but in the case of industries in category (c), may only be accorded after the consultations laid down in the Treaty have been carried out. The concessions include exemption from import duties on inputs, exemption from the *taxe unique* and from internal indirect taxes. In cases where the enterprise is of particular social and economic importance, exemption from profits tax may be given and depreciation may be accelerated. For industries in the remaining two classes, (d) and (e), the grant of fiscal concessions of a somewhat similar nature but including a favourable rate of *taxe unique* is in the hands of the Committee of Direction.

The second decision concerned the new tariff of the Union.[45] This was introduced in all five countries on January 1, 1966 except in West Cameroon, where its introduction was deferred until the following July. The new customs code was similarly agreed and came into force on January 1, 1966. At the same time the list of the common customs offices, of which there are 18, was laid down.[46]

The third important decision of the Heads of State was to adopt an act regulating the *taxe unique* in UDEAC.[47] The regulations for the operation of the *taxe unique* differ little from those in force in UDE except that the tax is obligatory for all establishments whose markets extend to the territory of more than one state whereas in UDE this system of taxation was applied only to certain products and establishments. The factors to be taken into account in fixing the level of the *taxe unique* are indicated in general terms as: the necessary degree of protection; the presence or absence of competing enterprises in the union, and the desirability of not interfering with the play of normal competition. At December 31, 1966, 95 enterprises were subject to the *taxe unique* in UDEAC, of which 47 were located in Cameroon; 19 in Congo, 18 in CAR, 8 in Chad and 3 in Gabon.

Finally the Heads of State agreed on the basis of the new Solidarity Fund. For the year 1966 specified contributions were prescribed, amounting to 1,900 mn. fr. CFA. The allocation of the contributions and the distribution of the proceeds are illustrated in Table 5:10 below, which also shows the effect of the decisions made at the second meeting of Heads of State at Fort Lamy in December 1966, with respect to the operation of the Fund for 1967.[48]

Comparison of Table 5:10 with the corresponding table relating to UDE (5:3) shows that for 1966 the gross contributions of the four UDE states was about 300 mn. francs more than in 1964. The rise was produced by an increase in Gabon's contribution of 500mn. offset by various reductions in the contributions of the others. Cameroon's contribution was fixed at 300mn. The total additional receipts thus available which amounted to about 600mn. accrued to CAR and Chad whose net receipts (column (c)) increased by 230 and 386mn. respectively. For 1967 the contributions are revised chiefly by reducing the gross contribution of Gabon by 300mn. and increasing that of Cameroon by 200mn. so that the total contributions will amount to 1,800mn.

The formation of UDEAC has thus been accompanied by

TABLE 5:10

UDEAC Solidarity Fund
(mns. of francs CFA)

YEAR	CAR			CHAD			GABON			CONGO			CAMEROON		
	(a)	(b)	(c)	(a)	(b)	(c)	(a)	(b)	(c)	(a)	(b)	(c)	(a)	(b)	(c)
1966	300	665	+365	300	1175	+875	500	3	−497	500	57	−443	300	—	−300
1967	300	630	+330	300	1170	+870	200	—	−200	500	—	−500	500	—	−500

SOURCE: Acte no. 12/65-UDEAC-34, and Acte no. 66/6-UDEAC-50

(a) contribution
(b) receipts
(c) net receipts

increased payments into the Solidarity Fund. Nevertheless the increase in net receipts by the benefiting states is not a measure of the true change, nor for the contributing states is the increase in their net contribution an appropriate measure of their true contribution. This is because as noted already, taxes and duties in respect of imports released in one state for consumption and subsequently transferred to another are, for a period of three years, to be paid over by the country of first importation to the country of consumption. For the Central African Republic the duty so transferred to Chad for 1966 was 233 mn. francs. Assuming there to have been no corresponding payments in favour of CAR, its true net receipts in 1966 would have been almost exactly the same as in 1964. Nevertheless, allowing for these payments, some additional redistribution of revenues will certainly have been brought about through the new Solidarity Fund. The main additional contributor is Cameroon, which was to receive no offsetting receipts through the Fund for 1966 and 1967 and which will only benefit to a very limited extent if at all from the provisions of Section 33. The main beneficiary is presumably Chad, which in 1966 received 875 mn. fr. through the Solidarity Fund in addition to payments, mainly from CAR, in respect of transferred imports recorded in the frontier checks.

8 ECONOMIC CO-OPERATION IN CENTRAL AFRICA: ACHIEVEMENTS AND PROSPECTS

A central question for any common market, concerns its impact on economic development. The question is seldom easy to answer, partly because it is rarely clear precisely what are the relevant alternatives. For UDE and for its successor, UDEAC, the main gains from integration are bound up with industrial specialization and the exploitation of scale economies which it facilitates, coupled with its effect on the inflow of capital, although benefits in the shape of a more effective and cheaper customs administration are probably of considerable importance also.

As far as the inflow of capital is concerned, it is probable that the inflows of foreign public aid to these countries might have been reduced substantially by their failure to co-operate. Until very recently, however, it is doubtful whether their inflow of private capital has been greatly affected by the common market for despite its existence most private capital has been directed to industries destined to serve the export market.

As to inter-country trade in local manufactures, it has been seen that although this grew rapidly among the UDE countries, nevertheless, as a share of total trade, it remains relatively small. Moreover its importance is at present greatest in a few commodities such as sugar, cigarettes and beer, in which trade could probably continue in the absence of a common market although its commencement might have been delayed without it. For most products the absolute value of inter-country trade is low, although it is significant that in some cases it represents a large part of the output of the establishments concerned.

From the statistics collected for trade in products subject to the *taxe unique*, it is also possible to get a picture of the developing level and pattern of inter-country trade in manufactures over a period which spans the incorporation of Cameroon into the customs union. Inter-territorial exports among the four UDE countries increased from 2,960 mn. fr. in 1963 to 4,010 mn. fr. in 1966, a rise of 30 per cent. Exports from Cameroon to UDE over this period have progressed rather more rapidly. They rose from approximately 300 mn. fr. in 1963 to about 650 mn. fr. in 1966, and in that year represented 14 per cent of total UDEAC inter-territorial trade. On the other hand, exports from UDE into Cameroon over this period merely kept pace with the growth of total UDEAC inter-territorial trade, and at a level of 110 mn. fr. in 1966 represented only 2 per cent of total UDEAC trade. The main constituents of the developing export trade from Cameroon were beer, clothing, shoes and aluminium ware. In the other direction trade consisted of a large number of items none of which was individually very important. Although Cameroon's exports to the UDE countries grew relatively rapidly in relation to the growth of common market trade during 1963–66, no dramatic increase occurred on the formation of UDEAC. This was not to be expected since trade between Cameroon and UDE was already enjoying a privileged customs regime. Cameroon's exports to its partners are likely to form an increasing proportion of UDEAC trade in the course of time, but major expansion will

TABLE 5 : 11

Inter-country Trade of UDEAC in Manufactures Subject to the Taxe Unique 1966 (000 francs CFA)

Exported from \ Imported into	CAMEROON	CAR	CONGO	GABON	CHAD	Total	% of Total Exports
CAMEROON	—	107,829	115,665	242,167	183,625	649,286	13·6
CAR	11,780	—	34,387	10,851	491,819	548,837	11·5
CONGO	62,048	1,130,223	—	701,219	1,555,970	3,449,460	72·3
GABON	38,366	15,903	36,868	—	20,853	111,990	2·3
CHAD	—	12,007	1,348	476	—	13,831	0·3
Total	112,194	1,265,962	188,268	954,713	2,252,267	4,773,404	
% of total imports	2·4	26·5	3·9	20·0	47·2		100·0

SOURCE : *Bulletin des Statistiques Générales de l'UDEAC* No. 18, April 1967.

be dependent upon the development of new industries in Cameroon, for which its relatively large home market places it in a favourable position, and on the completion of its rail extensions.

Since industrial development and the inter-country trade on which it must so largely rest has hitherto been rather limited in the equatorial common market, the contribution of economic integration to economic development can hardly have been of more than limited importance so far. The entry of Cameroon to the common market however virtually doubles the gross domestic product of the market and offers the prospect of greatly improved opportunities for industrial development based on import substitution. As economic growth proceeds and with increasing emphasis being placed on industrial development by all five countries the potential benefits to be anticipated from the market in the future should be much larger than they have been in the past. The transformation of potential gains into realized gains will, however, demand the continuance and effective operation of the framework for economic co-operation which has been established.

From this standpoint the recent evolution of economic co-operation in the area is on balance encouraging, although it is not the case that it has uniformly been in the direction of closer co-operation; tensions among the members have not been lacking; nor can it be said that the solution to several important issues is yet assured. So far, however, separatist tendencies have made themselves effective only in relation to the operation of certain of the common services, several of which have been replaced by national bodies.

The Equatorial Post and Telecommunications Agency began to break up as long ago as 1963 when CAR set up its own system. Today each country has its own Post Office and Savings Bank. The dissolution of the common agency in this case seems to have been precipitated partly by considerations relating to the control of savings funds, but it mainly gives effect to a widespread view that such vital agencies should be directly controlled by each state. In the field of internal air transportation the UDEAC countries have established their own internal air lines, although they continue to participate with other French speaking African countries in the jointly owned 'Air Afrique' which operates international and intercontinental services.

During UDE the administration of the common customs services also gave rise to dissatisfaction which was partly related to different views on the treatment which should be accorded to certain types of imports.[49] The new procedures described above on page 217 should safeguard the basic operation of the customs union but, despite the issue of detailed regulations, the separate customs administrations will under the new system be in a position to exercise some administrative discretion in relation to the interpretation of the customs code and the treatment of imports which was scarcely possible under the centralized system operated under UDE. Consequently it may be difficult to ensure the uniform treatment of imports as effectively as was the case in UDE. Close supervision by the Committee will be necessary if common standards are to be maintained and any differences which arise—and some will be unavoidable—are to be prevented from becoming large enough to impair the smooth working of the Union.

Finally, the case of the University of Brazzaville may be mentioned. Although it has not broken up, this institution, which was originally established to serve all four UDE countries, has become almost wholly a Congolese institution in terms of the composition of its student body, mainly as a result of the 1963 revolution in Brazzaville. The area is thus deprived of the cohesive force of a common institution of higher education which in other parts of Africa has been a helpful factor in maintaining co-operation by providing a common background for the new élites.

The prospects for the future of the enlarged economic union, and in particular for its industrial development must necessarily be a matter for conjecture. Plainly, if the common market is to have its maximum impact on the character and pace of industrial development there is needed a commitment on the part of each partner to its effective operation and confidence on the part of investors in that commitment. If this confidence is lacking, the establishment of plants of optimal size will not be encouraged. Investors will be more inclined to invest in projects of a scale which could if necessary be viable in the separate national markets and one of the main gains from integration will be lost. Also, any lack of confidence in the long-term maintenance of the market will tend to encourage unbalanced development which itself makes the maintenance of the market more difficult. Unless an investor is confident of continued free access to the market as a whole it is reasonable to suppose that he will be reluctant to establish a plant in any one country if the market is found chiefly in other states. Thus, in the absence of dominating advantages of a kind enjoyed by Congo by virtue of its economic infrastructure and coastal location, lack of confidence further weights the scales against location in the smaller members to the extent that their industries would have to rely heavily on their neighbour's markets. Even fairly favourable production conditions or the provision of offsetting inducements may not be sufficient to overcome this disadvantage. A commitment to the common market is inevitably bound up with the benefits which each member can anticipate. From this point of view several grounds support a belief that the self-interest of each member may encourage the continuance of economic co-operation and a commitment on the part of the members of the Union to make the system work.

In the first place, integration is likely to make possible a good deal of additional development. For instance, application of the comparative structural studies discussed in Chapter 3 suggests that the operation of the size factor, which reflects the economies of integration, might make feasible additional industrial incomes in the region as a whole of 35mn. dollars by 1970.[50] This would imply an increase in the annual regional rate of growth of GDP of a little less than 0·5 per cent over and above the forecasted rate for the period. The detailed industrial enquiries which have been carried out for the area perhaps provide a more dependable indication of the effect of integration. These enquiries have identified a substantial number of industrial projects which would only be feasible, except at great cost, if the common market is maintained.[51] Thus the primary condition for success appears to exist.

Secondly, most of the five UDEAC states appear to have a fairly clear economic interest in participating in the Union even if, for the time being, it continues to operate much as its predecessor.

230

For Cameroon, its largest and most advanced member, its planned rail links offer it the prospect of substantial additional market outlets for the industrial development which its relatively large home market virtually assures it of. The new rail links will also provide Cameroon with an opportunity to capture an expanding share of the transit trade serving the two inland countries.

Even the two inland and less favoured states, Chad and CAR have a strong interest in the wider grouping because the viability of their planned transport links with Cameroon will largely turn on its continuance. These new links will offer the two inland countries substantially improved development prospects from reduced transport costs and from the opening up of new and potentially highly productive areas. Apart from this, these two countries may justifiably hope to attract at least some industry which they would not otherwise get through the operation of the harmonization provisions of the treaty. In any event, despite the two land-locked members' often-expressed dissatisfaction with the market's operation, their withdrawal appears improbable because more attractive alternatives are not evident. The bargaining position of land-locked states in Africa is not strong.[52]

Gabon is perhaps the most viable of the four equatorial states. Hitherto, although it has drawn upon its partners for a labour supply, it has had limited trade links with them. Its exports to its partners have been negligible. Its small import trade, mainly with Congo, if anything, involved it in modest losses in the form of higher prices. In addition it made a small net contribution to the Solidarity Fund. Not surprisingly, enthusiasm for UDE was on the whole somewhat lukewarm although the cause of integration, both in equatorial Africa and more widely has found powerful support from André Anguilé, a former Minister of Finance and Planning and one of the ablest of the country's political leaders. Lately however there has been a more widespread interest in regional integration which is partly related to the changed emphasis of Gabon's development policy.

The lack of reciprocal trade between Gabon and the rest of the common market is bound up with the fact that since 1945 and during the early years of independence, the main weight of its development effort was placed on the expansion of export-oriented production, mainly of mineral and forest products. Although this has been successful in terms of the generation of domestic product, it has fostered the development of an economy characterized by an extreme form of economic dualism, in which a highly capital intensive export sector operates beside an agricultural sector which produces mainly for subsistence, and between which there is little else. Gabon's development policy now aims at producing a more balanced economic structure, partly by encouraging the development of a marketable surplus in its peasant agriculture, and partly by promoting the development of natural resource-based industries such as cement, steel and glass for which it possesses the necessary supplies of raw materials. These industries cannot be set up merely to serve Gabon's own extremely small internal market and can be feasible only on condition that they have access to the UDEAC market as a whole. Thus Gabon's new development policy gives it an economic stake in the success of the equatorial common market which it has hitherto lacked. The regional oil refinery has already been allocated to Gabon and she can reasonably look forward to developing other natural resource-based regional industries in the future. From these and other developments Gabon can anticipate substantial future economic benefit from UDEAC. Apart from such purely economic considerations, Gabon's present leaders also appear to see political advantage from associating Cameroon more closely with the equatorial states, and a strengthening of UDEAC should facilitate this objective.

For Congo, the remaining partner, the creation of UDEAC is of questionable benefit. Since 1960 Congo has suffered economic depression as a result of the loss of its position as the capital of the former Federation of French Equatorial Africa. The formation of UDEAC faces it with another challenge for it is placed in direct competition with the more developed and much larger Cameroon. Having regard to the transport-determined market areas which are presently focused on Brazzaville, this may not be very important in the near future. But if and when the extension of the trans-Cameroon railway to the north and east, and related developments are completed, the whole perspective for trade in the common market will be altered and the conditions will be created for Cameroon to play an increasingly important, and one day, assuredly, a dominant role in the markets of Brazzaville's economic partners. Nevertheless, assuming that an equatorial common market continues with Cameroon as a member, Congo's best prospect of maintaining its economic momentum appears to lie first in endeavouring to maintain the markets for its existing industries which would otherwise be severely hit, and beyond this to rely on attracting to Pointe Noire and Brazzaville a share of any new Union-oriented industrial plants by virtue of the advantages its location and infrastructure can afford. Almost certainly, its small population and infrastructure geared to the former UDE states place Congo in a better position to protect its economic interests inside the common market rather than by attempting to develop on the basis of its own market, which in the foreseeable future appears to be the only alternative.

Thus from various standpoints all five countries have a considerable interest in creating the conditions in which UDEAC can operate effectively. Whether it will be permitted to do so in the longer run is likely to depend increasingly on the achievement of an acceptable distribution of industrial development within the Union. How far do the arrangements set out in the Treaty promise to do this? The Treaty does not attempt in advance to allocate specific industries, which is certainly wise. Industrial allocation would only make sense, if at all, against the background of detailed studies of costs in alternative locations. A failure to undertake such studies prior to the allocation of industries among the East African countries was indeed one of the reasons for the initial failure of the Kampala Agreement. But although the omission from the Treaty of any attempt to allocate industries may be a matter for congratulation, it is certainly a matter for concern that the Treaty does not attempt to specify any framework of agreed differential incentives or other special measures on which the less favoured members could rely for benefits. Moreover, the ability of the members by unilateral action to create a favourable climate for investment within their borders even for industries serving their own markets is limited.

Admittedly the Treaty does empower individual states to offer investment incentives to industries serving their own markets, although even in this case, if a similar industry exists in another country, or even if one is merely envisaged, consultation is required by the harmonization provisions before the concesssions can be granted. The incentives which may be offered take the form, as described already, of exemption from duties on inputs and from duties levied in the form of the *taxe unique*, and possibly exemptions from profits taxes.

Incentives for industries serving the markets of more than one country however are determined by the Committee of Direction (except in the case of bilateral harmonization). The incentive takes the form chiefly of a favourable rate of *taxe unique* which is levied in substitution for other indirect taxes. The location of industry within the common market could conceivably be influenced by the grant of such an incentive in various ways. Firstly an enterprise producing a product new to the region could be offered a more favourable rate of tax if it were to agree to locate in, say, Chad rather than Congo. Secondly in the case of a product which is already in production it would be permissible for an enterprise to be offered a lower rate in respect of further production in designated areas. But this possibility must be viewed in the lights of the Treaty's provision that differences in tax rates for a given product are not to be large and are to be progressively reduced. It is also stated that after 1971 recourse to such differentials will be exceptional. Other permissible incentives which could vary according to the location of the enterprise include exemption from profits tax and the grant of accelerated depreciation.

Thus although the separate states are enabled to offer incentives to industries serving their own markets, subject to consultation in certain cases, the power to influence by the grant of incentives, the location of industries serving more than one country is firmly in the hands of the Committee of Direction to which the Treaty gives only general guidance as to the factors to take into account. Moreover, for expansion in existing industries as opposed to the initial establishment of industries in the area, the differential incentives which can be offered by the Committee are limited.

It thus appears that the individual members of UDEAC have less discretion to influence the location of industry by fiscal means than have the members of the East African Community, small as that is. In East Africa, as has been seen, deficit countries can impose a transfer tax under prescribed conditions at their sole discretion and products so protected will continue to enjoy access up to a point to their neighbours' markets. Moreover, in Equatorial Africa any proffered concessions to an industry serving one country imply forgone revenue to the country offering concessions, whereas in East Africa this is not so.

On the other hand, unlike the new deal in East Africa, the arrangements in UDEAC do envisage influencing the location of industry by administrative means so as to favour the less advanced members. How effective these attempts will prove to be in the absence of an agreed framework of differential incentives, and when domestic pressures force each country to look at its own interests first, remains to be seen. Of course, the requirement of unanimity in relation to the decisions of the Committee of Direction does mean that each state has a voice in relation to the location of new industries since any state can refuse to assent to the particular level of *taxe unique* which is envisaged for an industry which is proposed by another country unless it is assured of concessions on another which it seeks to attract. But this merely means that the distribution of industry in the union is to depend on the outcome of future negotiations. A framework for negotiation is certainly provided by the Treaty but the bargaining is yet to come and will be a continuous process.

It seems clear that the Secretariat is expected to play an important role in this process by reconciling the various projects which come up to it. To the extent that this is the case, experience in other areas where regional development policies are attempted suggests that an effective policy may demand a central agency having a less circumscribed initiative. Attempts to influence the location of projects and plans for industrial development which originate with private developers and the separate states may prove difficult even if major inducements can be offered. The initiation by the UDEAC authorities themselves of industrial projects might place them in a better position to influence the balance of industrial development, but they are unlikely to be able to do this unless they possess a strong agency, able to evaluate industrial projects independently and itself enjoying access to potential developers. It is doubtful if it could justly be claimed that the administration of UDEAC is yet adequately equipped to perform such a role. A strengthened central administration of UDEAC may therefore be an important condition for the success of its distribution of industry policy. The industrial development bank which is under consideration for the region could also perform an important role in contributing to balance. As industry develops in the area it will become progressively more important for a balanced pattern of development to be promoted in the interests of the cohesion of the union. It remains to be seen whether the present institutional arrangements will be effective in bringing this about.

REFERENCES: CHAPTER 5

1 For a general historical introduction to the development of AEF up to 1958 see V. Thompson and R. Adloff, *The Emerging States of French Equatorial Africa*, Oxford University Press, London, 1960.

2 See *Recueil des Conventions Relatives aux Organismes Communs aux Quatre États de l'Afrique Équatoriale*, Secrétariat-Général, Conférence des Chefs d'État de l'Afrique Équatoriale, Brazzaville, Fasciscule 2. *Convention portent Organisation de l'Union Douanière Équatoriale* (June 23, 1959), See also *Additif au Recueil des Conventions*.

3 The problems of integrating the two parts of this state are not discussed here.

4 See *Convention reglant les relations économiques et douanières entre les États de l'Union Douanière Équatoriale et la République du Cameroun* (June 23, 1961). Secrétariat-Général, Conférence des Chefs d'État, Brazzaville. Subsequent decisions and acts are listed at page B 14 of the Tariff des Douanes (UDE).

5 See *Traité institutant une Union Douanière et Économique de l'Afrique Centrale* (Dec. 8, 1964), Brazzaville.

6 All UDEAC countries are associated overseas territories of EEC under the Yaoundé Convention of 1963 which replaced Part IV of the Treaty of Rome 1957. See Chapter 2 Section 4 for further details.

7 See pp. 188–9.

8 See Recueil, Fasc. 1, *Convention Portant Statut de la Conférence des Chefs d'État*. Brazzaville (mimeo).

9 See *Convention et Réglementation de la Taxe Unique* (acte 12/60) of the Conference dated May 17, 1960, amended by Acte 36/60 of 10 November, 1960, Secrétariat-Général, Brazzaville.

10 See *Tarif des Douanes*, Direction des Bureaux Communs, Brazzaville, Table B. 10 for a list of UDE firms subjected to the *taxe unique*.

11 These include the company tax, turnover tax, etc. See Section 5.

12 The shares in 1959 were:

Gabon	21·92%
Chad	29·96%
Congo	28·24%
CAR	19·88%

13 See Conférence des Premiers Ministres, *Compte Rendu Analytique des Séances des June 22–3, 1959*.

14 See *Études Économiques, No. VII*, Bureau Centrale de la Statistique, Brazzaville, 1958.

15 Unpublished investigation, '*Fiscalité totale (douane et contributions directe) au 1. 1. 1965 par sous position tarifaire*'. (Brazzaville, 1965).

16 Currently at the official rate of exchange, the monetary product of UDE is only about two-fifths that of East Africa; if Cameroon is added, the proportion becames two-thirds.

17 In the immediate future, the position with respect to sugar may be affected by the decision taken by the Heads of State of OCAM in June 1966 to create an African and Malagasy Sugar Market. This involves an agreement amongst African producers and consumers of sugar to sell and buy agreed quotas of sugar at a fixed price. The operation is to be financed by an equalisation fund levied on imports of sugar from third countries. The headquarters of the organisation is at Fort Lamy. See *Rapport d'Activité*, 1965–66 Banque Centrale des États de l'Afrique Équatoriale et du Cameroun, page 75. Also: 'L'Organisation Commune Africaine et Malgache et le Marché Africaine et Malgache de Sucre. Banque Centrale des États de l'Afrique Équatoriale et du Cameroun', *Bulletin Mensuel*, July 1966.

18 See *Convention* dated Feb. 15, 1955.

19 See *Convention reglant les relations économiques et douanières entre les États de l'Union Douanière Équatoriale et la République du Cameroun*, June 23, 1961.

20 The Convention provides that this tax may vary between UDE and Cameroon for a given product, but that the differences must not be 'aggravated' and will be subject to progressive reduction tending to equalization unless one of the enterprises is placed in danger. In this case, the Mixed Commission may recommend safeguards.

21 For a list of the quotas for 1964, see e.g. *Annexe a la Décision No. 2/64 de la Commission Mixte Douanière Équatoriale-Cameroun.*

22 For the background to monetary development prior to the establishment of the Central Bank, see Thompson and Adloff, *op. cit.* Chapter II, *Currency and Banking*, pp. 117–23.

23 For a summary of the main provisions regulating the structure and operation of the Central Bank see *Dispositions Organiques,* Banque Centrale, Paris, 1962. The annexe lists the relevant texts.

24 Prior to November, 1965, there were only three, Congo, Chad and CAR, jointly sharing the 'Equatorial' Committee.

25 The external reserves which are attributable to Cameroon have been separately stated in the Annual Report for a number of years. (Two separate Annual Reports were, in fact, produced; one for Cameroon, and one for the other countries together). The external reserves for each of the UDE countries have been separately stated from 1964, and five separate reports are now published.

26 This approach to monetary harmonization is similar to that proposed by Newlyn for East Africa with the significant difference that in Equatorial Africa there is a shared currency whereas Newlyn's scheme envisaged separate currencies exchanging at par. See W. T. Newlyn, Monetary Systems and Integration, *East African Economic Review*, June, 1964, Vol. 1, pp. 41–58.

27 See Section 2, p. 178 above.

28 See *The Jeanneney Report*, Overseas Development Institute, London, 1964, p. 38. The original report is entitled *La Politique de Co-opération avec les Pays en voie de Developpement*, La Documentation Française, Paris 1963.

29 *Étude Monographique de trente-et-une Pays africaines*, Vol. 3, Cogrof, for UAMCE, Paris, December, 1964.

30 See *Customs Union Convention* of June 28, 1959, Articles 8–11.

31 This is also the criterion employed in the European Economic Community. See *Tax Harmonization in the Common Market.* Report of the Fiscal and Financial Committee (Neumark Committee), p. 14, Commerce Clearing House, Chicago, Trans., 1963.

32 See *Fiscalité de l'Afrique Noire*, No. 12, 1965, Paris, and *Droit Fiscal Comparé en Afrique Noire*, Pays de l'UDE, Cameroun, Senegal, Côte d'Ivoire, France, Paris, 1965.

33 *Convention sur le Régime des Investissements dans l'Union Douanière Équatoriale* of November 11, 1960.

34 See *Convention Reglant les Relations Économiques et Douanières entre les États de l'Union Douanière Équatoriale et la République du Cameroun.*

35 A convenient summary of the position prior to the coming into effect of UDEAC is provided in the United Nations publication, *Investment Laws and Regulations in Africa*, 1965, ref. E/CN.14/INR/28/Rev.2.

36 See *Étude des possibilités d'installation d'industries cotonnières et de confection au Cameroun, Congo, Gabon* RCA *et Tchad*, Syndicat Général de l'Industrie Cotonnière, Paris, 1963.

37 See *La Co-ordination des Industries dans la Zone Union Douanière-Cameroun*, Ministry of Co-operation, Paris, pp. 15–16.

38 *Ibid*, pp. 22–3.

39 The orders of magnitude involved are indicated in the following table:

Oil Refinery for Equatorial Africa
Per cent Rate of Return

	Port Gentil	Pointe Noire
Single refinery	3·7–7·5	2·2–5·5
Two refineries	0·3–1·1	

Source: Unpublished technical studies by Bureau de Recherches du Pétrole, 1963, and Gabonese Government.

40 See *Additif au Recueil des Conventions Relatives au Organismes Communs*, Tome 111, 'Harmonisation des Projets Industriels' (Decision of February 12, 1964).

41 On these relations, see A. Tevoedjre, *Pan-Africanism in Action*; *An Account of UAM*. Harvard University, Center for International Affairs, Occasional Paper No. 11. Ch. IV. The Dispute Between Gabon and Congo—Brazzaville.

42 See Statement of Gabonese industrial policy in *La Co-ordination . . .* p. 31.

43 The Solidarity Fund arrangements were agreed for an initial year. See *Acte no. 11/65–17 UDEAC–21 decembre 1965, fixant les conditions d'application du Fonds de Solidarité dans l'UDEAC pour l'année 1966. Journal Officiel (J.O.), UDEAC* Jan. 1, 1966. They were subsequently revised for 1967. See below ref. 48.

44 See *Acte no. 18/65-UDEAC-15 adoptant la Convention Commune sur les Investissements dans les États de l'Union*, J.O. No. 3 (l année) of March 1, 1966.

45 See *Acte no. 7/65-UDEAC/36-portant fixation du tarif des Douanes de l'Union douanière et economique de l'Afrique Centrale*, J. O. No. 1 (I année) of Jan. 1, 1966.

46 See *Acte no. 10/65-UDEAC-29 fixant la liste des bureaux des Douanes Communs de l'Union*, J.O. No. 1 of Jan. 1, 1966.

47 See *Acte no. 12/65-UDEAC-34 portant reglementations du Régime de la Taxe Unique dans l'UDEAC*, J.O. No. 2 of Jan. 2, 1966.

48 See *Acte no. 6/66 UDEAC-50 of fixant les conditions d'application du Fonds de Solidarité pour l'année 1967*, J.O. No .7 of Dec. 31, 1966.

49 Brazzaville at first refused to pay duty on goods received from China on the basis of bilateral barter deals. The issue of principle is resolved, but the problem of valuation remains. The problem of the treatment of these goods in relation to inter-country trade is a potentially thorny one.

50 This estimate is derived from an application of the formula developed in the United Nations study, *A Study of Industrial Growth*, New York 1963. Thus it was estimated in *Economic Co-operation in Central Africa* (ECN 14/L. 320 1966) that on the basis of the five country plans, value added in industry in the whole area in 1970 will be $225 mn. If this is increased in the relationship which the expected normal value for the area as a whole for 1970 bears to the sum of the expected normal values for the separate countries, industrial development planned to serve the whole region would amount to about $261 mn. This would mean that the industrial sector would grow at about 12·5 per cent instead of 10 per cent. GDP would correspondingly be 2 per cent higher at the end of the period for the region as a whole.

51 *La Co-ordination* . . . reviews most of the relevant technical and economic studies which have been made in the last few years. See also UNECA *Report of the Economic Mission on Economic Co-operation in Central Africa.*

52 The UN Conference on Trade and Development adopted the following principles for land-locked countries:—freedom of transit without discrimination, restriction of customs and transit fee other than for administrative needs, guarantees of reasonable rates, and adequate transport services in the transit states. If these principles were accepted the use of transit facilities by landlocked nations would become a right. These principles have yet to be embodied in an International Convention. See UN *Conference on Trade and Development*, Final Act and Report, UN 1964, Principles relating to transit trade of land-locked countries, pp. 25–6.

CHAPTER 6

OTHER INITIATIVES FOR ECONOMIC INTEGRATION IN AFRICA

1 INTRODUCTION

THE instances of effective economic co-operation in Africa to-day take the form of small groups of contiguous and normally culturally similar countries organised for co-operation in trade and industrial development or for functional co-operation in special fields. Two of the major examples, East Africa and Equatorial Africa, have been discussed in previous chapters. Other examples of this kind of co-operation are found in French-speaking West Africa and in Southern Africa.

Some new initiatives attempt to repeat this pattern in other parts of Africa, but others are directed towards promoting co-operation on a different basis. Sometimes this takes the form of attempting to widen the geographical basis of existing integration schemes so as to include all the countries in a natural economic region which may now be separated by different tariff, monetary and cultural systems. Thus ECA has initiated discussions on the formation of an Eastern African Economic Community which would embrace the countries of the present East African Common Market together with a number of neighbouring countries, including Zambia, Malawi, Sudan, and Ethiopia. Similarly it has attempted to bring about co-operation for industrial development in the West African subregion and it has also advocated economic integration for the UDEAC-Congo (Kinshasa) region. So long as the achievement of really effective co-operation within existing narrow groupings proves difficult, the pursuit of such wider groupings may appear impracticable, though it is of course conceivable that carefully selected wider groupings might be more cohesive than narrower ones if only because the causes of contention become dispersed.

Another kind of co-operation initiative is aimed at promoting strictly limited objectives for neighbouring countries in a single field such as, for instance, river basin development. One result of the development of schemes of this kind is that there are coming to be overlapping areas in the field of economic co-operation. Thus a country like Chad is a member of UDEAC, but co-operates with a different group of countries on the Chad Basin Commission, and with yet other countries for different economic purposes.

Finally some initiatives are being taken which from the outset aim at developing institutions of economic co-operation on a continental basis. The visionary hope of the early formation of an African Common Market has given place in the last few years to a more realistic emphasis on the promotion of regional market arrangements. Nevertheless, various forms of continent-wide co-operation of a functional nature continue to be discussed, and one has actually come into operation.

This chapter commences by considering briefly some examples of regional economic integration in French-speaking West Africa and in Southern Africa. It goes on to consider the unsuccessful bid to bring about the integration of Gambia with Senegal. Finally it considers two examples of actual or projected co-operation in the fields of banking and money.

2 ECONOMIC CO-OPERATION IN FRENCH SPEAKING WEST AFRICA

For more than half a century the French speaking West African states of today had close economic and political links within the administrative Federation of French West Africa (AOF).[1] In the economic field co-operation was expressed by a common currency, a range of common services and a customs union which was also the instrument through which resources were redistributed from the wealthier coastal states such as Senegal and Ivory Coast, to their less well endowed inland colleagues. When independence was in sight there was some support on the part of local federalists for a continuance of federal links in the area, but the territorialist view prevailed and in 1959, on French initiative, the Federation was dissolved.[2]

Nonetheless some attempts were made to create new political groupings to take the place of the old federation. In January 1959 the leaders of Dahomey, Senegal, Soudan and Upper Volta agreed to form a Mali federation, hoping in this way to prevent a total dissolution of the old AOF and also to provide a nucleus for some future French speaking West African Federation. Political pressure from France in the case of Dahomey, and from the territorialist Ivory Coast in the case of Upper Volta, led to the withdrawal of these two countries from the federation almost immediately, though there was for these two countries in any case no really solid basis for economic co-operation within this grouping. Upper Volta in particular was heavily dependent on Ivory Coast rather than Soudan for port facilities and communications, and also to provide employment on farms for migrant workers. Not long after, in 1960, the two remaining members of the Mali Federation finally parted company, with Soudan retaining the name of Mali.[3]

Meanwhile other former members of AOF were attempting to forge new political links. In 1959 Ivory Coast took the initiative in forming the Conseil de l'Entente together with Niger, Dahomey and Upper Volta. The members of this grouping lacked common frontiers and the economic interests of Niger and Dahomey lay with Nigeria rather than with the Ivory Coast. Not surprisingly the Entente has operated mainly as a loose organisation for the co-ordination of external policy but it was also intended to facilitate economic integration among its members and it has achieved a measure of functional co-operation in the economic field.

In 1961 Mali joined the Ghana-Guinea Union which itself had been formed in 1958 and which marked the first African initiative to break down the barriers between French and English-speaking African States. This loose grouping which was never effective in the economic field, finally liquidated itself in 1963 in response to the OAU prohibition on regional political groupings.[4]

While the former AOF area has effectively remained politically fragmented, a variety of arrangements for economic co-operation have been attempted between its former members in whole or part. The most successful of these relates to the monetary field.

When the Federation was dissolved, arrangements were made for the continuance of the existing monetary union, and soon after, in 1962, a West African Monetary Union was formally established.[5] It now includes all of the former AOF states except Guinea (Mali having rejoined) with the addition since 1963 of Togo. Its operations are very similar to those of the Equatorial African Union[6] and will not be separately discussed here.

Attempts were also made to retain an integrated market in the area. An agreement was signed on June 9, 1959 between all the former member states of AOF except Guinea which provided for a customs union and recognised the principle of free movement of goods among the signatory states without fiscal or quantitative hindrance. Except between Senegal and Mauretania, whose trade links have been particularly close, the 1959 Convention was never fully applied. Difficulties arose over the allocation of revenue for goods imported from outside and transferred from one member to another. As a result, customs barriers were established at the frontiers and indirect taxes on intra-regional trade were imposed, though attempts were made to harmonise the treatment given to such trade. Although its Committee of Direction continued to meet regularly to deal with transit problems and to discuss customs harmonization the Convention became virtually inoperative as a result of these infractions and deviations.

At last, a number of the members took the view that it would be more realistic and fruitful to enter into a new Convention which, by taking into account the diverse fiscal interests of the different states, might arrest the progressive deterioration of the economic links in the area. The outcome of these initiatives was that in March 1966 at the twelfth session of UDAO which was held in Paris, a new convention was adopted establishing the Union Douanière des États de l'Afrique de l'Ouest (UDEAO).[7] At Abidjan in the following June all of the former members of the AOF except Guinea signed the Convention. It came into force after the ratification of the Convention by five of the states.

The Union's central concern is to ensure the free circulation of local products of members within the area, subject to a certain measure of protection for existing industries and a fiscal tax. Partly with a view to facilitating this and the transit trade, there is to be harmonization of the law and practice relating to customs and a common external tariff is to be introduced, termed the customs duty, which is within the jurisdiction of the Union.

Three organizations have been created to implement the Union. The supreme policy-making body is the Council of Ministers. This is made up of one member of each government who is ordinarily the Minister of Finance. The Council meets once a year in ordinary session. Decisions are to be taken by a majority to be determined by the Council and are binding on all members. Beneath this there is to be a committee of experts composed of delegates from member states. It will hold two ordinary sessions a year to formulate propositions and recommendations or to advise on the questions submitted to it. Finally there is a Secretariat-General, which, however, has no powers of decision.

The main provisions of the Convention relate to the treatment to be given to local products and to products imported from overseas by one member and subsequently transferred to another member.

Local products are defined as products which are harvested, extracted from the ground or manufactured. The Convention provides that there is to be no obstacle to the free circulation of such products but they are subject to taxation in order to reduce revenue losses which would otherwise be involved. In principle, local products are subject to a fiscal tax equal to 50 per cent of the aggregate tax applied to a similar imported product. Simple assembly industries will only benefit from this preference within the limits of quotas fixed between the two interested states. Furthermore, in the case of competition between the industry of one member with a similar industry in another, the latter will be authorised by the Council to impose the fiscal tax at 70 per cent of the level on comparable products from outside.

The common external tariff to be imposed by all members will be known as the *droit de douane*. It will operate in addition to the other import charges imposed by the members which remain within their competence.

Where products are imported from outside the Union and are subsequently transferred to another member they are subject to the import charges which would normally be payable, according to their origin. This, however, is to be done in such a way as to prevent double taxation and may be effected by financial adjustments between the states not involving any collection of duties at the frontiers.

Difficulties have already arisen in connection with the implementation of this agreement. It is reported[8] that the Council of Ministers has not been able to reach agreement on the definition of aggregate taxation which is the basis for the reduction of duties on local products. Senegal and Ivory Coast have proposed that this should include internal taxes while the other members have rejected this because of the revenue losses involved. Some infractions of the agreement are also alleged in the import trade of the Ivory Coast with its neighbours. While an effective convention on the lines described could certainly serve very useful purposes in the area by rationalising customs procedures, avoiding double taxation, and providing a limited preferential trading area, it remains to be seen whether the new Convention will prove to be any more workable than its predecessor.

Some other arrangements for economic co-operation in the area operate on the basis of smaller groupings, though their achievements have been limited. The most important of these are among the countries of the Conseil de l'Entente. Basically the Entente is an informal instrument for policy co-ordination based on personal confidence between the Heads of State, and it has been widely publicised by its progenitor, President Houphouët-Boigny as a model for a realistic, gradualist approach to the achievement of greater unity in Africa.

Although the Entente is primarily a political grouping, the 1959 agreement which established it did contain two potentially important economic provisions. The first, which envisaged the harmonization of the countries' development plans has so far remained a pious aspiration. The second provided for the establishment of a Solidarity Fund. During the days of the AOF the Ivory Coast had consistently objected to fiscal redistribution through the federal budget from it and Senegal to the benefit of the poorer inland states. The establishment of the Solidarity Fund in 1959 reflected Ivory Coast's recognition that it was nonetheless not in its interests to remain an island of prosperity in a sea of poverty. In theory the fund was to receive for redistribution 10 per cent of the revenues of each member state. In practice the Solidarity Fund seems to have operated informally as the means through which the Ivory Coast (or its President) has subsidised the budgets of the other three countries as and when required, from resources not subject to public scrutiny in Ivory Coast. No provision for payment of the subsidies ever appeared in the Ivory Coast budget, though until recently, Solidarity Fund receipts were recorded in the budgets of the other members. The accounts of the Fund were not subject to audit.

Within the Entente a further attempt at economic integration is marked by Houphouët-Boigny's Convention of late 1965 on dual nationality and economic harmonization.[9] Reciprocal citizenship provisions in the Entente area derive their importance partly from the fact that a large part of the labour force of the Ivory Coast is made up of immigrants from other members of the Entente countries. The economic harmonization provisions reflect the pressure which has been building up, particularly from Upper Volta, to encourage a more equitable distribution of industrial development. The double nationality provisions aroused strong opposition in the Ivory Coast, particularly from white-collar workers, who saw it as a threat to their employment. In the event, to the chagrin of the other states, the President was forced by the Bureau Politique to withdraw his proposal and the convention was not ratified.

A still more recent development in the Entente countries has been the establishment of the Mutual Aid and Guarantee Fund which in 1966 formally superseded the Solidarity Fund. The object of the new fund is to stimulate foreign investment in the countries of the Entente through the establishment of a guarantee fund.[10] As with the old Solidarity Fund, the Ivory Coast is to be its principal source of finance. Thus of the annual total subscription of 650 mn. francs CFA the Ivory Coast will contribute 500 mn. francs, Upper Volta, Niger and Dahomey, 42 mn. each. Togo, which formally adhered to the Entente in 1966, will contribute 24 mn. francs. The benefits from the fund will flow initially to the less developed members of the grouping since the

Ivory Coast has agreed not to draw on it for the first five years of its operation.

The institution of the new Fund reflects the enhanced importance attached in the Ivory Coast (no doubt stimulated by the recent political instability of its neighbours) to helping its neighbours to get a larger share of economic development and it marks one of several signs of a new spirit of economic collaboration in the area. Whether it will materially influence the progress of the poorer members of the Entente unless they are also given preferential access to the Ivory Coast market is questionable.

It is from this point of view that the recently concluded Customs and Trade Agreement between Ivory Coast and Upper Volta is of some interest.[11] The agreement provides for a reduction of duty on Ivory Coast exports to Upper Volta of between 30 and 50 per cent. Upper Volta products on the other hand will enter the Ivory Coast duty free. Much will depend on how this agreement is interpreted but if it were lasting and liberally interpreted these inter-country preferences could provide a useful instrument for the expanded development of the very backward country of Upper Volta, whose domestic market alone is insufficient to support any but the most basic of manufacturing industries.

It is particularly difficult to foresee the future development of economic co-operation in the Entente area, in part because this has been very much the expression of the personal policies of President Houphouët-Boigny. The arrangements for co-operation just outlined find their justification from the Ivory Coast's point of view not so much from any promise of direct economic gain as from the encouragement which they may afford to the political stability of its neighbours. Among the other members there is some resentment of the Ivory Coast's dominance in Entente affairs which may ultimately have repercussions on the arrangements for economic co-operation. But in any case, it is unlikely that the present arrangements are so far making any significant contribution to the rate of growth of the Entente area as a whole, or to a more balanced distribution of economic activity within the area.

In the West African sub-region as a whole, co-operation at the levels of market co-operation or industrial co-ordination appears to be making little progress, although ECA has taken a number of initiatives, and many resolutions have been passed at international gatherings. Within the more limited area of the former AOF, however, various institutions exist for co-operation on a functional basis and new ones are being developed. Thus the operations of the Régie du chemin de fer Abidjan-Niger is regulated under a convention of 1960[12] from which Upper Volta (where the railway terminates) derives certain benefits.[13] A joint Dahomey-Niger governmental agency, the Organisation Commune Dahomey-Niger des Chemins de Fer et des Transports (OCDN) operates the port of Cotonou, and the railway from Cotonou to Parakou. This organisation also operates a subsidisation arrangement termed 'operation hirondelle' which subsidises the cost of exports from eastern Niger.[14] More recently, new functional organisations for inter-state economic co-operation have been established in the region like the Chad Basin Commission (1964), the Committee for the Improvement of the Senegal River (1964) and the Niger River Commission (1964).[15] To sum up, although economic co-operation is not highly developed in the area, for much of it there is a common currency and some common service organisations exist, as well as some trade preferences and other forms of mutual economic assistance. In addition, elements of a common labour market have continued beyond independence, up to the present time, though its operation has been interrupted by occasional bouts of xenophobia, mainly on the part of Ivory Coast, the chief recipient of migrant labour.

3 ECONOMIC INTEGRATION BETWEEN THE REPUBLIC OF SOUTH AFRICA AND BOTSWANA, LESOTHO AND SWAZILAND (BLS)

Introduction

An example of a long standing arrangement for economic integration in Africa which operates in a very special environment is the case of the former High Commission Territories of Bechuanaland (Botswana), Basutoland (Lesotho) and Swaziland (BLS). Geographically and ethnically these three countries, now, or, in the case of Swaziland, shortly to be independent, are closely related to the Republic of South Africa. For many years they have had the closest of economic ties with that country. Indeed, for most of their history as separate territories, it was assumed, both by Britain and by South Africa, that they would ultimately be absorbed within the latter. Provision for their incorporation was in fact made in the Act of 1909 which created the Union of South Africa, although it was subsequently made clear that this provision would not become effective unless the British Parliament was consulted and the wishes of the inhabitants were considered. During the following fifty years it was an object of South African policy to secure the incorporation of the territories into the Union.[16] With the development of *apartheid*, voluntary incorporation became out of the question, and by the early 1960's the dialogue about an ultimate transfer of the territories terminated. Britain began to prepare the territories for independence, and the South African government accepted that its future relations with the territories would be those appropriate to sovereign states. Nevertheless, economic links in the shape of legal and *de facto* integration arrangements continue to operate as in the past. As independence has approached, some consideration has been given by the Colonial Office and the local administrations to the merits of these arrangements and to possible alternatives. This has been stimulated partly by the need for the territories to determine their positions in relation to the intention of the South African government to produce new customs agreements for each of the territories in anticipation of their transition to independence. Discussions on new agreements are to take place at the end of 1967. Whatever form they take, which will partly if not mainly be determined by political considerations, it seems likely that geographical and economic considerations will point to continued close cooperation with South Africa on the part of BLS unless, indeed, no heed is taken of their justifiable claims to a new and improved financial deal.

The Economic Background

Table 6:1 sets out some of the salient economic and geographical features of the three countries and puts these

TABLE 6:1

Lesotho, Botswana, Swaziland and the Republic of South Africa: Economic Structure

	LESOTHO	BOTSWANA	SWAZILAND	REPUBLIC OF S.A.
Area—thousand sq. miles	12	220	7	472
Population—thousands, 1966	859	559 (a)	375	18,300
Population Density—persons per sq. mile	72	3	56	38
Gross Domestic Product 1965—R'000	37,425	27,890	55,000 (b)	7,881,000
G.D.P. per capita—Rand	44	50	160 (b)	430
Domestic Exports 1966—R'000	4,385	10,772	38,620	1,080,000 (c)
Imports 1966—R'000	22,917	18,858	26,471	1,645,600
Ordinary Revenue 1965/6—R'000	4,020	5,443	5,796	1,227,716
Customs & Excise Duties 1965/6—R'000	1,400	1,149	1,770	299,174
Customs & Excise as % of Ordinary Revenue	35%	21%	32%	24%
U.K. Grant in Aid—R'000	5,202	5,320	3,020	inapplicable
Total Revenue—R'000	9,222	10,763	8,816	1,227,716
Grants-in-Aid and Customs Revenue as % of Total Revenue	72%	60%	54%	inapplicable

SOURCES: Lesotho: *Annual Statistical Bulletin 1965; National Accounts 1964/5 and 1965/6; Trade Statement 1966,* Bureau of Statistics, Maseru.

Botswana: *National Accounts of Botswana 1965; Statistical Abstract,* Central Statistical Office, Gaberones.

Swaziland: *Annual Statistical Bulletin 1966; Gross Domestic Product 1960-64,* Statistical Office, Mbabane.

South Africa: *Statistical Yearbook, 1966,* Bureau of Statistics, Pretoria; I.M.F., *International Financial Statistics,* Washington, June 1967.

NOTES: (a) 1965.
(b) 1964 at 1960 prices.
(c) Excluding exports of gold.

251

against the similar magnitudes for the Republic of South Africa.

In area, the three countries taken together amount to more than half the size of the Republic, but a great part of the largest of the three countries, Botswana, consists of the sparsely populated and barren Kalahari desert. Lesotho is wholly an enclave within the boundaries of the Republic of South Africa and adjoins the Provinces of Natal on the east, Cape Province on the south, and the Orange Free State to the north and west. Most of its land is mountainous, and to the east, in the Drakensburgs, it attains a height of 11,000 feet. Swaziland is surrounded by the Republic on three sides but shares a border on the east with Mozambique. Botswana is bounded on the west and north by South West Africa, and on the north-east by Rhodesia. It also has a very small frontier on the north with Zambia.

The total population of the three countries in 1966 was approximately 2 million. This includes some 175,000 who were temporarily absent from their homes in the course of employment in South Africa.[17] By comparison, the population of the Republic of South Africa in the same year was 17·85 million. About 20 per cent of the Republic's population is European. There is no European settlement in Lesotho, but in both Swaziland, and Botswana there is a small settled European population which amounts to 3 per cent and 1 per cent of the respective populations. In Swaziland nearly one half of the land is owned by the European population.

Botswana is a vast arid table-land with an average rainfall of 19 inches varying from 12 inches or less in the drier portions to 27 inches in the extreme north. The greater part of the area consists of Kalahari sand veld and is largely uninhabited. Population is concentrated in the sub-tropical to temperate eastern region which is better watered and contains areas of higher elevation. The economy is based on agriculture and livestock. The main crops are maize and sorghum, much of which is produced for subsistence. Livestock is the most important source of cash income in agriculture. Mineral production is insignificant at present but surveys have revealed the existence of extensive coal deposits. Recently extensive copper nickel ore bodies have been discovered and their exploitation is likely to commence in

1971. Within the country paid employment amounts to only 30,000. In addition perhaps 35,000 persons, or some 20 per cent of the adult male population are temporarily absent, mainly in the Republic.

The economy of Lesotho is based entirely on the cultivation of crops, mainly for subsistence, and on the raising of sheep and goats on which the export of wool and mohair is based. There is also some export of cattle. Labour migration is a dominant feature of its economy. According to the 1966 census 97,000 or more than 35 per cent of the adult male population was temporarily absent in the Union or elsewhere. Known mineral resources are few and so far of little value. Industries are virtually non existent. The apparently viable Ox-Bow dam scheme on the Madimamatso river would permit the sale of fresh water and electricity to the Republic. If it is undertaken it may facilitate some small scale industrial development.

Swaziland is the smallest of the three countries, but the most generously endowed in terms of natural resources and minerals. It enjoys a variety of climatic and physical conditions and a good rainfall makes possible a variety of agricultural production. Although subsistence agriculture occupies the bulk of the population, cash crop production of a variety of crops, not only by European farmers but also on estates and by Africans, was valued in 1966 at seven times that of subsistence production and it is of growing importance. A rapid growth of irrigation projects in the low-veld region has contributed to this. Swaziland's important mineral resources include asbestos, iron ore, coal and kaolin. Apart from several large industrial units engaged in mining or the processing of local produce (sugar, pulp etc.) for export, little manufacturing development exists. The paid labour force within the country amounted in 1964 to about 25,000, many of whom were Africans from other countries.[18] About 19,000 Swazis find employment in the Republic. With the completion of the Swaziland railway the country now has a link to the coast through Mozambique. The railway was constructed primarily to facilitate the exploitation of the iron ore deposits, but should also make it possible to recommence coal mining and contribute to the more effective exploitation of the country's other resources. In recent years, Swaziland appears to have enjoyed a remarkably high rate of economic growth.

For some years the three territories have experienced budget deficits. With a quickening of the pace of political advance, rapid increases in the budget deficits have been experienced as revenues have failed to keep pace with increases in expenditure. The gap has been met by grants in aid from the British government. In 1965–66 these amounted to R3 mn. for Swaziland, or 54 per cent of ordinary recurrent expenditure. For Botswana the corresponding figures were R5·3 mn. or 58 per cent. For Lesotho £5·2 mn. or 72 per cent. This financial dependence of the three countries is bound up with the fact that their budgetary and fiscal policies are profoundly affected by their financial and economic relationships with South Africa. These relationships are described in the following section.

The Arrangements for Economic Integration between
South Africa and BLS

The economic integration of BLS with South Africa operates at several levels. In the first place there exists a form of common market and customs union between them and South Africa.[19] In the second place there is a *de facto* currency union, and banking and other financial links are close. Thirdly, a substantial part of the labour force of the three countries is employed in the Republic, mainly in the mines. Finally there are close links in transport and other services.

The origins of economic integration between South Africa and BLS go back to 1889 when the Cape Colony and the Orange Free State Republic, after declaring that it was desirable that there should be a general customs union between all of the colonies and states of Southern Africa, initiated a preparatory union which provided for free trade between the colonies and states, a common external tariff, and an equitable distribution among the participating countries of the duties collected. Political union in 1910 between the Cape Colony, the Orange Free State, the Transvaal and Natal made the terms of the economic union redundant for the members of the political union. The existing customs union was thereupon terminated and replaced by new agreements which took account of the position of those territories which were not parties to the political union. The Agreement signed at Potchefstroom on June 29 1910 between the newly established Union of South Africa on the one hand, and Basutoland, Swaziland and Bechuanaland on the other, was one of these.[20] At the time of writing it continues to regulate the economic relations of the participating countries.

The essential features of the 1910 Agreement were expressed in brief and general terms. It provides for:

The maintenance of the Customs Union tariff until altered by legislation enacted by South Africa or by the territories.

Free interchange of South African products and manufactures between the Union and the territories.

Payment by South Africa to the territories of an equitable share of the duties on goods passing through the Union to the territories and *vice versa.*

Conformity by the territories to the relevant tariff laws of South Africa.

Wines, beer and spirits of local manufacture were excluded from the free interchange clause. These goods are imported in bond from South Africa and the territories themselves impose and collect excise duties. Under the Agreement these must be at the rates in force in South Africa.

The Agreement specified the basis of the share of duties to be received by each territory. In effect, revenue from import duties and from excise duties on cigarettes, motor fuel and motor vehicles in the customs area (but excluding beers, wines and spirits of South African manufacture), is shared between South Africa and BLS on an assumed derivation basis, the figures used for the division being the relative customs revenues of each area in the three base years preceding 1910. The following

Distribution of Customs and Excise Revenue under the 1910 Potchefstroom Agreement

Country	% Share
South Africa	98·68903
Lesotho (Basutoland)	0·88575
Botswana (Bechuanaland)	0·27622
Swaziland	0·14900
	100·00000

shares, derived on this basis, have remained in operation as far as South Africa is concerned until today.[21]

Partly as a result of the customs union and partly for geographical reasons the three countries are closely linked in trade with the Republic. Although accurate data on the origin of imports and destination of exports is not available for the territories, necessarily a high proportion of their imports and exports passes through South Africa. Moreover, in all three countries South African products dominate the internal markets although in the case of Botswana a substantial part of its imports (estimated at a quarter in 1966) normally comes from Rhodesia. Botswana's trade with Rhodesia has been facilitated by a Customs Agreement which was concluded between the former High Commission territories and the Federation of Rhodesia and Nyasaland in 1956.[22] This agreement continues to be operated between BLS and Rhodesia, but it is of practical importance only for trade between Botswana and Rhodesia. Both Botswana and Lesotho market a high proportion of their exports, mainly of agricultural products, in the Republic. The bulk of Swaziland's exports on the other hand are destined for the outside world (80 per cent in 1966) though many of these are exported through the Republic.

Currency, Banking and Financial Institutions

Currency, banking and financial institutions are a second field in which there is economic integration with South Africa. A currency union exists and South African notes and coins are legal tender in each territory. Unlike the customs union the currency union does not rest on any agreement between the territories and the Republic.

The territories, like South Africa, are part of the sterling area and there are in consequence no restrictions on the transfer of funds from the UK to the territories. The territories allow their own residents to make payments freely to other sterling area countries. Their practice in this respect is more liberal than that of South Africa. Residents of BLS are treated by South Africa as residents of the rand currency area for current account transactions and there are in consequence no restrictions on payments of this kind between South Africa and BLS. For transactions involving the sale of South African securities owned by residents of BLS, South Africa treats such residents as non resident (to prevent evasion through BLS of South African controls on the export of capital) but it is prepared administratively to give special treatment. It is believed that South Africa administratively controls the export of capital in excess of amounts of R100,000 for investment in BLS. With these exceptions, capital can move freely between South Africa and BLS.

Because of the free flow of funds between BLS and South Africa, their interest rates and credit conditions generally are closely linked. When credit is generally tight in the Republic, commercial bankers tend to restrict their lending in BLS whatever the state of those economies and *vice versa*. The two commercial banks which operate in BLS are both branches of banks incorporated in the United Kingdom and are closely linked with banks in South Africa. Banks operating in BLS customarily employ in South Africa the reserve of liquid assets which is maintained against their deposit liabilities. At present there are no opportunities for employing such assets in BLS. South African building societies and insurance companies collect funds in BLS but invest no funds there.

The remaining field in which BLS are closely linked with the South African economy is communications and services. In Swaziland road haulage is undertaken mainly by South African Railways. The railway in Botswana is operated by Rhodesia Railways which is linked closely with South African Railways. In the past the Post Office Savings Banks and the Post Offices were operated by the South African authorities on behalf of the three countries but each now has its own system. All external mail, telephone, telegraph and international air services operate through South Africa. South African Airways provide part of the scheduled services linking the three countries with Johannesburg, though small internal air services also participate in this traffic.

The Costs and Benefits of Existing Integration Arrangements

Customs unions and common markets such as exist between South Africa and BLS may have a number of advantages. In the first place, costs of administration may be reduced and smuggling avoided. In this particular case the territories are spared the burden of administering their own customs and excise system which, other things equal, is an undoubted advantage, assuming that the attribution of customs revenue is approximately correct. It would be surprising if the proportions received by the three territories, based as they are on imports in 1906–8, accurately reflected current trade relations at the end of a period in which, as a result of protection and tariff changes, the character of import demand in South Africa has greatly changed and in which the rates of growth of the three territories appear to have varied considerably, particularly in recent years.

In 1963, in anticipation of proposals from the Republic of South Africa for the revision of the customs agreement on the independence of the territories, an enquiry was made into this matter. The British Government appointed a British statistician, Mr F. M. M. Lewes, to examine the workings of the South African Customs Union as it affected the three territories and in particular to examine the share of the customs revenue which they received. In his unpublished report he concluded, on the basis of admittedly meagre statistics, and estimates of trade movements of the main dutiable articles, that the overall share received by the territories continued to be about right, but that in the light of current conditions a reapportionment among the three countries would be appropriate.[23] The suggested reapportionment is indicated below and compared with the original allocation. It involved practically halving the share of the poorest of the three, Basutoland, and a more than threefold increase in the share of Swaziland, the richest of the three.

Customs and Excise Revenue

	Share under the 1910 Agreement	Proposed Reallocation
LESOTHO	0·88575	0·47093
BOTSWANA	0·27622	0·30971
SWAZILAND	0·14900	0·53033
TOTAL	1·31097	1·31097

The shares proposed by Lewes were imposed administratively by the British Government for 1965–66 onwards and the grants in aid to the recurrent budgets of the territories were adjusted in compensation. The present position therefore is that South Africa pays out to each country on the basis of the original percentages and transfers take place from Lesotho to the other two countries.

An important disadvantage of the South African customs union is that, in practice, BLS have no control over what is, in other less developed countries, a major source of government revenue and a powerful instrument of economic policy, namely customs and excise policy and rates. It is true that the agreement provides that the common external tariff may be altered both by South Africa and the territories, but in practice, alterations are initiated only by the South African government. During the colonial period informal consultations did take place between South Africa and Great Britain acting on behalf of the territories, but the effective voice was naturally that of South Africa.

Thus there is no direct relationship between economic growth in BLS and the growth of their customs revenues, for the latter depend on the state of trade in the Republic and the level of its duties. A recession in the Republic leading to a drop in imports and a fall in customs revenue would automatically reduce the revenue of BLS proportionately. A large proportion of tax revenue in BLS is effectively out of the control of the governments of BLS and cannot be influenced by any measures taken by those governments. As can be seen from Table 6:1 the percentage of ordinary revenue falling into this category in 1965–66 amounted to 21 per cent, 35 per cent and 32 per cent for Botswana, Lesotho and Swaziland respectively. This situation evidently greatly complicates the fiscal problems which accompany economic growth. Moreover, to the extent that the South African government limits imports by protective tariffs or quantitative restrictions for the purpose of building up its domestic industries, revenues in BLS will be lower than they otherwise would have been. It is these considerations, together with the heavy dependence of BLS on South African products which results from the customs union, which help to explain the relatively low contribution of customs and excise revenues to total revenues. In other African countries at comparable stages of development the proportion contributed by this group of taxes is commonly between 50 and 60 per cent.

Partly for this reason, even if the three countries receive their properly attributable share of South Africa's customs and excise revenues, it does not follow that the customs agreement necessarily results in a fair fiscal deal for them, still less that the arrangements are necessarily favourable to their economic development. Broader considerations are obviously relevant. They are particularly so in this case because of the great disparity in size of the members of the union and the high degree of trade dependence of the smaller members which is unparalleled in any other customs union in Africa. Market integration creates a wider market for manufactures and products in the customs area, which may benefit all partners. But the smaller non-industrialized members may not benefit in the absence of a redistribution of income towards them by fiscal means, some agreed means of directing industrial development towards them, or favourable markets for their primary products. The non-industrialized partners have to meet the higher costs of goods from their partners which accompany trade diversion and they are unlikely to be able to establish industries to enjoy access to the larger market without protection. Although in principle they may benefit from the spread effect or from preferential access to the markets of their partners for their primary products, the balance of advantage need not be favourable. The Lewes inquiry altogether neglected these considerations.

So far as concerns the market for local manufactures, there is little reason to believe that the operation of the common market has been other than detrimental to the three territories. Since 1925, South African policy has been designed to encourage her secondary industries behind a protective tariff.[24] Quantitative import restrictions have been used for the same purpose. The protection afforded to South African products in the markets of BLS has enabled them to assume a dominant position in those markets. Although in some cases the South African products are certainly competitive with imports, often the imported product would be cheaper. The excess cost falls on the three countries. As noted already, the protective nature of the South

African tariff and import restrictions have also operated to reduce the amount of revenue which would be available for distribution, although the Republic's need to impose duties for fiscal as well as protective purposes has ensured that there has been no absolute decrease in the yield of the South African tariff.

Although in principle the customs agreement offers BLS access to the large South African market for its manufactures, not surprisingly few manufactures have been established. Except in rare cases the establishment of manufacturing industry is unlikely in the face of the advantages of the economies of large scale production, modern technology and a developed infrastructure which are enjoyed by South Africa. Admittedly some such industries have been set up, but this has occurred mainly in Swaziland where development has been able to take place in fields which are not competitive with South Africa's protected industries. The absence of job reservation in BLS might appear to offer some offsetting advantages for the establishment there of labour-intensive industries serving the South African market, but the ambiguity of the present agreement, and the administrative discretion which can be exercised by the South African authorities in relation to capital export and other matters limit the possibilities.

In this connection it must be noted that although the present agreement provides for 'free interchange' of product and manufactures between South Africa and the territories, the term 'free interchange' is ambiguous. It has been interpreted to mean 'free of duty', leaving it open to South Africa to impose quantitative restrictions. This she has done in the case of primary products exported from the territories and in the case of manufactures the same interpretation could be employed. Admittedly, the same alternative is presumably open in principle to the territories but this is of limited interest since few industries are likely to be established unless they have access to the South African market.

Nevertheless, although in some cases South Africa has imposed quantitative import restrictions on primary products coming from the territories, within the limits of the quotas the products of BLS are treated on the same footing as products from

South Africa and enjoy access to its highly protected internal market. Wool, meat, citrus, and cotton are marketed through South African marketing boards[25] and so, until 1964, was Swaziland's sugar. In the absence of empirical data it is impossible to determine the balance of advantage to the territories in respect of their access to the South African domestic and overseas market for primary products, but they may have been quite favourable in terms of savings in marketing costs, and prices obtained. But the quotas imposed (as with livestock) limit the gains. Moreover, for some products not marketed through boards, such as timber, there appears to have been a tendency for the South African government to discourage the purchase of the products of BLS by administrative means when the interest of South African producers has demanded this.

Apart from the customs union itself, it is necessary to consider the costs and benefits which arise as a result of the monetary integration of BLS with South Africa. As already noted, the three countries use the notes and coins of the Republic and are served by commercial banks which are very closely linked to those operating in the Republic. These arrangements have both advantages and disadvantages as compared with the alternative of an independent monetary system. A most important advantage is that trade is facilitated by the absence of any exchange risk, restrictions, inconvenience or cost in transactions with the principal trading partners of BLS. In addition, membership of the currency union should facilitate the flow of private capital to BLS to the extent that the general credit conditions of the Republic permit this, and so long as there are no administrative interferences. Moreover, no foreign exchange problem arises in servicing external debts, which is a consideration which should facilitate the raising of loans for development purposes from places other than the Republic. Provided that a project is viable in the sense that it can produce an operating surplus sufficient to service the loans raised to finance it, there is no difficulty in securing foreign exchange as sometimes occurs in countries having their own currencies. These are important advantages.

Among the disadvantages of monetary integration are that outflow of savings and capital cannot be prevented and that money and credit conditions are determined by conditions in the Republic. In addition, the three countries derive no income from the capital which they, as holders of South African currency, are in effect making available to the South African authorities. Nor do these countries derive any capital finance from the currency circulation. Normally a currency union which is based on mutual agreement includes provision for distributing among its members the interest income made possible by the investment of the currency backing. Where a 100 per cent reserve is not maintained, some provision of fiduciary finance is also possible. In the Equatorial and West African monetary unions, profits from the currency are distributed on the basis of the known currency distribution. In the case of East Africa, the profits of the former East African Currency Board were distributed on the basis of a formula which attempted to approximate to the unknown currency distribution amongst its members. The amounts which might justly be claimed by BLS on this account cannot be ascertained precisely in the absence of firm knowledge of the currency circulation. Nevertheless, with the aid of national income estimates and using relationships between income and currency circulation which are found in countries at a comparable level of economic development elsewhere in Africa, a plausible estimate could certainly be made.[26]

The third important economic link between BLS and South Africa concerns the labour market. Here the balance of advantage of the present arrangements appears less open to doubt. The benefits are certainly important and on balance the arrangements are certainly advantageous to BLS. A substantial contribution to the national income of Lesotho and to a lesser extent in Botswana and Swaziland, is derived from remittances by or on behalf of migrant workers employed in South African mines and agriculture. It has been estimated that in 1964–65 R7,319,000 was sent or taken back to Lesotho on behalf of migrant labourers. In Botswana for the same year the corresponding total was R2,279,000. For Swaziland the estimate was R766,000.[27] To some degree such incomes are likely to be earned at the cost of forgone agricultural production in the territories since the migrants tend to represent mainly the more enterprising and able-bodied members of the male labour force,

263

but even so there is certainly a substantial net gain to the three countries.

A Revision of Economic Relationships in Southern Africa

It is only in the last few years with the approach of independence that there has been any attempt on the part of the Colonial Office or within the local administrations to evaluate the merits of the economic links with the Republic, the possibility of negotiating improved arrangements and alternative courses of action. In relation to the customs union itself, a stimulus was provided by the prospect of having to form a view on a new customs agreement for which the Republic produced a draft in anticipation of the forthcoming independence of the territories. The deteriorating budgetary position of the three countries also prompted economic surveys[28]. The reports which resulted gave some attention to fiscal policy but did not consider the possibility of improvement in the fiscal deal except for some changes which would make it possible for BLS to raise more revenue, primarily from their own consumers.

If the present economic and fiscal arrangements are deemed to be unsatisfactory and a satisfactory improvement is impossible to negotiate, it would in principle be possible for one or more of the three countries to opt out of them. They could establish their own customs system and possibly a tariff more suited to their own needs, and proceed to protect their infant industries. They could also establish their own monetary systems. The costs of administration would have to be borne by the country introducing them.

At the time of writing there has been no detailed evaluation of the practicability and the costs of operating separate customs services although rough estimates have been made of the likely capital and recurrent costs involved in the operation of border posts which would have to be counted against any additional revenue made possible by a separate system. It would also be necessary to negotiate a transit agreement for goods in bond with South Africa and the cost of its operation would have to be borne by any territory seeking to establish its own service.

Clearly the benefits from operating separate customs services would depend on the character of the tariff structure established and the effectiveness with which duty on the major dutiable imports could be collected. In discussing the possibility of separate customs services, the report on *The Development of the Swaziland Economy* suggests that the revenues derived by Swaziland from the existing customs agreement 'are not less than she would raise if she had her own customs administration levying the same rates of duty'.[29] A similar statement is found in the Botswana Report.[30] These statements presumably reflect the findings of the Lewes Report and imply that South African products would not be taxed. But there would clearly be little purpose in having a separate customs administration if South African products were not taxed. A more relevant question would be how much revenue could be raised if a non-discriminatory tariff were imposed on all imports.

Obviously the revenue raised from a separate customs administration is not the only consideration to take into account in deciding the policy options. Except to the extent that the prices of South African goods fell as a result of the tariff or it resulted in a diversion of demand to cheaper sources outside South Africa, the increased revenue would not represent a real income gain but merely a transfer from consumers in the three countries to the exchequers. On the other hand, at the present time the prosperity of the three countries depends, though in varying degrees, on free access to the domestic or overseas markets of South Africa. Any income gain from a change in the fiscal system would have to be weighed against the corresponding income losses which might ensue if access to markets in the Republic were to be limited as a result of a change in the customs union. Important factors in this respect are the proportion of their exports which are marketed in the Republic; the prospects for the development of additional production which could only be marketed profitably in the Republic; and alternative markets outside the Republic. The lack of empirical data on these questions and uncertainty about the response of the Republic make it difficult to form a judgement on this issue.

Currency and banking is a second area where in principle alternative arrangements could be considered. The advantages and disadvantages of the present arrangements have been noted above. On the eve of independence in 1966 both Lesotho and Botswana sought expert advice about their future currency arrangements.[31] The issue of a separate currency for any of the three countries would present no great difficulty. The main advantage would be that if it were backed by the Rand or a major international currency, the income from the assets backing the currency could be expected to yield a small profit after deducting operating costs. New currencies could be introduced without reference to South Africa if the backing were Rand deposits or securities. On the other hand if sterling or some other international currency were employed, it would be necessary because of the operation of exchange control in South Africa, to enter into negotiations with that country in order to arrange for withdrawn South African currency to be converted into the chosen international currency. In the circumstances, use of the South African Rand would be a natural choice. It would be the best way of avoiding the possibility that South Africa would introduce exchange control on transaction with BLS. Moreover, if agreement were reached on the interchangeability of notes within BLS and South Africa little, if any, inconvenience for trade would result. Bearing in mind the fact that the establishment of a separate currency would create very little scope for the pursuit of independent monetary or credit policies the conclusion of the experts called in to advise Lesotho on this question was that 'it seems highly questionable whether the advantage Basutoland could derive from a separate currency at the present time would compensate for the disadvantages',[32] but they avoided trying to quantify the gains.

The common market and the currency are the principal fields in which there is likely to be on balance some net disadvantage to BLS from the existing arrangements. In the labour market there is on the other hand a large positive gain. Evidently the possible repercussions of a change in present customs and currency arrangements on the earnings of migrant labour in South Africa would have to be weighed up. Nevertheless there is no reason to suppose that a revision of the customs and currency arrangements would in themselves entail major changes in the present or prospective position of these countries' nationals working in South Africa. The long run policy of the South

266

African government with respect to foreign 'bantu' labour is quite clear. During the Verwoerd government a committee was appointed to examine the position of 'foreign' Africans in the Republic.[33] Among the Committee's main recommendations was that the dependants of foreign workers should be immediately repatriated and that the long term aim should be the repatriation of the workers themselves. It was recognized that this would be impracticable immediately and an exception was therefore proposed for workers in mines and on farms by means of an annual quota for admission, in which BLS would receive preference. The principal recommendations of the committee were later accepted by the South African government and indicate the long term framework in which, in the absence of change in South Africa, the labour policies of BLS must be formulated.

In the immediate future however, BLS need probably have little fear of a curtailment of employment opportunities in South Africa, for although these benefit BLS, the addition to the labour supply also benefits South African industry and agriculture substantially and these benefits are not likely to be forgone. It seems to be widely agreed in South Africa that it would be impossible at present for her to replace much of this labour from domestic sources. The effect of any substantial reduction in the supply of foreign labour on the wage level in mines and farms in South Africa could therefore be considerable and this repercussion is unlikely to be overlooked by a government whose internal price level is somewhat inflexible, geared as it is to the fixed price of gold. When it becomes in the domestic interests of South Africa to repatriate workers from BLS or to reduce the inflow this will no doubt be done. A failure to recast the customs arrangements may well impede the development which will ultimately be necessary not only to absorb displaced migratory workers from BLS but also to provide a living for their steadily growing labour forces.

In the light of all the uncertainties concerning the benefits from opting out of the existing arrangements it is not surprising that thinking in BLS has centred not on removing but on improving the existing arrangements on the most favourable terms possible. Evidently access to the large markets of South Africa could be a major asset to the three countries although the need for South Africa to look after its Bantustans[34] first may sharply limit what can be hoped for in this direction. Nevertheless there is no indication that South Africa may not be persuaded to support a substantially more favourable arrangement than the present one.

The foregoing review of the working of the existing arrangements has indicated some of their more important disadvantages from the standpoint of BLS which may be summarized as follows. It is not in practice possible for BLS to protect their infant industries. The present agreement provides only for free interchange of products and manufactures and has been interpreted to permit the imposition of quantitative restrictions which have been imposed on primary products. There is no consultation on fiscal or monetary policies. The attribution of revenue though probably correct overall (and, after the administrative reallocation, for each territory individually) does not provide a fair fiscal deal. And no revenue is derived from the use of the Rand as currency. Many matters are undoubtedly settled to the disadvantage of the territories in the field of trade as a result of the exercise of administrative discretion by the Republic. Import prohibitions in particular may operate to the disadvantage of the three countries. These disadvantages indicate the general lines of the new deal which the territories should seek. Four important changes seem to be desirable in any new agreement.

In the first place, some formal provision should be sought for the establishment of a consultative body to be concerned with the operation of the customs union. Evidently the great disparity between the economic power of the Republic and the three territories makes it unreasonable and unrealistic to suppose that the territories can have any important voice in the determination of fiscal and tariff policies, and the machinery employed in the East African Common Market and elsewhere is hardly likely to be acceptable to South Africa. Nevertheless, a situation in which the territories have no right even to be informed of prospective changes in tariff policy by South Africa or to represent their own needs is clearly unsatisfactory and hardly consistent with the new status of these countries. Consultation may improve the chances of avoiding at least some changes which are clearly detrimental to the interest of BLS and could facilitate consideration of their needs for certain protective tariffs which may be of decisive importance for their own development. For instance, a protective tariff on soda ash could be of considerable benefit to Botswana by reserving the South African market and the cost to the Republic might be relatively small.

In the second place, it is highly desirable that a revision of the agreement should include a provision permitting the three countries temporarily to impose either quantitative import restrictions or a tariff upon South African products which compete with prospective infant industries. The chances of BLS being able successfully to establish manufacturing industries in the absence of such provisions are small. It is understood that the draft agreement first proposed by South Africa contained no provision for protecting infant industries in BLS but would, on the contrary, have permitted protection for South Africa's already established industries against competition from BLS.

In the third place an upward revision of the fiscal payment to the territories should be sought. The grounds for this are that the customs agreement results in the replacement of lower cost foreign products by higher cost products from the Republic. Although the case for some additional compensation seems strong, the amount which might justly be claimed is difficult to determine. Moreover, as we have seen, each of the countries probably enjoys some offsetting gains from its access to the markets of the Republic for their primary products. A further complication is that South Africa's gains from the present arrangements need to be equal to the losses which may be incurred by the territories.

One commonly advocated method of dealing with the cost of trade diversion to the smaller members of a common market involves providing fiscal compensation based on the revenue losses assumed to be incurred by the country importing the duty-free products of its partners. Such a basis was employed in the Trade Agreement of 1964 between the Government of Nyasaland and the Government of Southern Rhodesia.[35] Under this agreement the Government of Southern Rhodesia agreed to pay to the Government of Nyasaland 10 per cent of its trade surplus with that country after excluding certain products such as those subject to excise in Nyasaland (beer, cigarettes, etc.)

and unmanufactured local products. The rate of 10 per cent appears to have been fixed as a rough approximation to the average rate of duty forgone by Nyasaland as a result of the maintenance of the customs union between the two countries after the break-up of the Federation of Rhodesia and Nyasaland.

Of course, customs revenue forgone is not necessarily a relevant basis for fiscal compensation if the objective is to provide compensation for real income losses. There is no reason to suppose that forgone revenue measures such losses as may be involved in buying South African products rather than those of the rest of the world, in part because of the operation of import restrictions, in part because some South African products are 'competitive' with imports. Moreover, to the extent that domestic production of certain commodities would be feasible with protection, the loss involved in buying South African products, rather than those of the rest of the world, becomes irrelevant. In addition to the points mentioned on pages 260 and 265, the analysis of Chapter 4, Section 7, is pertinent.

An alternative base for providing compensation suggested by Professor D. V. Cowen[36] would involve allocating the shares of South African import revenues to the territories on the basis of the ratios of the total net manufactured imports of the four territories, irrespective of whether these imports come from abroad or are manufactured in South Africa.

Yet another suggestion entails retaining the shares indicated by the attribution procedures currently employed, and giving the territories in addition a share of the income tax on the profits of the manufacturing and commercial sector in South Africa. There is a precedent for this in the arrangements adopted in East Africa for the Distributable Pool which was set up on the recommendations of the Raisman Commission.

Data are not available to show the effects of these alternative bases except for that based on the ratios of net manufactured imports, the effects of which are indicated in Table 6: 2. As can be seen this basis would result in nearly doubling the shares received by the territories as a whole.

Fourthly, in considering the terms of any revised agreement it would be desirable to try to provide increased scope for the territories to increase their direct tax revenues by autonomous

270

action. For instance, it would be desirable to authorise the territories specifically to impose export taxes on their primary products. Almost certainly the incidence of these taxes is on the producers and the tax represents a very convenient way of taxing cattle producers. Two out of the three territories already impose such taxes, although it is doubtful if their actions are consistent with the Customs Agreement. Apart from this it would be desirable to give the territories flexibility to determine their own excise duties on beer, wines and spirits, instead of requiring them to conform to the rates in force in the Republic which are on the whole low. There may even be grounds for going beyond this and permitting the territories to impose levies taking the form of a turnover tax on a limited range of other commodities[37]. If such levies were imposed on a non-discriminatory basis they would not upset South Africa's privileged position in the markets of the three and, since the incidence would be largely on the consumers, the levies could not be represented as seriously harmful to South Africa's interests or inconsistent with the spirit of the integration arrangements. Evidently the scope for major differences *vis à vis* South Africa would be limited by the need to prevent smuggling.

Finally, it would be desirable to seek either as part of a broader economic agreement, or separately, provisions which would meet some of the problems on the monetary side. In the first instance some machinery needs to be established for consultation between the monetary authorities in South Africa and the Finance Ministries in the three countries. Possibly

TABLE 6: 2

The South African Customs Union

		BOTSWANA	LESOTHO	SWAZILAND	TOTAL
(i)	Present Effective Proportion of S. African Customs and Excise Revenue	0·30971	0·47093	0·53033	1·31097
(ii)	Amount 1965-6: R.000	1,149	1,222	1,393	3,764
(iii)	Share based on Ratios of Net Manufactured Imports (excl. wines, beers, spirits)	0·84	0·76	1·46	3·06
(iv)	Amount based on (iii): R.000	1,918	1,735	3,333	6,986

representation on the board of the Reserve Bank of South Africa might be sought. One of the main purposes of this consultation would be to acquaint each party with the thinking of the others on monetary and credit policies, and in particular to try to ensure that credit in BLS was adjusted as far as possible in conformity with the needs of the local situation rather than that in the Republic. Scope could easily be provided for the exercise of a differential credit policy. In addition, measures might be discussed which would lead to a greater proportion of the savings of BLS being invested locally rather than in South Africa. Finally efforts should be made to obtain an annual payment from South Africa in consideration of the circulation of South African currency in the territories. The annual income which might be obtained from separate currencies backed by the Rand might be of the order of R160,000 for Lesotho, R80,000 in the case of Botswana and R80–160,000 in the case of Swaziland. [38]

A successful outcome to the negotiations might be encouraged if the British government were to give assurances that its budgetary assistance to the territories would not be cut immediately in proportion to any increased payments from South Africa. If this is not done, any increases will not immediately benefit the territories and could be represented as transferring funds from South Africa to Britain, which is hardly a helpful background for negotiation.

Evidently the scope for improving the terms of economic association between South Africa and BLS is greatly influenced by the interplay of political factors and the greatly disparate bargaining power of the interested parties. The absence of empirical data on a range of important matters also makes it difficult to base the negotiations on hard facts and increases the uncertainty of the outcome. It is unlikely that any future arrangements will be satisfactory in all respects to every party and it will be necessary for each to make a judgement on their overall effects from their own standpoint. A generous response on the part of South Africa to the changes which considerations of economics and equity seem to justify need cost relatively little but could make the maintenance of economic association of decisive advantage to the territories. In the absence of such a response, some at least of the territories seem likely to have alternatives open to them which on further analysis may turn out to be more attractive than the maintenance of the *status quo*.

4 THE ECONOMIC INTEGRATION OF GAMBIA WITH SENEGAL*

Gambia is an extreme example of a country which owes its existence entirely to colonial policy. It forms an irrational intrusion into the much larger country of Senegal, stretching from the coast inland along both sides of the Gambia river, and making up a strip about 200 miles long and only twelve or thirteen miles wide. Although roughly following the course of the river, Gambia does not extend to the natural limits of the basin on either side, nor does it reach the source which lies in Guinea. The frontiers of Gambia cut through both natural features and human settlement patterns. Wholly surrounded by Senegal except on its seaward margin, Gambia largely isolates the southern region of Casamance from the rest of Senegal. Ethnically the people of Gambia and Senegal are the same. For a brief period, in fact, from 1765 to 1783, much of what are now Gambia and Senegal formed the single British colony of Senegambia.

From that time until very recently the two countries have been subjected to the separate influences of the French and British colonial systems. This has created differences in administrative, cultural and economic patterns which are important obstacles to a closer association of the two countries.

The anomalous position of Gambia, both in itself, and in relation to Senegal, received a good deal of attention in the nineteenth century, and there were several abortive British and French proposals which envisaged the exchange of some other French colony for Gambia, so as to permit its incorporation into Senegal. Economic factors had something to do with these proposals, although on both sides, wider issues of areas of colonial influence and general colonial policy played the major role.[39]

Following Senegal's independence in 1960, and the prospect

* An earlier version of this section was published in the Journal of Modern African Studies, 1965. I am indebted to the editors for permission to make use of that article.

of early independence for Gambia there was a revival of interest in the possibility of a closer relationship between the two countries. This new interest seems to have been the product of three main considerations. The first is doubt as to whether Gambia by itself is economically viable. At present it has a budget deficit and is dependent upon a substantial grant in aid from the UK. The second is the view that the present economic frontiers are disadvantageous to both countries. For Senegal it means a partial isolation of its southern province of Casamance and an inability to exploit the Gambia river fully. For Gambia it is contended that it cannot exploit its main natural asset, which is the river basin, and that Bathurst, the capital, is deprived of the opportunity to serve as the port for a large economic area to which it is particularly suited. In short, it was argued that it is impossible to make adequate use of the economic resources of Gambia and Senegal without close co-operation which is hindered by political and economic frontiers. A third reason for seeking association is political. There is some fear in Senegal that Gambia could become a base for the operations of banned political parties or for subversion from outside. For its part, Gambia, which lacks an army, recognises its extreme vulnerability from a military point of view.

It was against this background that the possibilities of association began to be explored towards the end of 1961 when the two countries established an Inter-Ministerial Committee to discuss matters of joint interest. Among other things this Committee considered such matters as posts, telecommunications and feeder roads. By all accounts it was not particularly successful. Subsequently the two governments discussed the possibility that when Gambia achieved independence some form of association between the two countries might be entered into. In these talks the Gambian government made it clear that it would only consider association on terms which would guarantee it a high degree of autonomy in internal affairs—which amounted in effect to a willingness to consider only a weak confederal relationship. These talks led to the commissioning from the UN of a report to consider the various possibilities of association. To help matters along the UK government indicated that no discussions on Gambian independence would be entertained until the governments of Senegal and Gambia had considered the UN recommendations.

The Economies of Senegal and Gambia

A brief review of some salient economic features of the two countries will be helpful to an understanding of the economic issues involved in their possible association. Table 6:3 summarises some of the relevant data.

TABLE 6: 3

Economic Features of Gambia and Senegal[1]

	GAMBIA	SENEGAL
Area: sq. miles	3,978	77,060
Population	300,000	3,000,000
Rate of population increase	2·3 per cent p.a.	
Density of population per sq. mile	75	39
Gross Domestic Product	£9,000,000[2]	£167,000,000[3]
G.D.P. per head	£30	£56[3]
Total exports	£3,232,000	£43,984,000[3]
Groundnut produce as percentage of total exports[4]	95	81[3]
Exports per head	£10	£15
Balance of trade	−£1,158,000	−£10,760,000[3]

NOTES:
1 All figures refer to 1962.
2 This figure is based on calculations of the Economic Adviser, Gambia, since no detailed estimates are available.
3 CFA francs have been converted to sterling at the official rate of exchange of 696 to £1. The CFA franc, however, is overvalued, and this should be borne in mind in comparing these figures.
4 In Gambia, only groundnuts are exported; but in Senegal, shelled groundnuts and oil are of roughly equal importance.

In size, the two countries are very different. Senegal is twenty times as large as Gambia and its population is ten times as large. In terms of basic economic structure on the other hand, the two countries are very similar. Both are mono-crop agricultural economies which rely mainly, in the commercialized sector, upon groundnut products. Both have an external trade deficit. In both countries the greater part of the population is engaged in agriculture. In Senegal there is a small nucleus of industrial development which dates from the days when Dakar was the capital of the federation of l'Afrique Occidentale Française (AOF) and its products circulated freely throughout the area. Although the federation has disappeared, and its economic successor, the West African customs union, is ineffective, Senegal still exports a number of manufactured products—mainly food, drink and tobacco and consumer goods of various kinds—to her former fellow members, and continues to enjoy a substantial transit trade.

Although the two countries are so alike in basic structure and resources, their economies are organized on very different bases. The differences manifest themselves in the first place in foreign trade policy. Whereas in Senegal imports are subject to administrative restriction and tariffs are high and discriminatory, Gambia's import policy is liberal and non-discriminatory, and import charges are relatively low.

Thus in Senegal a complex system of import duties produced in 1962 an average rate of duty of well over 30 per cent despite the very substantial margins of preference enjoyed by a high proportion of imports. Apart from this, imports are generally controlled by a system of licensing. Goods from France may be imported without either restriction or licence, and together with goods from the other EEC countries, they enjoy a substantial preference margin. Also Senegal binds itself to buy from France a certain minimum total value of goods and minimum proportions of important types of imports. In most cases these proportions exceed 50 per cent. Partly as a result of these arrangements, France is Senegal's chief supplier, providing in 1962 about two-thirds of her imports. In due course, goods from all EEC countries will, as a result of Senegal's association with the Community, enter on level terms administratively as well as tariff-wise and this should eventually bring about some increased diversity in import sources.

In return, France provides preferential markets for the products of Senegal. A market for a large part of Senegal's groundnut output is guaranteed and until recently under the *surprix* system the price paid was about 25 per cent higher than world market prices, representing an annual subsidy of 8,000 mn.

francs CFA. Under the EEC association agreement this subsidy will disappear. In 1962 85 per cent of Senegal's exports went to France.

By contrast with Senegal, Gambia has a very liberal import policy. Goods may be imported from most countries under freely granted open general licences. Compared with Senegal, import charges are relatively low. During 1960–62 the average rate of duty on all imports, including a 4 per cent purchase tax, was about 20 per cent. The tariff is non-discriminatory except for a Commonwealth Preference margin which on most goods is very small. In 1962 about 40 per cent of Gambia's imports came from the United Kingdom.

A second important difference between the two countries, partly a consequence of the divergences just mentioned, is that there is a substantial difference between the structure and level of their internal costs and retail prices. Many imports are relatively expensive in Senegal because import quotas and payments restrictions divert demand from the cheapest source. Gambia's liberal import policy on the other hand enables it to buy its supplies from the cheapest source. Once landed, relatively high import tariffs in Senegal add to the difference. In addition, the *surprix* system has given rise in Senegal to some inflation of domestic costs of production. At the present exchange rate which overvalues the CFA franc, food prices have been estimated to be 100 per cent higher in Dakar than Bathurst, wages up to 80 per cent higher and in general the cost of living to be 50 per cent higher.

Given these differences and the difficulty of policing the frontier it is not surprising that there is a good deal of smuggling from Gambia to Senegal. In March 1960 an unofficial French estimate put the value of smuggled goods c.i.f. Bathurst at over £500,000 or £700,000 including customs duties and profit margin. A similar Gambian estimate broadly confirms this. For some categories of goods, for which price differences are very large, it is estimated that a very high proportion is transferred – up to 80 per cent for tobacco, 50 per cent for textiles and 60–70 per cent for shoes. On this basis, goods imported into Gambia and subsequently smuggled into Senegal represent about 10 per cent of Gambian imports and produce about 15 per cent of Gambia's total revenue from import duty. Smuggling is thus quite important to the Gambian economy. By contrast, legitimate trade between the two countries is negligible. On the other hand although Senegal complains much about smuggling, it is really of relatively small importance to her. Smuggled imports amount to less than 1 per cent of total imports, and the value of customs duties lost by Senegal from smuggling has been estimated at 250 mn. francs, which is, currently, about 1 per cent of total budget revenue or 2 per cent of revenue from import duties.[40]

The United Nations Report

Early in 1964 the commissioned UN report was submitted, dealing with political, economic, and fiscal aspects of association.[41] It was followed by a supplementary report by FAO on the integrated agricultural development of the Gambia River Basin.[42]

After reviewing three possible forms of political association between Senegal and Gambia ranging from the full incorporation of the latter as a Senegalese province, through federation to a loose entente, based on a treaty, the UN report concluded that it might not be practicable in the existing climate of opinion to go beyond the third alternative. This judgement, which events have so far borne out, is the background to the following discussion of economic association.

With economic as with political association it is also possible to conceive a number of alternatives ranging from complete integration – probably feasible only with political unity – to various degrees of association which might be compatible with an absence of any formal political links.

Total economic incorporation need be considered only briefly since it would involve political integration which is probably unfeasible on a voluntary basis in the foreseeable future, and in any case is outside the scope of this book. As compared with economic association between independent states it was thought to have two main advantages. First, with French concurrence, Gambia could benefit from French guarantees and preferential markets for groundnuts. But

278

preferences are of diminishing importance as France reduces its support prices to the free market level as required by EEC. Second, Gambia could as part of Senegal presumably expect to enjoy the status of an associated overseas territory. But this is also largely irrelevant since, following the precedent set by Nigeria, Gambia could expect to be able to negotiate an association agreement. Such an agreement may be of some potential importance since, although Gambia's main export – groundnuts – at present enters EEC duty free, its Development Plan indicates the intention to process an increasing proportion of the groundnut crop into oil. On present plans groundnut oil from non-associates will face a 10–15 per cent tariff in EEC by 1970. Of course, as part of Senegal, Gambia might also expect to benefit from financial assistance from the Development Fund of the Six which would not otherwise be forthcoming.

With this possibility ruled out, the alternative of some form of economic integration between two separate states was then considered. Here the general approach was to advocate integration in the sense of customs union, fiscal harmonization and ultimately monetary integration, with Gambia making the adjustments. It was recognized that economic integration could not occur immediately for a variety of reasons. In the first place administrative problems would make it impossible to introduce the complicated regulatory system of Senegal into Gambia overnight. Even if these were not present the changes would impose too large a burden on Gambia in the shape of a sharp rise in the cost of living and other adjustments. The UN report therefore advocated a gradual economic association of the two countries beginning first with areas in which agreement is easy to reach and gradually building up to a more advanced form of association.

As the first essential move towards economic integration it was suggested that customs frontiers should be abolished. They are difficult to police properly, and involve Senegal in communications and transport difficulties with the Casamance. Since immediate unification was ruled out for reasons just stated a device was proposed which would make possible the abolition of the customs frontier without the need for immediate tariff unification. It amounts basically to a transitional free trade area with import restrictions in Gambia. Customs frontiers would be abolished and Gambia given an overall import quota, based on recent import levels, to which reduced rates of duty would apply, corresponding initially to the rates hitherto levied. Special quotas would be laid down within the overall limit to cover the items in which there is most smuggling at present, namely, textiles, cigarettes, tobacco, shoes and matches. After this, it would be for the governments to agree on the stages by which the tariff should be subsequently unified.

On monetary matters the report took the view that while ultimately the currencies would have to be unified this was not urgent. Senegal is not autonomous in the monetary field but forms part of the West African Monetary Union, which currently includes Ivory Coast, Dahomey, Upper Volta, Mauretania, Niger and Senegal. Gambia at the time was a member of the West African Currency Board, but has now set up its own Central Bank. The implications of monetary unification are not discussed, but the purely technical aspects should not present any great difficulties. A comparable operation in Cameroon was carried out quite smoothly.

The Gains from Economic Integration in Senegambia

What in fact are the specific economic gains to be anticipated from integration in Senegambia as a whole? In the first place the Gambia river could be used to bring down the Senegal groundnut crop for export. The UN report quotes estimates that this could save Senegal 1 to 3 francs per kilo on groundnuts. On a crop of 80,000 tons this would come to between 80 and 240 mn. francs (£120,000–360,000). While this is a useful gain, it is not clear that it is necessarily bound up with the abolition of the frontier. Many other countries in Africa use the transport systems of others, without unifying tariffs. The expanded use of the river would, no doubt, be made very much easier if the price policies of the two marketing boards, the Agricultural Marketing Board in Senegal and the Gambia Oilseeds Marketing Board were fully harmonized. This should not present any great difficulties when France ceases to pay more than the world market price for Senegal's groundnuts.[43]

The other main field to which much importance has been attached in the discussions on closer association concerns the integrated development of the Gambia river basin in relation to irrigation and hydrological development, a matter which receives lengthy discussion in the FAO report. Construction of a storage dam in the upper catchment area of the Gambia river could make it possible to irrigate about 100,000 acres in the middle reaches, to protect 160,000 acres of potential rice land in the estuary, and to improve conditions for another 160,000 acres. It would also be possible to generate several hundred million kwh. of electricity.

While these projects may be practicable from a technical standpoint, their economic feasibility is more questionable. One difficulty is that it seems likely that unless the returns were very high, a labour supply to undertake the intensive cultivation of the additional acreage would be very difficult to obtain, so long as land continues to be readily available in these countries. In addition, for the proposed electricity production a market of the size called for does not exist at present, and is not in prospect for the next few years. Finance of the order required will certainly not be readily forthcoming and will in any case depend on prior feasibility studies. For these and other reasons these development possibilities must therefore be regarded as very long term and few effects could be expected for at least ten years.

But in any event it is once more far from clear that the proposed developments hinge on a substantial measure of market integration, still less on customs union. In other parts of Africa, useful initiatives are being taken in river basin development on the basis of intergovernmental authorities, as with the Chad, the Niger and Mono basins.[44] Senegal itself already participates with Guinea, Mali and Mauretania in an intergovernmental Committee which is concerned with the improvement of the Senegal river, the building of a dam and other matters, and a basic convention was recently submitted to the participating governments for ratification. A similar intergovernmental Gambia river authority could probably go a long way in advancing the development outlined in the FAO report independently of either political or market integration. It is true that in the past, schemes depending for their economic viability on inter-state economic co-operation have been notoriously difficult to finance from international agencies and other aid providers. The situation, however, may improve as a result of the establishment of the African Development Bank which is specifically enjoined to give assistance to such schemes.

Apart from these gains, integration would also mean ultimately administrative savings from abolishing the customs frontiers, the avoidance of smuggling—which, however, at present benefits Gambia substantially—and possibly very slightly improved possibilities for industrial development for the area as a whole.

Like many other recent reports on integration, this one largely took for granted that a customs union would be a good thing for all. But theory and experience both suggest that whether a small country like Gambia would benefit in terms of additional incomes will depend on 'backwash and spillover effects',[45] the balance of which on general grounds can be expected to be unfavourable for a very small country joining a larger area. A positive gain to the smaller country will very likely depend upon negotiated benefits in such fields as fiscal compensation, industrial development, labour movement and so on. It would be more practical to negotiate these as an integral part of a deal about customs than separately. The possibility that Gambia may be better favoured than some other small territories in as much as the Gambia river may form a potential natural growth point is hardly a reason for failing to consider these matters.

There are in fact a number of reasons for supposing that, whatever its merits for Senegal, in economic terms, a transitional free trade area, and ultimately, a customs union of Gambia with Senegal has little to commend it *per se* to the smaller territory.

In the first place the proposed transitional free trade area would be difficult to administer and would produce economic problems for Gambia. No doubt imports through Bathurst could be readily controlled; but without a rationing system the incentive to divert quota goods to Senegal would be considerable. The introduction of a rationing system would impose increased costs of administration on Gambia; without it a sharp rise in living costs could be expected. What happens when the quotas are exhausted? Would additional imports bear the full burden of the higher Senegal tariff? Would the proposal be consistent with GATT?

More importantly, a consequence of tariff alignment in the longer run must inevitably be a shift towards the products of Senegal which already possesses industries producing phosphates, tinned goods, cement and building materials, cigarettes, beer, soap, shoes, textiles. This shift would gradually involve a loss of revenue for Gambia as rising tariffs accompanied by rising prices make an increasing range of Senegal industry competitive in Gambia. It is most unlikely that Gambian revenue would increase as customs duties are unified, as the report suggests. The only circumstance in which this might occur, and in which gain might automatically be derived from the transitional arrangements, is if Gambia were able during this period to attract some new industries to serve the customs union, profiting from its initially lower wage and price level.

In short, it is not evident that many of the more important economic gains anticipated from integration in this particular case depend on Customs Union. Moreover a customs union *per se* is almost certain to involve Gambia in revenue losses. Finally the transitional proposals seem likely to be difficult to administer and the burden would fall on Gambia.

There are, however, three alternative possibilities of which surprisingly no mention is made in the report, possibly because of its preoccupation with smuggling and the administrative savings from abolishing the customs frontier. These other possibilities would require the maintenance of customs frontiers, but they could otherwise permit a substantial measure of economic integration in most of the areas discussed in the report, with advantage to both sides.

The first of these possibilities is a simple free trade area which would permit each country to maintain its own tariff. In general a free trade area must be regarded as second best to a customs union in terms of potential economic gains from integration, but in this particular case, where the fiscal systems are so different, and the additional opportunities integration offers for industrial development are probably limited, it may have a lot to be said for it. Under a free trade area local agricultural products would be freely exchanged, without restrictions or duty, and so would any local manufactures, subject to tax on their import content.

Such a free trade area could be of benefit to both sides. It would permit most of the gains from agricultural integration to be achieved. For instance, groundnuts from each area could go to the nearest decorticating plant making possible savings in transport costs and more effective utilization of capacity. Also it would facilitate the expanded use of the Gambia river as a transport artery. This kind of free trade area would of course require internal customs checks to be maintained and it would not eliminate the incentive to smuggle. But even the UN proposal involves accepting the continuance of smuggling for an indefinite period. In any event smuggling is confined to a limited number of articles which have a high duty and are portable. Finally a free trade area does seem to be an arrangement to which several other nearby countries in Africa are turning.[46] It might ultimately offer Gambia the more attractive prospect of economic integration within a larger grouping.[47]

The establishment of a free trade area for Senegambia might conceivably require some changes in taxation in Gambia. For instance, since Senegal cigarettes might well displace imports, a consumption tax might have to be imposed to avoid a large revenue loss. In other directions, however, the present smuggling trade and other factors suggest that, while large external tariff differences and price level differences remain, Senegalese manufactures would be unlikely to displace imports for Gambia. In the longer run attention would also have to be given to internal fiscal harmonization if full advantage were to be taken of any of the probably modest opportunities for expanded industrial development which might be offered by the wider market area.

If a full free trade area were not acceptable to either country, a second alternative would be to institute a free trade area in local agricultural produce only. This again could be advocated on a wider African plane for those countries where marketing arrangements permit it, as an important and possibly practicable step towards wider economic co-operation in Africa. A third possibility would be to enter into *ad hoc* agreements for free trade in certain industrial products as experience with co-operation develops.

Such arrangements would be likely to offer a reasonable prospect of long term advantage and no immediate disadvantages. But a transitional free trade area as the prelude to a simple customs union offers Gambia no obvious advantages, and some evident immediate disadvantages in the form of higher administrative costs. It would not be sensible to enter such an arrangement without some more equitable distribution of the direct costs and benefits of the changeover to the two countries, or without collateral agreements in other fields.

Recent Developments

Developments since the UN report was considered by the two governments do not justify a belief that far-reaching measures for closer association are likely in the near future, even in the economic field, unless new proposals are forthcoming. Following the report in March 1964, talks between the two Governments were held in Dakar in May. At these meetings the Gambians put forward proposals on the political side—which envisaged a confederal structure in which responsibility for defence, foreign affairs and overseas representation would be vested. This was not acceptable to Senegal which appears to have countered with proposals envisaging the eventual integration of Gambia into Senegal. This in its turn was not acceptable to Gambia and eventually it was decided by the two governments to enter into agreements on foreign affairs and defence only.[48]

As to the economic proposals, although the Gambian government did not accept the proposals for a transitional free trade area with quotas, its view seems to have been that levels of taxation and import duties should be gradually assimilated to those of Senegal, if there were an assurance of countervailing benefits in the form of increased trade and economic activity in Gambia.[49] On the other hand the Senegal view appears to be that any acceptable form of economic association must lead in the not too distant future to the full incorporation of Gambia into Senegal.

Nevertheless, several modest steps have been taken towards

functional co-operation between the two states in several fields. These include the continuance of the Inter-Ministerial Committee, and the joint request for aid from the UN Special Fund for the joint development of the Gambia River. In February 1965 the agreements on defence and diplomatic representation were signed. Other agreements between the two countries cover the movement of persons and co-operation in matters of health. With the recent establishment of a distillery in Bathurst there is now also some prospect of negotiating protection for Gambia's products in Senegal, in return for similar protection for some of Dakar's products, and conceivably the scope for such *ad hoc* agreements might increase.

In addition, a formal treaty of association was signed in Bathurst on April 19, 1967. Its purpose is to promote and extend co-ordination and co-operation between Gambia and Senegal in all fields. The inter-state Ministerial Committee is to examine the means for promoting these objects and will submit recommendations to the two Governments.[50]

In a situation in which Senegal seems committed to ultimate political integration as a condition of close economic association, and Gambia to substantial political autonomy, and in which, moreover, the economic gains from integration are likely to be modest, the *status quo* could well continue in substantially its present form in the absence of fresh politically-motivated initiatives. It is conceivable that Senegal may come to accept that a broad form of economic association may be the best way of promoting political integration, and thus be induced to offer Gambia the economic incentives it should demand, in the form perhaps of a fiscal compensation or broad industrial development agreement, before agreeing to integrate for economic reasons alone. At the moment, however, with the defence agreements implemented, Senegal's main worry has been resolved and it seems in no hurry to press the merits of political integration unduly, apparently confident that its advantages will come to be seen and accepted in the longer run. That this may be an optimistic view is suggested by the many examples of the obstacles in the way of bringing about political or economic union after lines of separate development have been allowed to harden. On the other hand, Gambia is not interested in becoming a province of Senegal, and although there is admittedly a fairly widespread feeling among the Bathurst élite that some form of economic association could be in Gambia's interests, even this is felt to be unlikely as long as the Senegalese economy remains highly regulated. One factor which might cause Gambia to reappraise its attitude would be a decision by the British Government to taper off its substantial budgetary grant-in-aid, but this seems a remote possibility.

5 AN AFRICAN TRADE AND PAYMENTS UNION

A persistent theme running through African initiatives for integration concerns the desirability of monetary co-operation, and in particular the formation of an African clearing and payments union. In 1961 the now defunct Casablanca grouping decided to set up a payments union and, as we have seen, the establishment of such a scheme forms part of the objectives of the OAU. In 1963 the Fifth Session of ECA and the conference of African Heads of State both resolved to request a study of the establishment of an African Payments and Clearing Union.[51] Outside Africa these initiatives have been greeted coolly—as were comparable initiatives in Latin America—because of the fear that they may pave the way to a move away from convertibility and so hinder development.[52]

Clearing and Payments Unions may serve three main purposes.[53] In the first place, where inconvertible currencies exist, a clearing arrangement may facilitate the multilateral off-setting of surpluses and deficits and so expand trade. In the second place, it is possible that a clearing agreement may facilitate a reduction in the cost of exchange transactions. In the third place the arrangements might be used to provide credit to countries in temporary balance of payments difficulties, either on the introduction of an integration scheme or for other reasons subsequently, and so contribute to the better operation of such schemes.

Suggestions for an African Clearing and Payments Union appear to have been promoted in part by the success of the European Payments Union (EPU) which was set up with the first purpose in view. Europe emerged from the war with virtually every currency inconvertible and with rigid national exchange control regulations. These would have paralysed trade altogether had it not been for the conclusion of bilateral payments agreements which regulated the settlements between each European country and its trading partners. However, although these bilateral agreements facilitated settlements between each pair of countries separately, they did not permit any country to use its surpluses with one trading country to finance deficits with another. The main purpose of EPU was to permit such mobilization through the multilateral clearing of bilateral surpluses and deficits against one another and to facilitate in this way the gradual elimination of exchange controls and restrictions on European trade and other transactions. The success of EPU paved the way to the restoration of currency convertibility on a broader, world-wide basis in 1958, and it led to the simultaneous liquidation of EPU whose initial main function had become unnecessary.

If a similar purpose is to be the main justification of an African Payments scheme it is a weak one because there is no parallel between the payments problems of Europe after the war and the situation in Africa today. In the first place, as we have seen, trade among African countries themselves constitutes only a small fraction of their total trade (around 10 per cent) whereas intra-European trade amounts to about two thirds of total trade. Moreover the bulk of intra-African trade is concentrated among small and widely separated clusters of countries such as those of North Africa and East Africa. The most important reason which limits the value of an African payments union is that, as we have seen, virtually all intra-African trade is stipulated in terms of the convertible currencies of the major trading countries. The earnings of any one of these countries can readily be converted into other currencies needed for payment. Where this is not the case, as with the franc earnings of some of the countries belonging to the franc zone, the mere introduction of a clearing union would do nothing to solve the problem which is bound up with the over-valuation of the local currencies and special trading arrangements with France. The main problems in the currency field for African countries at present is not inconvertibility—as it is or may in the past have been in Latin

288

America—but rather overall balance of payments difficulties which give rise to exchange controls and restrictions, and these are not so far widespread or severe, except in one or two cases. These factors evidently limit the feasible scope and significance of an African clearing union in the immediate future and would point if anything to a regional rather than a continental union.

It is nevertheless possible that the establishment of an African Payments Union might be of value if it could serve the second purpose and permit a reduction in the cost of exchange transactions. This might be achieved in the following manner. For trade with non-African countries each member country could be allowed to exchange convertible currencies earned or accumulated by it for other foreign currencies needed for payment. This could conceivably reduce African countries' exchange transaction costs, by, for instance, offsetting the sterling surpluses and French franc deficits of some countries or currency areas with the sterling deficits and French franc surpluses of other members. As regards trade among African countries or monetary areas, any member could be credited by the Union with its convertible currency claims on another member or area and these credits could be used to settle any convertible currency debt incurred towards another member. This type of transaction would minimize the actual use of foreign currencies in the settlements to be effected. The most efficient use of such clearing facilities would call for the maintenance by each member of minimum working balances in convertible currencies with the Union so that payments could be effected by debits to the member's account instead of requiring simultaneous and equivalent transfers of other currencies by the payer to the Union. Such arrangements might also make it possible to invest more profitably some portion of each country's foreign exchange reserves.

A clearing agreement of this kind would not in itself involve any credit operations among the members. Exchange resources transferred by a country to the Union would be fully used for each payment, or retained abroad as exchange reserves in convertible currencies on behalf of members. In this way no credit or exchange risk would be assumed by members which are not already involved in their holding of foreign exchange reserves separately and directly rather than through the medium of the Union.

Whether any economies would in fact be affected by a Payments Union having such limited objectives would clearly depend on the extent to which any economies in the use of foreign currencies would be offset by the administrative costs of operating the new institution. These costs could well be large and certainly cannot be disregarded in evaluating the case for a union.

A Payments Union for Africa on these lines was in fact advocated by Professor Triffin in a recent report to ECA.[54] The main justification of such a union in his view, however, would be not so much its possible economies but rather that it would 'give concrete expression to Africa's groupings for effective co-operation in this field, and (would) set up immediately on an *all-African* basis, and *without costs or risks to anybody*, an institutional machinery susceptible of far larger and more fruitful developments in the future'.[55] His proposal was subsequently endorsed by an expert group whose recommendations were later submitted to the Sixth Session of the Economic Commission for Africa in early 1964.

The general arguments for the development of a payments union to serve the third purpose have already been discussed in Chapter 2 and need not be repeated here. As trade liberalization and integration commitments develop in Africa there will be an increasing need to develop arrangements of this kind in order to safeguard the progress and continuance of integration. At the present time, however, the need for such measures is limited by the low level of intra-African trade. The formation of new free trade areas or customs unions inside Africa are unlikely in themselves to create balance of payments difficulties for their participants, though they might create revenue difficulties. By the same token, the imposition of restrictions amongst the members of existing groupings is unlikely to make any significant contribution to a solution of their balance of payments difficulties, though this is not to say that they may not be introduced.

The Report of the Experts mentioned above also contained recommendations for other forms of monetary co-operation amongst African states, including the formation of an African Monetary Council and an African Monetary Centre of Studies and Co-operation. At the Sixth Session where this report was considered caution prevailed. It was decided simply to convene an initial meeting of monetary authorities and to submit recommendations to this meeting. As to the payments union, the Executive Secretary was merely requested to carry out further studies in the context of industrial harmonization and the development of intra-African trade. Opinion at the meeting seemed to favour the development of co-operation with IMF to achieve many of the monetary objectives under discussion rather than the creation of new Pan-African institutions. Most African countries belong to IMF and by virtue of their membership already have access to credit facilities. Bearing this in mind, and also the very limited contribution which an African Payments Union could make unless it could provide credit facilities for which no obvious source is in prospect—postponement of the establishment of a payments union certainly seems the course of wisdom. This is not to rule out the possible utility of some special arrangements between the central banks of the groups of adjacent African countries between which the level of trade is fairly high, and to some extent this takes place, though in the franc zone short term credit facilities are more often provided by France. Short term credit agreements between central banks might well contribute to substantial economies in the use of reserves. For instance, the requirements of seasonal crop financing in the three East African countries tend to follow each other. If funds for this purpose could continue to be shifted within East Africa (as occurred through the operations of the commercial banks when there was a single currency) a greater volume of credit can be made available in each country than would otherwise be the case.

6 THE AFRICAN DEVELOPMENT BANK

While no significant action has yet been taken to promote African monetary co-operation outside the regional groupings already existing, in the field of banking an institution of some potential importance for integration was established towards the end of 1964—the African Development Bank (ADB). Indeed its establishment is something of an historic event since it is the first institution for functional economic co-operation in Africa to result from an all-African initiative. The idea of establishing a development bank for the continent of Africa can be traced back to the All African Peoples Conference at Tunis in 1960 when a resolution was passed which envisaged 'the setting up of an African investment bank to promote development projects'. Subsequently in 1961 ECA convened a panel of experts to study the feasibility and possibility of establishing an African Development ment Bank.[56] Following its qualified approval, ECA established in 1962 a Committee of Nine Member States to make all the necessary arrangements for the establishment of the Bank.[57] A conference of African Finance Ministers was held in Khartoum from July 31st to August 4, 1963 under the auspices of UNECA[58] at which the text of the Agreement Establishing the African Development Bank was approved. The agreement entered into force on September 10th by which date twenty signatory Governments had deposited their instruments of ratification and the necessary proportion of the authorized capital stock of the bank had been assured. By mid-1966, twenty-seven independent African countries had become members.

The purpose of the Bank is to contribute to the economic and social development of its member countries either individually or jointly. To accomplish this, the Bank is to promote the investment of public and private capital in Africa; use its own resources to make or guarantee loans or equity investments; and provide technical assistance in the preparation, financing and implementation of development plans and projects. The Bank may operate alone or in concert with other financial institutions or sources; it can help to formulate projects and loan applications, whether for submission to the Bank itself or to other lending agencies.

The Bank is a wholly African institution in the sense that its membership is confined to African countries, its capital is provided by African countries and its voting power is wholly African, as is its administration[59]. Its authorized capital is 250 mn. dollars. Membership is acquired by subscription to the capital stock in proportions laid down. Subscriptions to the paid up capital stock (one half of total subscription) is to be made in six instalments, and to the callable capital as and when required by the Bank. As to voting power, each member has 625 votes plus one additional vote for each 10,000 unit share of the capital stock of the Bank held by that member.

The Bank's administrative structure is modelled on the International Bank for Reconstruction and Development. It consists of a Board of Governors to which each member appoints one Governor and one Alternate, a nine man Board of Directors elected by the Board of Governors, and the President, elected by the Board of Directors by a majority of the total voting power of the members. In addition at least one Vice President is elected by the Board on the recommendation of the President. The President of the Bank is elected for five years and the Directors for three years. The Bank is empowered to borrow funds in member countries and elsewhere, furnishing such collateral or other security as may be required. In the resources of the Bank a distinction is made between ordinary capital resources and special resources. Ordinary capital resources include principally the subscribed capital of the Bank together with funds raised by borrowing. Special resources are made up of grants or unguaranteed loans made to the Bank. These funds are subject to special rules and regulations to be agreed between the Bank and the donor or sponsor. These Special Funds must be kept separate from the ordinary capital resources of the Bank.

Operations of the Bank

The basic operating principles of the Bank were described in the African Development Bank Agreement. Its loan and investment policy and procedures have subsequently been set out in more detail for the approval of the Board of Governors.[60] As to loans, the general principle is that the Bank will finance specific projects which clearly contribute to the economic development of its member countries. From the standpoint of integration an important provision is that a special preference is to be accorded to all projects which benefit two or more member countries and which thus stimulate intra-African measures of co-operation.

Such projects may include transportation links, telecommunication links, irrigation and flood control, joint production and distribution of electric power and other forms of energy, or, in certain cases, industrial and agricultural projects. This provision has considerable potential importance for integration since multinational projects have been particularly difficult to finance through the international agencies. Any loans for multinational projects will normally be made to national governments with specific responsibility assigned to particular ministries. The Bank will also provide loan finance for pre-investment and feasibility studies, again with particular attention to studies required for multinational projects.

In general, the Bank will make loans for a given project only to the extent that alternative sources of finance are not reasonably or readily available. Loans will normally be made only for projects in which the borrower itself makes a contribution from its own funds of approximately 50 per cent of the project. Although Bank operations will principally finance specific projects, global loans to support the operations of sub-regional or national development banks will also be considered. Finance will ordinarily take the form of loans but equity finance is envisaged in special cases. It is also envisaged that at a later stage the Bank may guarantee loans for economic development. Provision is made for two rates of interest on loans. To first-class economic projects—industrial plants, public utilities—a fixed rate of interest approximating to the market rate for international loans of this type will be applied. In the case of agriculture and social projects the Bank hopes to be able, on the basis of special funds, to lend on concessional terms. Initially the upper limit for ordinary loans is fixed at 8 mn. dollars for multinational projects and 3 mn. dollars for national projects. Loans under 100,000 dollars will not be considered except for pre-investment studies.

The proposals for the establishment of an African Development Bank have not met with unqualified enthusiasm. Doubts as to its potential value have been widely expressed both within the continent and outside, and are reflected in the various reports which have been made on the subject after consultation with African governments, international institutions, and governments and the capital markets of the developed countries. The concern has been that the creation of the Bank might deprive its member countries of resources of manpower or finance which could be better used at home, and that the Bank's operations might be hampered by political difficulties.

Considerable effort has in fact been made to ensure, in the structure of the Bank, that it should be free from political influence and local pressures and run on sound banking lines. As to the first point, it is recognized that the Bank will be useful only to the extent that it can mobilize new resources for African development or can direct resources to new fields of investment —the principle of 'additionality' of which much was made in the preliminary discussions. The Bank would not serve a useful purpose if it merely duplicated the work of other financial institutions or financed projects which others were prepared to finance. This point is particularly important since it has been decided that the share capital of the Bank and its control is to be wholly African. This means that the Bank necessarily has a relatively small share capital. On its own credit it is unlikely to be able to borrow large amounts and it will probably not be able to borrow at all in the private capital markets of the developed countries for many years. For some time to come, therefore, the Bank will have at its disposal relatively small resources from its own share capital and any funds it may obtain through its ability to attract funds from national and international agencies.

These considerations suggest that the Bank's main effort would be best directed to stimulating, rather than itself undertaking, investment. Its success will then be judged by the amount of additional investment which its activities bring about. This view of the Bank's functions seems to have been accepted and it is reflected in the two principal lines of activity which are to be emphasized in the operations of the Bank. The first is the systematic discovery and creation of investment opportunities and their formulation and presentation to the point where they can be financed. There is much evidence to suggest that a lack of well worked out projects rather than a lack of finance *per se* has been a major constraint on the inflow of international funds to many developing countries in Africa and elsewhere.[61] Hence, sponsorship of studies of projects to be financed could be one of the most useful fields of activity for the Bank. The second line of activity to be emphasized by the Bank involves the systematic search to find funds, from private or governmental sources, as projects are demonstrated to be viable. These two kinds of activity could help substantially to increase the flow of productive investment in Africa.

It might still be argued that instead of setting up a new institution it would have been better to persuade existing institutions to give more attention to Africa by, for instance, setting up Africa departments as the International Bank itself has done. The case for an African institution presumably rests on the hope that it will achieve a higher degree of identification with African countries and problems and also develop a more intimate knowledge of African needs and opportunities than any such alternative. What is not so clear is that the establishment of several sub-regional development banks might not have been an even better approach.

REFERENCES: CHAPTER 6

1 For the early background, see V. Thompson and R. Adloff, *French West Africa*, Stanford and Oxford University Press, 1958.

2 For the background to break up and the factors which produced this situation, see R. S. Morgenthau, *Political Parties in French-Speaking West Africa*, Clarendon Press, Oxford 1964, pp. 300–29 'From AOF Federation to Sovereign Nations'.

3 Morgenthau, p. 327.

4 See Colin Legum, The Changing Ideas of Pan-Africanism, *African Forum*, New York, Vol. 1 No. 2, p. 57.

5 See *West African Monetary Union*, published by the Banque Centrale des Etats de l'Afrique de l'Ouest, Paris, no date.

6 See Chapter 5 for a discussion of the operations of the Equatorial Central Bank.

7 See *Bulletin de l'Afrique Noire*, Paris No. 424, 1966, pp. 8568–9.

8 See *Marchés Tropicaux et Méditerranéens*, Paris, April 22, 1967, p. 1200.

9 See *Convention on Dual Nationality and Economic Harmonization*, Abidjan, 1965.

10 See *Convention Creating a Fund for Mutual Assistance and Loan Guarantees*, 1966, Abidjan.

11 See *Customs and Trade Agreement*, Ivory Coast and Upper Volta, Abidjan.

12 See *Convention entre la République du Côte d'Ivoire et la République de Haute Volta, fixant l'organisation et le fonctionnement du chemin de fer Abidjan-Niger*, April 30, 1960.

13 It was announced in October 1966 that Ghana and Upper Volta have set up a joint commission, to be known as the Ghana-Upper Volta Transport Commission, to control commercial road transport between the two countries.

14 On its operations, see UNECA, *Transit Problems of African Land-Locked States*, E/CN.14/TRANS/28, 1966, pp. 56–60.

15 On these organisations, see the references cited in footnote 44 below.

16 See Hailey, *The Republic of South Africa and the High Commission Territories*, OUP 1963, and *Basutoland, the Bechuanaland Protectorate and Swaziland; History of discussions with the Union of South Africa, 1909–1939*. HMSO, Cmnd. 8707, 1952.

17 See G. M. E. Leistner, 'Foreign Bantu Workers in South Africa; Their Present Position in the Economy'. *South African Journal of Economics*, Vol. 35 No. 1, March 1967. The 1966 *Censuses of Population* of the three countries also have data bearing on this question.

18 ILO *Report to the Government of Swaziland on Manpower, 1964.*

19 See *Customs Agreement-Union of South Africa-Territories of Basutoland, Swaziland and the Bechuanaland Protectorate*, Potchefstroom, June 29, 1910. High Commissioner's Notice 65 of 1910. South-West Africa is also part of the South African Customs area.

20 Similar agreements were entered into between South Africa and the Rhodesias and between the three former High Commission territories and the Rhodesias. These are no longer in force although a form of customs agreement between the High Commission territories and Rhodesia still operates. See footnote (22) below. The historical background to the 1910 agreement is described in J. van der Poel, *Railway and Customs Policy in South Africa, 1885–1910*, London, 1933.

21 See pages 258–9 for a discussion of the reallocation of the overall share among the three territories by decision of the British Government.

22 See *Customs Agreement Between the Federation of Rhodesia and Nyasaland and Basutoland, the Bechuanaland Protectorate and Swaziland*, High Commissioner's Notice 63 of 1956. High Commissioner's Office, Capetown, May 24, 1956.

23 See Report of the Ministry of Overseas Development Economic Survey Mission, *The Development of the Basutoland Economy*, Ministry of Overseas Development, London, 1965, para. 237.

24 On this, see H. M. Robertson and M. Kooy, 'The South African Board of Trade and Industries'; 'The South African Customs Tariff and the Development of South African Industry', and references therein cited. *South African Journal of Economics*, Vol. 34, No. 3, Sept. 1966.

25 The arrangements for Swaziland are discussed in *Report on the Marketing of Agricultural and Livestock Produce in Swaziland*, by H. C. Biggs, Ministry of Overseas Development, London, 1966.

26 An IMF Staff Paper quotes an estimate for Botswana of 2·5 mn. Rand for August 1966.

27 All these figures are derived from Leistner, *op. cit.*

28 *The Development of the Swaziland Economy*, *The Development of the Basutoland Economy*, *The Development of the Bechuanaland Economy*, Ministry of Overseas Development, London, 1965.

29 *op. cit.* para 35.

30 *op. cit.* para 40.

31 See, for instance, H. Kessels and H. J. Tomkins, *Report to the Basutoland Government on a National Savings and Development Bank, the Monetary System and Certain Aspects of Land Tenure*, Maseru, April 1966.

32 *op. cit.* p. 23.

33 See *Report of the Committee re Foreign Bantu* (Froneman Report), Pretoria 1962 (mimeo).

34 Some of the economic problems of these areas and the South African government's policies towards their industrial development are discussed in C. R. Hill's book *Bantustans—The Fragmentation of South Africa*. Institute of Race Relations and OUP, London 1964.

35 Southern Rhodesia Government Notice No. 25A of 1964, *Trade Agreement* between the Government of Nyasaland and the Government of Southern Rhodesia. (Supplement to the S. R. Government Gazette Extraordinary dated January 7, 1964, Government Printer, Salisbury. See also A. Hazlewood, The Malawi-Rhodesia Trade Agreement, *Bulletin of the Oxford University Institute of Economics and Statistics*, May 1965.

36 See D. V. Cowen, Towards a common market in Southern Africa, *Optima*, Johannesburg, June 1967.

37 See the three reports on the economic development of the three territories cited above, in which some suggestions are made for the introduction of new taxes and levies in the territories.

38 If currency per head in BLS were the same as in East Africa, the respective circulation would be approximately R 4 mn. in Lesotho; R 2·5 in Botswana and R 1·75 in Swaziland. Assuming a return of 5 per cent and agency costs of, say, 20 per cent gives the above figures. The higher figures for Swaziland are based on an alternative, more plausible estimate of currency requirements in relation to national income. The initial cost of the currency would also have to be taken into account and might well absorb the whole of the annual income for an initial year.

39 On these antecedents to the recent initiatives, see the extremely inter-

esting study by J. D. Hargreaves, *Prelude to the Partition of West Africa*, Macmillan, London, 1963, especially Chapter 4, pp. 145–95.

40 The problem of smuggling, of course, is not peculiar to Senegal and Gambia. There is evidence to suggest that in former French West Africa it was a large-scale phenomenon. See Chambre de Commerce de la Cote d'Ivoire, *La Contrabande par Terre en Afrique Occidentale Francaise* (n.d.)—based on a Franc Sterling Study Mission for 1956. See also, E. J. Berg, Socialism and Economic Development in Tropical Africa, *Quarterly Journal of Economics*, November 1964, pp. 566–70.

41 See *Report on the Alternatives of Association between the Gambia and Senegal*, United Nations, New York, Department of Economic and Social Affairs, March, 1964. This report was also published by the Gambia Government as Sessional Paper 13, June 1964, Government Printer, Bathurst.

42 See *A Report to the Governments of Gambia and Senegal; Integrated Agricultural Development in the Gambia River Basin*, Food and Agricultural Organisation, Rome, February 1964.

43 See Chapter 2, Section 3.

44 For a note on the Chad and Niger Authorities, see *Natural Resources Newsletter*, No. 5, January 1965, UNECA, Addis Ababa. See also Moustapha Seck, *L'aménagement du bassin du fleuve Senegal* (Guinea-Mali-Mauretanie-Senegal) and Pierre Renier, *La mise en valeur commune du bassin Tchadien*, in *Europe-France Outre-Mer*, Paris No. 412, pp. 50–6.

45 See Chapter 2, pp. 43–5 for a discussion of the operation of these effects.

46 See, for instance, the proposals for a West African Free Trade Area covering Sierra Leone, Liberia, Guinea and Ivory Coast.

47 A similar free trade area (with the East Africa Common Market) was once suggested for Zanzibar, a country whose economic problems before its union with Tanganyika had many similarities with those of Gambia— a local market too small to attract industry, a relatively low tariff, *vis-à-vis* its neighbours, and heavy reliance on customs as a source of revenue. See *Report on the Economic Development of Zanzibar*, Government Printer, Zanzibar, 1962, pp. 9–10.

48 See Prime Minister's speech at Opening Session of House of Representatives on July 1, 1964, in *Gambia News Bulletin* No. 80, July 9, 1964 (Supplement), p. 3, Government Printer, Bathurst.

49 Prime Minister's Speech, *op. cit*, p. 4.

50 *Afrique Nouvelle*, April 20, 1967, quoted *Africa Research Bulletin*, Vol. 4, No. 4, Exeter, England.

51 See *Report of the Expert Group on an African Payments Union*. UNECA, E/CN.14/262, p. 1.

52 An instructive review of proposals for Latin America is found in Barry Siegel, Payments Systems for the Latin American Free Trade Association,

in Wionczek (ed.) *Latin American Economic Integration*, Praeger, London 1965.

53 They may also be used as a policy means for influencing the pattern of trade and developments within a regional or continental scheme for economic co-operation on a continuing basis. Siegel's essay, referred to above, contains some comments on the payments proposals of the Economic Commission for Latin America for the Latin American Free Trade Association from this point of view.

54 See R. Triffin, *Report on the Possibilities of Establishing a Clearing and Payments Union in Africa*, Annex VI to the Report of the Expert Group on an African Payments Union.

55 *op. cit.* para 9.

56 See *Report on the possibilities of establishing an African Development Bank*, E/CN./14/129, 196.

57 See *Final Report of the Committee of Nine on the Establishment of an African Development Bank* (January 14–23, 1963), E/CN.14/FMAB/I.

58 See *The Conference of Finance Ministers on the Establishment of an African Development Bank and its Preparatory Meeting*, E/CN.14/FMAB/39 (Sept. 6, 1963).

59 The Asian Development Bank, by contrast, inaugurated in November 1966, at Tokyo, has found about one-third of its capital from countries not belonging to the region. Three of the Board's ten directors represent the non-regional subscribers.

60 See Board of Governors, African Development Bank, *Text Concerning the Loan and Investment Policy of the African Development Bank and its Procedures*, Abidjan, Dec. 18, 1965.

61 See, for instance, A. Waterston, *Development Planning: Lessons of Experience*, Johns Hopkins Press, Baltimore and Oxford University Press, 1966.

CHAPTER 7

CONCLUSION

THE main purpose of this book is to discuss the rationale of regional economic integration in less developed countries and against this background to look at the functioning, achievements and problems of existing integration schemes in Africa. It is hoped that this may provide some insight into the possibilities and problems of projected groupings in the continent, and the kinds of institutional arrangements necessary if potential benefits from economic co-operation are to be achieved.

The case for regional integration in Africa, as in most other less developed areas, rests on the fact that industrial development and a more balanced economic structure are major policy objectives in most countries, partly because these objectives are seen as the best way of achieving economic growth and stability, and partly for non-economic reasons. Regional integration offers the prospect that it may enable these objectives to be achieved more effectively through specialization. At the present stage of economic development in most African countries, industrialization must be based on import substitution. Beyond a point the small scale of most national markets makes this an expensive process. By basing import substitution on a regional, rather than a national market, integration should increase the feasible rate of growth of manufactured output for any given level of protection. In this way it should contribute to economic growth directly and indirectly.

One of the major difficulties in maintaining and promoting integration hitherto has centered on arranging an equitable distribution of benefits—which in practice means an acceptable distribution of industrial development. African countries are interested in promoting industrial development and diversification not so much within the boundaries of a regional grouping as within their own borders. Existing schemes are unlikely to be

301

cohesive, still less are new ones likely to come into existence if regional groupings do not incorporate the means for making possible an acceptable balance of development.

Although this is by now widely recognised, and attempts have been made to take it into account, the recent history of economic integration in Africa is not wholly encouraging, and in some regions long standing arrangements for co-operation through common markets and common services which originated in the colonial era have been largely liquidated. At the same time the extent of continued co-operation in finance, common services and trade should not be under-rated, and the prospects for effective co-operation in the two major remaining market groupings are not unpromising.

The extent to which further African economic integration will come about is difficult to gauge. It seems safe to assume that its progress will be related to opportunities for economic gains, which are bound up with economies of scale, size of local markets and individual national preferences for industrial development. Opportunities for gain from the operation of these factors already appear to exist for several regions and their potential importance may in the future be even greater. Because of this, integration is likely to continue to form a major concern of economic policy for many African countries, though its progress may well suffer setbacks.

At the same time, while economic benefits may be necessary, they may not be sufficient in themselves to bring about integration even where gains are clearly in prospect. Cultural differences between francophone and anglophone African states present one hindrance to integration which is largely absent in Latin America where comparable initiatives are being undertaken. No proposals for economic integration between African states of different language groups have yet come to anything. Apart from cultural differences, political factors are operative. Effective economic integration demands a willingness to co-operate intimately with other countries, perhaps to the extent of accepting a substantial measure of dependence, which may be difficult to reverse. It may entail a willingness to rely on another country for essential services or for key manufactured products and will certainly imply gearing the infrastructure to some extent so as to support the integrated market. Economic gains from integration will thus have a price in terms of a reduction of flexibility and autonomy. In African conditions where political change is rapid, and regimes and alignments can alter overnight, the impact of political instability as a brake to the development of economic integration should not be underrated.[1]

Another factor relevant to the assessment of future integration prospects is the *magnitude* of gains from integration and their distribution over the continent. Although these gains are extremely difficult to quantify, it appears that they have so far been modest. Moreover, plausible estimates of future potential gains do not encourage the belief that these will be dramatic. Estimates quoted in earlier chapters of this book suggest that, over a five or ten year time horizon, an increase in annual growth rates of GDP of about 0·5 per cent might be attributable to integration. If these estimates are anywhere near the mark, integration is not in itself a panacea for underdevelopment. Of course, the estimates can hardly be regarded with confidence. Even so, the assumptions underlying the ECA estimates are hardly pessimistic. Still, the gains may be underestimated, because the dynamic factors at work may be under-rated. Moreover, even though past, or short-term future gains may be small, the potential benefits may in the longer run become substantial as incomes and industrial potential grow. Nevertheless, policy makers may understandably be reluctant to limit their freedom in economic policy and to involve their countries in the inevitable uncertainties of untried co-operative arrangements for what may appear to be modest gain.

However, if integration is thought to be ultimately advantageous, then even if its gains may not be large in the foreseeable future, an early start may be desirable since it may be much more difficult to bring about integration later. For if once high cost industries are established to serve national markets, the countries concerned may be reluctant to subject them to outside competition later. Sidney Dell has put this point succinctly:

'Experience in Latin America shows that once a country begins to move along the path of economic self-sufficiency, it becomes very difficult later on to change direction. It would be much easier today to get agreement on a reasonable division of labour in Latin America if there had not already been substantial autarkic development in many parts of the Continent. In this respect Africa has an advantage over Latin America—its need for an integration of markets may be less immediately pressing, but integration may be easier now than at a later stage, when vested interests become much stronger'.[2]

For advocates of integration in Africa, this consideration inevitably raises the question of the best means of stimulating it. Many recent initiatives have sought to promote co-operation between sizeable groups of countries, by establishing from the outset organizations and programmes with far-reaching objectives. In part this may be because the forms are valued as symbols of the sought-for unity and in part because it is felt that their existence may favourably affect the path, speed and efficiency by which eventual integration is achieved. Tactical considerations may also have played some part—if GATT demands a customs union as a condition of approving preferential trade arrangements, it is not surprising to find this written into the objectives of regional groupings.

An example of this approach is the scheme which has been put forward for an Economic Community of Eastern Africa, embracing Kenya, Uganda and Tanzania, Malawi, Zambia, Mauritius, Ethiopia and Sudan, with a Treaty, a Council of Ministers, and calling for co-ordinated sub-regional planning and the creation of a customs union by way of a free trade area within a period of ten years. These proposals came forward at a time when the tightly knit East African Common Market was itself going through a phase which made its continued survival look doubtful. Similarly proposals have been put forward for linking UDEAC with its huge neighbour, Congo (Kinshasa), and for a co-ordinated industrialization programme based on this wider grouping—although UDEAC itself is not yet firmly consolidated. Other suggested schemes look to industrialization based on a large West African sub-regional grouping including both anglophone and francophone countries.

Such ambitious schemes for sub-regional integration assume that large groups of less developed countries—some of which are without any past experience of integration—can be induced to harmonize their development plans and fiscal policies, but a realistic appraisal of these schemes must surely view them against a background which includes weak and ineffective national planning machinery in many African countries, shortages of administrative and entrepreneurial resources, a lack of the technical and economic data necessary for the development of rational sub-regional plans, and the dependence of most large-scale industrial development on foreign capital and skill. Although it is conceivable that the establishment of grandiose institutions and programmes may develop a desirable inbuilt dynamic for integration, attempts to establish them at this stage may only hinder progress to integration by making any advance conditional on agreement on a very broad front and beyond what is at present negotiable. The apparent widespread enthusiasm for such proposals should not be misinterpreted, for while general expressions of support for these initiatives can be elicited without too much difficulty in international conferences by practised international civil servants, experience in Africa suggests that genuine national political commitment to very broad and far-reaching groupings and arrangements is rare. These resolutions are, as Kitzinger has unkindly but not unfairly remarked, seldom more than 'Decisions taken in the void and honoured in desuetude'.[3]

If integration is to be effectively promoted in Africa it will probably be necessary, in general, to think in terms of much more limited objectives on which effective decisions might be more readily taken. No doubt some regions with past experience of co-operation, and with similar traditions, and which are not made up of countries at rather different stages of development, may in the future find it possible to achieve *ab initio*, or to maintain, free trade areas, customs unions or even economic unions. In other cases where such experience is lacking and intraregional disparities in development may be considerable, less ambitious arrangements may be more practicable but nonetheless capable of producing substantial benefits.

To the extent that the major source of gains from integration lies in the field of large-scale industry it would clearly be desirable to identify industries where economies of scale are present and to allocate these among the participating countries on an equitable basis so that each country in the group provides markets to the others for this kind of product. In doing so, the comparative advantage of different national locations would have to be taken into account if potential gains are not to be dissipated, but considerations of regional balance must also come into play. These regional industries might eventually form the foundation for the development of separate national industrial complexes. Sub-regional development banks could play an important role in initiating and establishing these possibilities.

For industries serving a regional market, the desirability of minimizing uncertainty would suggest that access to the markets of the countries in which the plant is not located should be provided for by some form of interstate agreement. But it is doubtful whether the exploitation of economies of scale in Africa today demands the establishment of complete customs unions, for it is commonly the case that sectoral interdependences are presently limited and will probably remain so for some time to come. The progress of regional specialization might further be facilitated if 'regional' industries could be given a special legal status and could operate under a tax regime guaranteeing each participant country shares in the profits—as is done in some cases in UDEAC. Joint financial participation by the governments of the region, as is practised in the UDEAC bilateral harmonization agreements, could also help to provide a greater assurance of continued access to markets in the region by providing a financial deterrent to unilateral action on the part of any country. The promotion of a common market for selected 'regional' industries may also stand a better chance of success if decisions on the allocation of a group of regional industries could be taken together on a basis which would promise all participants some advantage from the industrial development made possible by regional co-operation. The fate of the West African Steel Community is an indicator of the likely outcome if this is not done.

Initially arrangements for regional industries could be confined to a limited number of products but they might later be extended to free trade or even simply preferential market access for a range of other products. Such a limited approach could provide an opportunity for developing with respect to particular projects the habits of co-operation which may be a necessary condition for the development of effective co-operation over a wider area and in other fields. Exponents of comprehensive sub-regional planning may look askance at such tactics because they may, by comparison with the ideal, represent a second-best solution in terms of path and scope. And it is certainly necessary to bear in mind that just as the development of protected national industries may itself hinder the formation of initial regional groupings, so may separate integration schemes on a narrow geographical basis place obstacles in the way of the later establishment of wider groupings unless regional projects are confined to those which would have a good chance of viability in any eventual wider grouping. At the same time, if integration has to wait upon comprehensive schemes drawn up on a wide geographical basis and involving a total integration of markets as well as integration in other fields, it may be indefinitely delayed.

But the difficulties first of agreeing on market integration for regional industries and subsequently of implementing an equitable allocation of these industries among the countries making up the region may themselves be formidable. Often these industries will be financed wholly or mainly by foreign capital. Even given a desire on the part of the interested governments to share industrial development, it may be difficult to induce investors to go ahead in locations other than those which seem most profitable. A regional investment bank may be able to make some contribution to the achievement of regional balance but this is hardly likely to be great unless finance is a limiting factor in relation to the projects, or unless the bank has special resources from which projects in lagging regions can be subsidized.

Thus, even with good will, it may be difficult to provide the less developed countries with a share of regional industries. But the attempt to ensure the co-operation of initially lagging countries by trying to get large-scale 'regional' industries to locate there is not the only approach to the problem. Within a common market the more backward areas are not only at a disadvantage in attracting regional industries, but in the face of competition from established producers of the more advanced countries they also find it difficult to set up smaller-scale industries even where these would be viable in terms of their own national market, except in those cases where transport costs provide some natural protection. For many less developed countries contemplating membership of a regional grouping it may be even more important to have arrangements which permit them to provide some initial protection for potentially viable national industries which may be started with local resources than for them to rely on attracting large-scale externally financed regional industries to what may be, initially, a very unfavourable location. For one thing, the immediate gains from a development of such national industries in terms of expanded income and employment may be larger. In addition, such a progression represents a more normal sequence of development and should help to make the country a more attractive location at some later date for the establishment of regional industries. Perhaps this consideration may explain some aspects of the new arrangements which have emerged in both Equatorial and in East Africa. In these groupings it is no longer the case that there is automatic free access to the markets of all their members. In the case of regional industries in East Africa, free access is to be provided, but, as we have seen, a country is to be permitted to impose temporary surcharges on the products of other East African countries which compete with industries it wishes to set up. In Equatorial Africa free access to the market of partner countries is conditional on the performance of the harmonization arrangements.

Of course the distinction between a regional industry and a national industry is necessarily arbitrary and a question of degree, and it by no means follows that several national industries will be able to produce as efficiently as one larger industry located in one country only. But the loss of some production economies is almost certainly an unavoidable cost of maintaining a reasonably satisfactory balance of industrial development.

Whatever approach is chosen, the central problem, given the political preconditions, is how to arrange things so that any long-term possibilities of economic gain to the region are not lost in the pursuit of separate short-term advantage on the part of individual members. Basically this is a problem of providing firm

assurances rather than mere possibilities of balanced development within the region. Very largely the solution to this problem must be found by African countries themselves, which
must first be willing to seek agreement. But given this willingness, there may be an important role for international support
in at least two directions. First of all, international support is
necessary to ensure that the rules hitherto applicable to international trade by those countries which are members of GATT
will not hinder regional integration schemes which may be
economically well founded and practically negotiable. The rules
deserving special attention in this connection are first that of
unconditional most favoured nation treatment in relation to
tariffs; and secondly, the principle of the non-discriminatory
application of quantitative restrictions.

Countries may depart from the most favoured nation principle and enter into discriminatory arrangements only if these
establish 'on substantially all the trade' between them a customs
union or a free trade area, or an interim agreement which includes a plan or schedule for the establishment of such an
arrangement within a reasonable length of time. Opposition to
less inclusive forms of trade co-operation has been based on the
view that it will encourage uneconomic development in the
countries practising them, and harm the trading interests of
leading trading nations. In practice GATT rules on discriminatory
arrangements have been applied with some flexibility. The
establishment of the European Iron and Steel Community was
permitted, even though it represented a clear departure from the
principle that approval should be conditional on freeing substantially all trade. Likewise no attempt was made to impede the
trade preferences involved in the arrangements for association
between EEC and certain African states.

Since the UNCTAD conference of 1964 the climate of international opinion in relation to the formation of discriminatory
trading arrangements among less developed countries has
certainly become more favourable. Not only did the conference
recommend that regional integration should be promoted
among developing countries but less inclusive forms of co-
operation also received support.[4] It was also recommended that
developing countries should not be required to extend to

developed countries preferential arrangements in operation among themselves. UNCTAD thus marks the acceptance of, and widespread support for, forms of integration in less developed countries which fall short of customs unions. Consonantly the Trade Development Committee of GATT later conceded that 'the establishment of preferences among less developed countries appropriately administered, and subject to the necessary safeguards, can make an important contribution to an expansion of trade among those countries and to the attainment of the objectives of the General Agreement'.[5] These developments suggest that the door is now more widely open for the conclusion of less inclusive integration arrangements among less developed countries though the details have still to be worked out and concrete cases put to the test. Less developed countries cannot yet count on automatic approval of integration arrangements falling short of customs unions and free trade areas which they might negotiate among themselves.

Apart from supporting a modification of the rules of the game, external support may be important on the financial side. If short term and long term interests are to be made to harmonize, substantial amounts of public money may have to be spent to ensure an equitable distribution of benefits both through the creation of an appropriate infra-structure and in other ways. Although for a wide range of modern industry it may be true that the advantages of location are man-made and can thus be created, to do this costs money. Even where such investment may be justified in the long run, it will often be difficult, if not impossible, for the necessary resources to be found from the region itself in which even the most advanced member may nevertheless be very poor. If developed countries and the international agencies could be induced to assume some responsibility for helping the less developed countries to deal with this problem, the progress of integration might be hastened. Such support might take a variety of forms ranging from the provision of finance for payments schemes, to financing infra-structure investment. The provision of finance for low cost factories may also provide an incentive to a more balanced regional development which may be far more important, given the time horizon of investors, than any fiscal incentives related to current earnings. In these various ways it may be possible to create conditions in which justifiable integration initiatives have a greater chance of reaching fruition.

Time alone will reveal the future of economic integration in Africa, but, as has proved to be the case with political regrouping, time may not be on its side. But even if far-reaching schemes for regional economic integration may not at present be widely negotiable, important economic gains may still be derived from the initiation of more limited forms of co-operation for the joint promotion of selected regional projects, or even from the establishment of preferential trade groupings falling short of a common market. These beginnings may subsequently provide the foundation for more intimate and profitable co-operation later. To achieve and maintain even these more limited forms of co-operation, however, will certainly pose a formidable challenge to African leaders.

REFERENCES: CHAPTER 7

1 See, for example, the forceful statement of Mr Jamal, former Minister of Communications, Power and Works in Tanzania, and now Minister of Finance, in Leys and Robson, *op. cit.*, Appendix II, p. 214. The relevance of this consideration is perhaps greater to common services and infrastructure services (cf. Zambia and Kariba) than to manufacturing industry though in that case too it is by no means irrelevant.

2 See Sidney Dell, *Trade Blocs and Common Markets*, Constable, London, 1963, p. 215.

3 See U. Kitzinger, Nairobi Conference Report, *Journal of Common Market Studies*, Oxford, Vol. IV, May 1966, p. 259.

4 See *Conference on Trade and Development*, Vol. I, *Final Act and Report*, p. 11.

5 See *Report of the Committee on Trade and Development*, GATT Document L/2614 of March 28, 1966.

SELECTIVE READING LIST

1 VINER, JACOB, *The Customs Union Issue*, New York, Carnegie Endowment for International Peace, 1950. The basic work for the static theory of customs unions.

2 MEADE, J. E., *Problems of Economic Union*, London, Allen and Unwin, 1953. A valuable general survey which covers not only trade, but also the balance of payments and movements of labour and capital. Emphasis primarily static.

3 MEADE, J. E., *The Theory of Customs Unions*, Amsterdam, North Holland Publishing Company, 1956. An extension of the static theoretical work contained in (2). A classic work which should be required reading for any student of the subject.

4 MEADE, J. E., *Trade and Welfare*, London, Oxford University Press, 1955. This is the second volume of a fundamental treatise on the theory of international economic policy. Part IV covers problems encountered in the formation of Customs Unions and other preferential systems. The analysis is comparative, static in character, and is conducted on the assumption that the twofold objectives of full employment within countries and of equilibrium in the balance of payments between them are successfully achieved.

5 LIPSEY, R. G., 'The Theory of Customs Unions: A General Survey', *Economic Journal*, Sept. 1960. A valuable survey of the development of customs union theory from Viner to 1960 with a rather brief consideration of some empirical work relating to EEC.

6 JOHNSON, H. G., 'An Economic Theory of Protectionism, Tariff Bargaining, and the Formation of Customs Union', *Journal of Political Economy*, 1965. An attempt to provide a logically coherent explanation of why commercial policy is conducted as it is. The paper departs from the conventional assumptions of international trade theory and welfare economics by positing a collective preference for industrial production. A most important contribution to the theory.

7. COOPER, C. A., and MASSELL, B. F., 'Toward a General Theory of Customs Unions for Developing Countries', *Journal of Political Economy*, Chicago, Vol. 73, 1965. This important article also starts from the standpoint that there is a social preference for 'industry' and explores the implications of this for static customs union theory.

8 MIKESELL, R. F., 'The Theory of Common Markets as Applied to Regional Groupings Among Developing Countries', in (ed.) R. F. Harrod

and D. C. Hague, *International Trade Theory in a Developing World*, London, Macmillan, 1963. An attempt to look at the case for customs unions in less developed countries against 'dynamic' assumptions.

9 KITAMURA, H., 'Economic Theory and the Economic Integration of Underdeveloped Regions', in (ed.) M. S. Wionczek, *Latin American Economic Integration*, London, Praeger, 1966. A representative example of the attempts to analyse integration in less developed countries against the background of dynamic protectionist assertions.

10 HIRSCHMAN, A. O., *The Strategy of Economic Development*, Yale 1958, Ch. 10 'Inter-regional and International Transmission of Economic Growth'. A brief general statement of the problem of the inter-regional and international distribution of economic growth.

11 *East Africa, Report of the Economic and Fiscal Commission*, 1961, London, H.M.S.O. CMND: 1279. A classic on East Africa, and of interest for students of common markets in less developed countries generally.

12 BROWN, A. J., 'Customs Union Versus Economic Separatism in Developing Countries', Parts I and II, *Yorkshire Bulletin of Economic and Social Research*, May and November, 1961. Two path-breaking articles concerned with the market limit on industrial development and the working of 'spread and backwash'. Of particular interest to students of the East African Common Market. A first attempt at quantification.

13 GHAI, D. P., 'Territorial Distribution of the Benefits and Costs of the East African Common Market', in (ed.) C. Leys and P. Robson, *Federation in East Africa. Opportunities and Problems*, Nairobi, Oxford University Press, 1965. An empirical analysis which attempts to quantify the inter-country distribution of benefits and costs in East Africa.

14 NEWLYN, W. T., 'Gains and Losses in the East African Common Market', *Yorkshire Bulletin*, November, 1965. An attempt to quantify the short-term gains to Uganda and Tanzania from leaving the East African Common Market.

15 NDEGWA, P., *The Common Market and Development in East Africa*, East African Publishing House, Nairobi 1965. A valuable account of the development of the East African Common Market with a detailed analysis of trade statistics.

16 BALASSA, B., 'Trade Creation and Trade Diversion in the European Common Market', *Economic Journal*, March 1967. This study is not directly relevant to Africa but reviews a number of empirical studies relating to EEC and puts forward new estimates. Of methodological interest.

INDEX

314

INDEX

INDEX

318

INDEX